THE BUDDHIST VISION

SUBHUTI

THE BUDDHIST VISION

A Path to Fulfilment

WINDHORSE PUBLICATIONS

Also by Subhuti:
Buddhism for Today
Bringing Buddhism to the West
Sangharakshita: A New Voice in the Buddhist Tradition

Published by Windhorse Publications
11 Park Road
Birmingham
B13 8AB

© Subhuti 1985 and 2001
First published by Rider, 1985
First Windhorse edition 2001

The right of Subhuti to be identified as the author
of this work has been asserted by him in accordance
with the Copyright, Designs and Patents Act 1988

Illustration on p.42 by Aloka
Illustration on p.44 by Simon Perry
Cover design Karmabandhu
Cover photo John Bigelow Taylor
Printed by Interprint Ltd, Marsa, Malta

A catalogue record for this book is available from the British Library

ISBN 1 899579 36 2

The publishers acknowledge with gratitude permission to quote from
the following: p.54: Bhikkhu Nanamoli (trans.) *The Path of Purification*,
Buddhist Publication Society, Kandy 1991

Since this work is intended for a general readership, Pali and Sanskrit
words have been transliterated without the diacritical marks which
would have been appropriate in a work of a more scholarly nature.

CONTENTS

LIST OF ILLUSTRATIONS

About the Author

Dharmachari Subhuti was born Alex Kennedy, in Chatham, England, in 1947. He became a member of the Western Buddhist Order in 1973 and has been involved in teaching, writing, and working in this context ever since.

Among other things, Subhuti established the London Buddhist Centre, a major urban centre for teaching meditation and Buddhism, as well as the Guhyaloka Retreat Centre in Spain. He has written a number of other books concerned with the development of Buddhism in the West. As one of those responsible for the induction of the Western Buddhist Order's new members, he developed and for some years directed the 'training process' for men preparing to join the Order.

He is Chairman of the eight-person college that constitutes the headship of the Western Buddhist Order now that its founder, Sangharakshita, has stepped down from official responsibilities. Subhuti travels widely, spending part of each year in India, and is much in demand as a speaker and study leader.

Preface

I wrote *The Buddhist Vision* during the winter of 1984, while staying on the Greek island of Skopelos in the North Aegean Sea. The sun was sinking low when my friend and I arrived at the remote bay where we were to pass the four months set aside for writing. I had stayed here three years before, writing another book, and I knew just what I had to do on arrival so as to inaugurate my work. I had to climb alone to the top of a small hill near our house to watch the deep red ball of the sun dip behind the distant mainland coast, the mountains of Greece, abode of the gods and muses, a jagged purple outline on the horizon. As I made my way up through the heavy-scented Mediterranean pines and the prickly holm-oaks, past the Cyclopean walls of an ancient acropolis, I heard a rustling in the undergrowth and an angry screeching. In a tangle of thorn-bushes thrashed a large long-eared owl, caught by its tail feathers. As I approached it shrank back from me, hissing with terrified fury. With a long stick, I cautiously prised apart the branches that trapped it and in an instant it flew off into the gathering dusk. Two or three times over the next weeks, that owl (or one very like it) would accompany me as I walked through the olive groves, flying away before me, then perching on a branch a few yards ahead, waiting for me to catch up.

Whether or not these auspices did indicate that the bird of Wisdom had been released from the thicket of confusion, I generally wrote in a very inspired mood. Every day I was practising meditation, contemplating especially the figure of Manjushri, the embodiment of ultimate wisdom, and this would give me the perspective for the day's work. The act of writing was in itself a meditation: a deep reflection on the themes I was trying to communicate. I had to find my way closer to the heart of Buddhism and apprehend the Buddha's message more directly for myself. In many cases I felt I understood things for the first time as I wrote about them, although I had learned them many years earlier and even taught them many times to others. Over the weeks of effort I felt more and more convinced of the essential truth of the Dharma, the Buddha's teaching, and a strong and growing desire, almost overpowering at times, to make it known to others. Naturally, this fervour was sometimes a little hard to live with, not merely for my companion but for myself, and I had to struggle with the extreme discrepancy between my spiritual vision and rational understanding on the one hand and the actual state of my being on the other. But this is the stuff of spiritual life, the purificatory tension between the ideal and the real.

This intense and exalted mood perhaps explains the tone of my book, which I am told is unambiguously convinced and committed – although inevitably in the end the product could not live up to my own high expectations and is but a modest achievement. The book emerged out of my attempts to communicate the Dharma over some ten years, especially to those who knew little or nothing about it, principally through courses of six or ten classes, given once a week at urban Buddhist centres, mainly in London, or during one-week residential courses held at various Buddhist retreat centres in England. All these courses were sponsored by the Friends of the Western Buddhist Order, the new Buddhist movement founded by my teacher, Urgyen Sangharakshita, in London in 1967, and run by members of the Western Buddhist Order, which Sangharakshita initiated in 1968 and to which I belong. In conducting courses over these years I had developed a presentation that seemed to appeal to a wide range of people and that gave me scope to talk about everything that I wanted to communicate. This book is closely based on those courses.

People who come to learn about Buddhism at a Buddhist centre run by members of a Buddhist order are almost always considering that they might become Buddhists themselves or at least that Buddhism might play some active part in their own lives. Idle curiosity or academic interest do not usually lead one to step through the door of a Buddhist centre. I therefore presented my courses very much as one committed to the Buddhist way of life, offering it to others as a path that they too might want to follow. In a certain sense my approach was unashamedly 'missionary' – it was my hope that people would respond to the Buddha's message through my words by applying it to their experience and even by committing themselves to it for the rest of their lives. I believed that if I was able to show people what in Buddhism had led me to dedicate my life as a disciple of the Buddha, some would want to do the same. This book, then, is the record of my attempt up to that time to communicate what inspired me to become a Buddhist.

The tone of my book emerged from my desire to share my own conviction. But what of the content? Any book that purports to communicate the Buddhist vision of existence must be selective, since the total Buddhist tradition contains an unimaginably vast array of teachings. Two-and-a-half millennia have passed since the Buddha himself lived, and what he taught has been evolved by countless successors to suit many different temperaments and cultures. Each land where Buddhism has flourished has its own distinctive forms – indeed, each will often be host to a number of schools and traditions. Most modern presentations of Buddhism are based on one or other Asian school. My own teacher, Urgyen Sangharakshita, has taken a different approach. He was born and brought up in England, and spent some twenty years in India as a Buddhist monk, where he had direct experience of several major traditions before returning to England to teach the Dharma. He always considered himself to be first and foremost just a Buddhist, drawing on the entire tradition for his inspiration rather than any one particular school. He has responded to the spiritual needs of his disciples with whatever teachings and practices seemed appropriate, no matter what their provenance, so long as they conform to the basic principles of the Dharma. This book is based mainly in his presentation.

Much of what I discuss will be familiar to Buddhists of all schools, although I have emphasized strongly a perspective that is not fully shared by one major school of Buddhism, the Theravada of South-East Asia. All the rest – the Mahayana schools – accept the rich imaginative realms of the Bodhisattva Ideal, which is an important element in this work. Since mine is an attempt to communicate the living spirit of Buddhism, rather than a source-book of facts, I have not shown the affiliation of each and every teaching or given alternative renderings and readings. I fully accept that the Buddhist vision could be unfolded in quite different, and equally valid, ways. I do not pretend to a definitive and uniquely correct presentation. Not every Buddhist might agree with the selection I have made or the interpretation I have given – although I would be surprised if they quarrelled with the broad picture. What I have done, however, is surely not unusual. Although all Buddhists may see the same Buddhist vision, we each see it from our own point of view and tell it in our own words. We may aspire to let that vision live for itself in the hearts of our hearers, but in trying to bring that about we must select and craft. This is my attempt to communicate the Buddhist vision, based on my own understanding and experience in the light of what I have learned from my teacher. I hope it will be a useful introduction for others.

Until the twentieth century, Buddhism was practised almost entirely by Asians within Asian cultures. It has therefore spoken the languages, literal and metaphorical, of those cultures. The images and metaphors, symbols and myths, references and allusions, the casts of thought and styles of expression, the concerns and issues dealt with, are all particular to various Asian societies and civilizations – each of course often very different from the others. The fundamental message of the Dharma is universal, but its expression must always be culturally specific. Buddhism has now come to the West, and even in its former Asian heartlands it encounters very different worlds. It must therefore respond to these new worlds in new ways. We who are among the first generations of Western Buddhists have the difficult task of understanding Buddhism through forms that are largely determined by Asian cultures of the past and then putting it into practice within our own culture. We are all of us, perforce, translators, both in our own understanding and in our communication of what we have learned to others.

In this book I have taken an image as my framework – or rather a complex of images. Those images are unmistakably Asian. However, it has seemed to me that the combination of words and images is uniquely powerful and that we must come to terms with the images, absorbing them into our own imaginative vocabulary. Cultures are porous and are capable of making once alien influences entirely their own – after all, the images of Christianity were once Eastern and alien. This process, however, takes time and these are early days. I have therefore attempted to assimilate the images as much as I can by explaining them in terms that I think will seem familiar to Westerners, whilst being true to the Dharma. I have especially used a number of concepts I have learned from my teacher that derive from Western usage but that seem to convey very adequately the meaning of certain Buddhist ideas. The three principal ideas of this kind, on which I depend quite heavily, are evolution lower and higher, individuality, and the creative and reactive mind. I am quite aware that these do not directly translate any terms found in traditional Buddhist texts. They are interpretive. None the less they do quite closely communicate the essential meaning of some traditional concepts. For instance, the notion of evolution that is so familiar in modern discourse because of the use it has been put to in the sciences is very helpful in expounding the path of Buddhism. And metaphors of growth and development are explicitly and significantly used many times in texts that almost certainly derive directly from the Buddha. I have not argued the case for these terms in this work, but it is not hard to see how they do relate to traditional expositions.

Given that the book emerged out of my teaching newcomers at Buddhist centres run by the Friends of the Western Buddhist Order, it introduces Buddhism from the point of view from which we in that spiritual movement commonly understand it. It will therefore be useful to those who are beginning to involve themselves in our spiritual community, since many of the practices and teachings of that community are described and some of its institutions are implied. It is of course fully possible to practise Buddhism outside our fellowship, and I hope that what I have written will be relevant to those who are following a spiritual path within other contexts, whether Buddhist or not, or without any context at all.

I wrote this book sixteen years ago and much has changed since then. The world is a very different one – after all, it was then still dominated by the confrontation between Communism and Capitalism, now seeming but a distant memory. Buddhism in the West has developed much further in this time, both in the Friends of the Western Buddhist Order and outside it, so the ways in which the Dharma is presented have also changed. Finally, I am not quite the same person I was then. I have a great deal more experience of teaching the Dharma and I have thought about it and practised it for longer – and I hope more deeply. If I were to try to communicate the

Buddhist vision now I would probably do it in a very different way. However, I still stand by what I wrote then and consider it to communicate what needs to be said. Since many people have told me that the first and second editions were useful to them, I am happy to see it republished in a third. I am especially happy because this new and revised edition has had to meet the exacting editorial standards of Windhorse Publications – I received little or no editorial comment from my previous publishers. The book has therefore been greatly improved. Dharmacharini Jnanasiddhi in particular has expended much effort in revising the work, virtually rewriting it in many places, giving it the attention for which I had neither the time nor the skill. I have been impressed by her clarity, sensitivity, and dedication. She has also been very patient, since at times it has been quite difficult to get hold of me.

The improvements to this new edition made by her are almost entirely in terms of style: clarifying presentation of ideas, improving sentence structure, unmixing metaphors. It has not been necessary to alter the ideas themselves at all in the main. The discerning among those who read the earlier editions may notice that one or two points have been left out or made rather differently – either because I thought the original presentation led to confusion or else because I have gone into the issues more fully in a more appropriate context. It is not, however, that I have changed my position on what I originally said.

I owe Jnanasiddhi a great debt of gratitude – the lion's share of work in preparing this edition has been hers and the credit for improvement is entirely hers. I would also like to thank all those at Windhorse Publications who have made republication possible and also Dharmachari Ratnaprabha for his very perspicacious comments. My principal gratitude, as ever, must go to my teacher, Urgyen Sangharakshita, from whom most of the teaching in this book originally came and who inspired and encouraged me to write it, uncomplainingly putting up with the inconvenience of my absence since I was his secretary at that time. There is finally someone else I want to thank, who played a crucial role. All those years ago when I did put some work into this book I lived on that beautiful Greek island accompanied by Dharmachari Jayadeva. While I sat, pen in hand (it was another world indeed), gazing out over the rocky bay to the wine-dark sea beyond, struggling to understand and communicate the Dharma, Jayadeva looked after my every need, whilst immersing himself in the classics of Ancient Greece. His stimulating companionship was an important basis for my work. I will not forget what he and many other people have given me that has made this publication possible.

Dharmachari Anagarika Subhuti
Sadhamma Pradip Retreat Centre
Bhaja
India
January 2001

1

Everyone Has a View

Everyone has a view, a perspective on existence. These views govern
the direction of our lives; they are often almost entirely unconscious,
forming a substructure to our minds, made up of unthinking
assumptions about ourselves and our world. Though we may be
unaware of our views and may never give them articulate expression, nevertheless, in everything we do and say, we betray our basic
perspectives. It might even be said that we *are* our views. Our views
may be self-contradictory, unfounded, untrue, but because we are so
closely identified with them we may never see them for what they
are.

Views range from the most casual opinions about everyday matters
to theories about ultimate metaphysical issues. At bottom, everyone's system of values is founded upon some view about the purpose
of life, however vague, inarticulate, or inconsistent; for example, we
consider life to be the survival of the fittest, or a test for a higher life
to come, or simply without any point at all. Usually, our views
remain a more or less loosely associated jumble of assumptions,
prejudices, opinions, and beliefs; occasionally they may be elabo-
rated into complex and dazzling philosophies.

Even when built up in this way into finely-spun structures of
thought, the basis of our views is deeper than thought. Our most
fundamental views are not so much concepts – though they may find
conceptual expression – as powerful myths that give form to our
desires and passions: myths such as Aryan supremacy, or of the
historical process inevitably leading to the perfect society, or of the

redemption of man by a saviour god. 'Myth' here does not mean a mere legend or fiction but an archetypal patterning of the psyche that shapes reason and emotion into a whole, thrusting in a single direction. It is these myths, which may be in contradiction to each other, together with the whole mass of our views, that move us.

Broadly, views are acquired in two ways: either we generate them for ourselves or we inherit them from the culture that surrounds us. The acquisition is usually unconscious and we exercise little discrimination in what we allow to structure our minds and lives. The views we develop for ourselves are often but rationalizations by which we provide ourselves with reasons for following our desires. Those we inherit from others are often picked up, partly from a felt need to conform to the views of our families, friends, and the social groups within which we live, and partly because they suit our wants. We are being fed with views all the time: by our educational institutions, mass media, and our everyday contacts. The very shapes of our houses and manner of our dress affect the way we see the world.

We may pick up views indiscriminately; however, once adopted, they can have a very strong influence upon the whole course of our lives and be hard to shake off. Having given shape to our emotions and thoughts, they mould our actions. We order the world in conformity with our longings, and then we live in the world that we have ourselves created. Clearly, the views we hold have consequences for us, either good or bad. They may lead us into everrecurring cycles of confusion and pain, or they may give rise to greater freedom and happiness. It is of the greatest importance that we clarify our minds and distinguish those views that are wholesome and helpful from those that are diseased and harmful, since our very lives depend upon it.

Such a clarification of our mental states requires intensive selfexamination. We need to learn to be aware of our thoughts and motives; to see what it is that influences us and to what end. We then must begin to take responsibility for our own views, to see what emotions underlie them and where they tend to lead us. Thus far, the work is negative and consists largely in clearing away confusion. But how *shall* we see the world? – that is the question that now confronts us.

Choosing a View

Again we have basically two choices. We can either try to develop for ourselves a more comprehensive and satisfying view of things, or we can open ourselves to the influence of one that is already developed. Both options have their attendant dangers and difficulties. We may be deceived by ourselves in the first case and by others in the second. Both may have either a successful or a disastrous outcome. It is, however, to the guidance of others that we must, almost inevitably, turn. Unless we cut ourselves off from human society altogether (which is almost impossible to do today, even were it desirable), we must always be under some cultural influence from which it will be hard to disentangle ourselves. Besides, if others have, with great effort perhaps, and even suffering, managed to achieve a breadth of view far greater than our own, we would be foolish not to allow ourselves to be taught by them. Our own efforts would be greatly accelerated if we, wisely and with circumspection, let ourselves be influenced by the most enriching views in our human culture.

Our own times are probably unprecedented in the diversity of views of life available to us. In the West, our traditional Christian-based culture is still extant, though now much on the defensive, and there is the new 'consumer culture', with its instant material satisfactions, which finds more and more adherents the world over. Besides these, a vast range of 'alternative' views is developing, drawn from Eastern religion and Western science, psychology and philosophy, or various combinations of these. Among all these views we must choose what influences we want. But how can we evaluate? Would not our evaluation itself be based upon a view? Are we not simply predisposed to select what most suits our own immediate desires, for better or worse?

How then can we evaluate values? We will find we are thrown back on our own experience – but our own experience carefully and critically examined. To begin with, we must be sure that we have correctly understood the view we are investigating and that we are not prematurely judging it in the light of our preconceptions about it. That done, we can ask ourselves whether or not it makes reasoned sense; whether the view is self-consistent; and whether it conforms to experience. Then we can try to see what the likely consequences of that view might be if put into practice. We can examine the lives of those of its adherents we might encounter. We can even experiment to see what its effects are within our own lives.

Not only can we make a very cool and reasoned examination, but we must also take into account our own immediate responses to the view. Here we must, of course, be self-critical, distinguishing our own superficial partialities from a genuine intuition. If we are healthy and straightforward, we will find that some views seem to constrict and confine us, as if we cannot think and feel at our fullest within them. Such views are too narrow to do justice to our potential as human beings. Other views, we will find, seem dark and twisted, distorting our natures into bizarre and unnatural shapes. Others again seem to lighten our hearts, open up our minds, and give us room to expand and breathe new air. They reveal vistas of limitless horizons and undreamt-of possibilities towards which we feel irresistibly drawn.

The evaluative criterion is therefore within our own experience. If we know ourselves well enough and are sincere in our enquiry, we will find that we recognize an increase in genuine happiness, friendliness, and mental clarity from some views, and of suffering, alienation, and confusion from others. We can see what views tend to the former and what to the latter. Those that tend to produce more positive and wholesome states are, in Buddhist terms, 'right views', and those that engender negative states are 'wrong views'.

The Buddhist View

The view that is to be presented in this book is a Buddhist view of life, and it is upon the above criterion that it asks to be evaluated. It offers itself as a way of viewing life that will help the individual to become happier, to experience greater harmony with others, and to see things with a purer understanding. In essence, this is Buddhism: a view of the infinite possibilities of human development. No ceiling confines us; there is, for Buddhism, no God for ever above and beyond man's reach. We may, if we choose to make the effort, break through barrier after barrier in our lives, in an unending spiral of intensifying happiness, wisdom, and love.

The founder of the Buddhist tradition – known by the title 'Buddha', meaning 'Awakened One' – required no blind belief from his disciples but expressly urged them to 'test my words as the goldsmith tests gold in the fire'. In the Buddhist texts we are again and again called upon to weigh up what we hear before we place any reliance upon it. We will then approach this Buddhist view wide awake, responsibly, separating our own thoughts and feelings from the mass of our inherited assumptions. We should be careful neither to accept blindly and uncritically nor to reject through prejudice. After listening to the view carefully and sympathetically, we can evaluate it in the light of our own reason, intuition, and experience.

Essential as this initial appraisal is, it is only the first step. Critical evaluation and intellectual assent are not enough, for Buddhism demands action of its followers. They must put it into practice, act upon it, and make it their own. Yet even this is not enough. The Buddhist view may enable one to cultivate higher and nobler states of mind and to function more and more beneficially, but still, at this stage, it is not something one sees directly for oneself. It is reasonable, intuitively one responds to it, and all experience bears it out, but it is still, as it were, an influence from outside. The ultimate aim of the Buddhist view is to produce in those who respond to it a corresponding *vision* so that they see for themselves, by direct experience, the truth of that view. In a sense, then, one no longer has a view at all, for view has been replaced by direct vision.

For Buddhism, therefore, the final criterion for evaluating views is whether or not they lead to the transcendence of views, that is, to vision. Wrong views distort and stunt the lives of those who hold them, right views promote the cultivation of more and more positive mental states, but, above all, followed to their conclusion they lead to that direct experience of the nature of things which is vision. Vision lies at the heart of Buddhism. For Buddhists, it was first seen by a historical individual, Siddhartha Gautama, some 2,500 years ago, in northern India. In attaining that vision he became the Buddha. He saw that every human being has the potential to become a Buddha, and he spent the remainder of his life trying to help others to realize his vision. The tradition we know as Buddhism is the continuing attempt of the Buddha's successors to attain that vision of reality themselves, and to communicate it to others.

The Buddha's vision is beyond particular time and place. It is as relevant today as at any point in the long history of the tradition that he founded. In accordance with the changing cultures and ages within which it has been conveyed, it has been constantly renewed and re-expressed. The tradition is a rich treasury of the many forms that its communication has taken. Each of these forms has had its own power to move us to make profound changes in ourselves and our world.

Our own times are characterized by a disintegration of common values. We are faced with a melting-pot of views about which there is no general agreement. An increasingly prevalent view is the materialist one. The supernatural and the other-worldly, heaven and hell, or other possible dimensions of being, play little part in the conscious attitude of most people today. No doubt much superstition and unreason has been cleared away, but we are left with drastically limited horizons. It is a flat, one-dimensional world in which we live out our brief span between birth and death. Much of our time is taken up with elaborate housekeeping and the business of physical survival, albeit in ever-increasing comfort and convenience, at least in the West. Whatever time is left we devote to entertainment. To those who feel that such a view of life leaves something in them unanswered, this Buddhist vision is offered.

2

A Vision of Existence

The Buddha's Vision

The ascertainable historical facts of the Buddha's life provide but a bare outline. We know that he was born Siddhartha Gautama, in the sixth century BCE, at Lumbini on the modern Indo-Nepalese border. His father was a leading nobleman (sometimes, it is said, the head) of a prosperous warrior clan, the Shakyans. His mother died a few days after his birth and he was nurtured by his aunt. He was married to a cousin at an early age and had by her a son, Rahula. He underwent, in his early manhood, a deep spiritual crisis which he later spoke of in these terms:

> And I too, before awakening, being liable to birth because of self,
> sought what was likewise liable to birth; being liable to ageing,
> disease, dying, sorrow, and impurity sought what was likewise
> liable to ageing, disease, dying, sorrow, and impurity. Then it
> occurred to me, 'Why do I, being liable to all these things myself,
> seek after them? Why don't I, liable as I am to birth, ageing, decay,
> dying, sorrow, and impurity, seek the unborn, the unageing, the
> undecaying, the undying, the sorrowless, the pure, the uttermost
> security from the bonds – Nirvana?'*

Siddhartha Gautama felt a deep revulsion for the emptiness of his life as a prosperous citizen and, leaving home in accordance with the

* *Ariyapariyesana Sutta, Majjhima-Nikaya i.163*

practice of the times, took up the life of a wandering seeker after truth. After studying under various teachers from whom he failed to gain effective guidance, and after practising austerities for a number of years, he decided to make his effort, on his own, by the path of meditation. Beneath a peepul tree at what is now Bodh Gaya, he gained Enlightenment and became a Buddha.

We are told that, after his Enlightenment, he could not at first see any way to communicate his experience, the gap between his own Enlightened mind and that of the rest of humanity being, in a sense, infinite. Yet the very essence of his experience was a deep feeling of compassion for every living creature. He knew that his vision would remove for ever all their sufferings if only they could perceive its full depth and splendour. He now saw, in imagination, the whole of humanity like lotus plants growing in a vast lake. Some were buried deep in the mud at the bottom of the lake; some pushed their buds up through the water; whilst others stood clear of the water, their petals beginning to open to the radiance of the sun. So beings were, he saw, in different stages of development. There were some whose hearts were already ripe for his teaching and others, again, whom he must encourage to mature until they could absorb the full experience of Enlightenment. For the remainder of his life he devoted himself solely to this task, and with great skill and unfailing patience he developed a whole system of teaching to suit all temperaments and levels of development. According to tradition, many of his immediate disciples did gain Enlightenment and, throughout the ages, many more have done so under his inspiration. For 2,500 years Buddhism has retained within itself, despite decay and atrophy in some of its institutional forms, a living tradition of direct spiritual experience stretching back to the Buddha himself.

What was the Buddha's vision of existence? Both the vision itself and the attempt to communicate it to others, by whatsoever means, are known to Buddhists as the Dharma. This is a Sanskrit word (in Pali, another important language of early Buddhism, it is *Dhamma*) with a number of complex meanings. For present purposes, Dharma means the Truth as experienced by the Buddha and as taught by him. This is a key word in Buddhism, best left untranslated. It is as the Dharma that Buddhists speak of Buddhism, and they themselves are really better referred to as 'followers of the Dharma'.

Our question, then, becomes, 'What is the Dharma?' In a sense, of course, it is not possible to say. The Dharma cannot be known by the intellect alone; it must be experienced, face to face. Yet expression of the experience in conceptual terms may help us to gain, at least, a rational understanding of its scope. We can also use symbols and images to stir in us the deeper faculty of imagination and to help us appreciate something of the beauty and range of the Buddha's insight. In this book we will be using a blend of both concepts and images to convey a general account of the Dharma. We will be examining, primarily, three great symbols, or rather groups of symbols: the Wheel of Life, the Spiral Path, and the Mandala of the Five Buddhas. These will form the framework of our exposition. First of all, however, it is necessary to explain some basic principles of the Dharma.

The Nature of Things
The main conceptual formula used by the Buddha to convey his vision is known as the 'principle of universal conditionality' or, more strictly, though less intelligibly, the 'law of conditioned co-production':

> This being, that becomes; from the arising of this, that arises; this
> not being, that does not become; from the ceasing of this, that
> ceases.

These words are deceptively easy to comprehend with the intellect, yet they contain a depth of meaning that few attain. They teach us that the entire universe is made up of processes, each of which arises in dependence on a network of conditions. When the conditions that have brought about any particular process are no longer present, it ceases. Each process, itself the product of conditions, in its turn conditions new processes. The Buddha saw everything, both in man and in the world, as a complex of these interrelated processes. Life is a ceaseless swirl of motion. Nothing remains still for a single instant: either it is forming or decaying. What we call 'things' are, in reality, processes. The world appears to us as if it consisted of solid, stable entities, virtually permanent and unchanging. This way of seeing things is necessary for everyday practical purposes but we proceed to turn practical convenience into rigid belief and behave in the world as if we, and it, were fixed, everlasting entities. But everything, human beings included, is a process and, though there may be continuity within that ever-changing process, there is nothing that is eternally stable.

From one point of view the impermanent nature of conditioned things is horrifying. It means we can never wholly rely or depend on anything conditioned, because whatever we depend on is liable to inevitable decay. Material objects can be lost, stolen, or broken. People are subject to shifting moods and will themselves, at some point, die. Nothing in the phenomenal universe is ultimately substantial. There is nothing that can, as it were, take the full weight of our reliance. If we do build ourselves upon things that are conditioned, we are doomed, sooner or later, to experience frustration and pain.

The fact of impermanence has, however, another side to it. It means that everything must change and, if it must do so, it may change for the better; for the flow of conditioned processes may function in two different ways: it may, on the one hand, form a continuous oscillation, an ebb and flow of generation and decay, or, on the other, it may move in a mounting curve of increasing development. It may function in cycles, going round and round like a wheel, or wind higher and higher in the manner of a spiral. Since we are ourselves conditioned processes, then we, too, may function in the cyclic or the spiral fashion.

In the cyclic kind of conditionality the play of conditions brings elements together for a while to form, say, a stone, a tree, or a horse. Sooner or later, conditions alter and the cohesion ceases. So growth and decay follow each other inexorably. Though vast planets and organisms of astonishing complexity may be produced, sooner or later decay will set in and they will be scattered. This kind of conditionality is mechanical; once conditions are established, the consequence follows automatically just as does the turning of a clockwork motor from the winding of the spring. It is cyclic in that, though there is a rise, it is a rise that falls again. Like a great wheel the chain of conditions rolls around. Fixed at the hub, it cannot move beyond its own circumference. Nothing new has come into being, only infinite rearrangements of the old.

Much of our own functioning is of this kind. Not only are our bodily processes governed by the cyclic type of conditionality, but so is much of our mental activity. We think, speak, and act as the product of a complex of conditions: physical, biological, and social. We are largely what our environment has made us. In fact, much of our behaviour, though we like to think otherwise, is explicable in terms of a stimulus–response model of Pavlovian simplicity: we simply react to things around us with little self-awareness. This type of mental functioning has been termed the 'reactive mind'.

The workings of the reactive mind do not account for all human behaviour. There is yet another way in which we can operate: by means of the 'creative mind'. This kind of mental functioning is characterized by ever-increasing *quality*, in accordance with the spiral type of conditionality. Rather than operating in cycles, the chain of conditions rises by successive augmentation, gaining in quality at each new level. Each factor surpasses the preceding one and is surpassed by the one that follows it. Each forms the basis for, but does not limit, the stage that grows out of it. When we function in this spiral-like way, we are creative. We take the conditions as presented to us – the world around us, our own feelings and emotions – and we invest them with some new value drawn from our own depths. A clear example of this spiral or creative mind is seen in the work of the artist. A sculptor, for instance, takes raw stone and the head of his subject as his conditions and produces a bust that is not merely a good likeness, displaying his technical skill, but also, at its best, conveys a deeper insight into the nature of man. Not only has there been a material change in the block of stone but also a qualitative change in the mind of the artist which he has managed to convey to his sculpture.

The creative mind is by no means the exclusive property of the artist. Whenever we transcend our conditioning to any extent, we act creatively. Whenever, for instance, we are activated by genuine altruism or generosity, whenever we bring new harmony and clarity into the situations in which we find ourselves, then we act creatively. Creative behaviour is characterized by self-awareness, inspired spontaneity, and positive experiences like friendliness, happiness, and vigour. It is a continuous transcending of the boundaries of our conditioning at higher and higher levels.

The choice between reactive and creative behaviour faces us at every moment. We can either continue the cycle of our reactions or, by cultivating self-awareness, we can gradually establish a flow of creativity. The Dharma encourages us to make that transition from the reactive to the creative mind. It shows us that to function reactively is to experience continuous frustration and pain, while the creative leads to ever-increasing happiness and fulfilment.

The reactive mind is represented by the symbol of the Wheel, the creative by the Spiral. The Wheel and the Spiral exist in different degrees in different people. Some make no effort to cultivate higher states within themselves. Their minds are dominated by the cyclic kind of conditionality, by the Wheel. Others do make some effort although they still function reactively to a greater or lesser extent. These belong partly to the Wheel and partly to the Spiral. Finally, there are beings whose lives are a continuous process of creative expansion. They are wholly of the Spiral. Buddhahood is the point at which the spiral process separates itself completely from the cyclic and there is nothing but creativity.

From those who are making their first faltering steps on the Spiral to those who are on the threshold of Buddhahood stretches the path of human development. Those treading that path must be constantly watchful to allow the creative mind within them to unfold and to keep at bay the reactive mind. Time and again, they will falter and, over and over, they must renew their efforts. Midway on that path there is, however, a vital point of transition. It is the point at which the Spiral within one just outweighs the Wheel. It is called the point of 'Stream Entry' because it is where one enters the stream that inevitably leads beyond the Wheel towards Buddhahood. It is a point of no return because, although the reactive still functions within, it can never possess one wholly again and one cannot but go forward on the path. Up to that point, one can slip back, even give up the attempt altogether. The point of Stream Entry is an important intermediate goal for Buddhists because it is only from that point onwards that progress is assured.

Buddhism, then, holds up this vision of the universe as a process with two tendencies: the reactive and the creative. It shows us that human beings may ascend a path of development that stretches from the Wheel to the point of Buddhahood, at which the Spiral unfolds free from all cyclic tendencies whatsoever. Buddhism not only has a vision of human potential, but also offers guidance on the path: it describes the stages along the way and it has a vast treasury of methods that help us to tread it.

The Threefold Path: Morality, Meditation, and Wisdom

One of the most basic teachings of early Buddhism divides the path into three successive stages, and shows the work to be done at each. The 'Threefold Path' consists of the stages of morality, meditation, and wisdom. We will be exploring each of these in later chapters of this book, so only a preliminary account is necessary at this point.

When we first set our feet upon the path, there is a vast gulf between our higher aspiration and our everyday behaviour. However sincerely we want to cultivate creative states of mind, our actions and our way of life are little different from those of anyone else. Sometimes our work and the people we are closest to do not assist our efforts. It may even be that our friends and relations actively deride our interest in developing ourselves. We must, therefore, examine our lives to see what does and what does not contribute to our development. Not only may our way of life be hindering us to an extent, but our own behaviour may be working against our desire to grow. We may be acting so as to harm others, whether in great or small ways. In acting thus, we confirm the negative tendencies in our mind that keep the Wheel spinning. Such behaviour is defined as *unethical* in Buddhism, because it binds us more and more tightly to the reactive mode of conditionality. So we begin our higher development by bringing our way of life into harmony with our pursuit of the path, that is, by examining and improving our morality.

As aids to the cultivation of morality, Buddhist tradition gives various lists of precepts. Precepts are not commandments imposed upon us by an external authority. They are a description of the behaviour of one who is completely creative, and they act as guidelines by which we may test and work upon our own actions. The commonest set of precepts is fivefold and describes what one who is perfectly creative does *not* do. Each one is taken as a principle to underlie our actions as we tread the path:

> I undertake the training principle of abstaining from
>   harming living beings.
> I undertake the training principle of abstaining from
>   taking the not-given.
> I undertake the training principle of abstaining from
>   sexual misconduct.
> I undertake the training principle of abstaining from false speech.

> I undertake the training principle of abstaining from
> intoxicants that lead to heedlessness.

Once freed of the grosser unethical acts, and once one's way of living has begun to enhance development instead of detracting from it, one's mind will begin to settle and clear, for the consequence of a truly ethical life is mental lightness and ease. Now is the time to begin to work more directly upon the mind through meditation. In Buddhist terms, meditation is a way of raising the level of consciousness so as to experience an unceasing progression of positive states. Through meditation, one purifies the mind of all distraction, superficiality, and negative tendencies. It is usually practised systematically by sitting in a secluded place and carrying out a simple exercise. Two basic practices of this kind are common to many of the different schools of Buddhism. The first is known as the Mindfulness of Breathing, in which, in a number of stages, attention is concentrated more and more upon the breath as it passes in and out of the body. As we become skilled in the practice, the ceaseless chatter that usually dominates our minds gradually calms down, leaving a feeling of deep stillness and harmony that is intensely pleasurable. The mind is poised and clear, vividly aware without any object to be aware of.

The second, complementary, practice is called the Development of Loving-Kindness. One develops feelings of love and well-wishing towards oneself, first of all: then, stage by stage, towards a friend, a neutral person, an enemy, and finally one gradually expands one's feelings of love outwards to embrace all creatures in all the directions of space. As we persist regularly with the practice of meditation, we become more and more accomplished, becoming quite quickly absorbed in these lofty and joyous states. Eventually, not only will we be enjoying them at the time of meditation but all the time, whatever we are doing.

Once this degree of skill in meditation has been reached, the mind will be in a very elevated state. All subconscious energies will be resolved into consciousness, all rigidity and prejudice will be overcome, and fear, hatred, and craving will be suspended. For the time being we will not be experiencing any inner conflict and we will be free enough and concentrated enough to bring the full weight of our being to bear on comprehending the very nature of existence. So the stage of meditation provides the basis for the stage of wisdom.

This stage is characterized either by reflecting upon some saying of the Buddha's that sums up his insight, by contemplating some symbolic expression of his vision, or by any of a number of other methods. Eventually, breaking through from view to vision, we see things as they really are. The attainment of wisdom is not merely a process of understanding. Integral to the experience is a dissolving of the barriers between ourself and other beings. No longer are we exclusively bound up with self; rather, experiencing no essential difference between ourself and others, we feel unbounded love and compassion equally strongly for all beings. The understanding of wisdom and the fellow-feeling of compassion are but two aspects of the one experience of vision.

The arising of vision marks the point of Stream Entry, the point at which the spiral tendencies outweigh the cyclic. From here until the final extinction of all reactive, wheel-like currents within one, at Buddhahood, one must permeate with vision every part of one's life. Gradually, vision transforms and re-orders every level of one's being.

Buddhahood itself is not truly the end of the Path. In a sense, it is only the beginning, for it is at Buddhahood that one is completely free of all fetters, even the subtlest, tying one to the Wheel. Buddhahood is the point at which the Path passes completely beyond our comprehension. Our own most exalted moments provide but the palest analogies for the sublime progression that now ensues.

The picture we have given of the Threefold Path offers a glimpse of the stages through which we can ascend and the means by which we can travel. It is obviously a rather simplified picture. Few people's lives unfold in quite such an orderly manner; many people nowadays start their efforts on the Path with the practice of meditation before they have properly undertaken the stage of morality. It is also a picture from one particular viewpoint that stresses the individual's work to *change*. Taken by itself, it can make the following of the Spiral Path seem a rather isolated and self-concerned life. Far from this being the case, our interaction with other people and the deepening of our relationships with them is crucial to our development. Through our contact with those more advanced than ourselves we gain the inspiration and the understanding to progress. Through contact with our peers we gain stimulation and challenge, encouragement and criticism and, above all, that indispensable feeling of fellowship without which life is not truly human. In our contact with those less developed than we are, we learn to nurture and care for others. Other people prevent us from becoming lost in the fog of subjectivity where we see nothing but ourselves and our own needs. The Spiral Path could be seen as, essentially, consisting in the deepening of our friendship and love for others. The higher we climb on the Path, the more we will be able to enter into fellowship with others.

The Three Jewels of Buddhism

The ideal of friendship is of such centrality to Buddhists that, in its highest form, it becomes one of the three chief objects of veneration. These three, the 'Three Jewels', are the Buddha, Dharma, and Sangha. The Buddha is reverenced as the goal towards which all beings are moving and also as the historical individual, Siddhartha Gautama, the founder of the whole Buddhist tradition. The Dharma is both the Truth that the Buddha perceived and the Path that he set forth in his teachings. The Sangha is the spiritual community. These Three Jewels, or 'three most precious things', are the basis of Buddhism. What renders one a Buddhist is 'Going for Refuge to the Three Jewels': making a personal commitment to realizing in our own lives the ideals that the Three Jewels represent.

The spiritual community or Sangha, then, is one of the foundations of Buddhism. At its highest level it is the indescribable accord that exists between the spiritually attained – those who have reached or surpassed Stream Entry. Sharing the same creative vision and yet each a unique expression of it, they are the sublime example of harmony. Complete trust and perfect understanding mark their relations with one another. In Buddhist scriptures there are many very moving examples of this type of love and sympathy existing between the various members of the Buddha's company.

On a lower level, the sangha refers to the community of all those who have gone for Refuge to the Three Jewels. They all experience the Buddha's vision as the ultimate meaning of their lives and they are all committed to its realization. Since the sangha at this level includes both those who have, and those who have not, passed the point of no return, many of its members are subject to the buffetings of the still-unquieted reactive mind. The bond between them may therefore be of a more fragile kind, but it is none the less deep and heartfelt. Having expressed one's Going for Refuge to the Three Jewels in a simple ceremony, one is then a member of a sangha: a body of men and women, devoted to the Three Jewels, who form a spiritual community (though not necessarily living together under one roof). The word sangha is sometimes used in a more restricted sense to refer to monks and nuns alone, but membership of the sangha – Going for Refuge to the Three Jewels – does not enjoin the following of any particular way of life, except that it should be one that genuinely helps the individual to grow. Members of the sangha have a variety of lifestyles; for instance, some live in residential communities, often for either men or women, monastic or otherwise; others will be married and have families; still others may live on their own. What they have in common is not their lifestyle but their common commitment to the Buddha's vision. That common vision makes the sangha potentially a very powerful force for the transformation of the world.

The sangha, on all its levels, makes up the Buddhist community and, whenever time and circumstances will permit, it manifests a whole culture that has the treading of the Path as its basis. Institutions and practices, customs and ceremonies, arts and crafts: a whole way of life for men and women at all stages on the Path and of all temperaments and talents gradually evolves to help them in their development. Such Buddhist cultures have flourished at many times and in many different forms in the East with great beauty and richness. A Buddhist way of life is beginning to emerge here in the West, unique in its manifestations yet based upon the same principles as those of the past.

An Evolution of Consciousness
So far I have presented the Buddhist vision of existence in terms derived from traditional expositions of the Dharma. But there are currents in Western thought that suggest close analogies to the Dharma and that can certainly be broadened to convey its message. For instance, a number of modern thinkers have suggested that the concept of evolution explains more than just the origins of species. There are still some people who contend that the world was created by God with all the species now on earth in the form we find them. These 'creationists' are few, however, and it is now widely accepted

that all existing life-forms on the planet evolved from simple organisms over very long periods of time. That much seems to be more or less beyond controversy. The manner by which that evolution took place is still an open debate. Whether the mechanism of evolution can be explained in terms of the adaptations of natural selection or by some higher order of meaning working itself out through the evolutionary process is, of course, of the greatest significance. For present purposes, however, we may confidently assert the generally accepted thesis that man has evolved from life-forms that are lower, in the sense that they are of far simpler biological structure, without entering the lists of the debate about how it happened.

It has often been pointed out that the concept of evolution can be used to describe many of the phenomena in our universe. Do galaxies and stars evolve in a similar way to the individual human being, from conception to adulthood? That whole evolutionary trend running through the universe seems to culminate in man, the most complex and adaptable form of which we have empirical evidence. But is the mature human being the final product of evolution?

Here, we need broader terms of enquiry for, so far, we have seen evolution as an increasing complexity of physical and biological organization, or what could be termed quantitative evolution. But when we look at mankind we see that human cultures too may be seen to be in a process of evolution or decay. Furthermore, when we look at individual men and women, we find that though they may share within broad limits a common physical form, they have very different psychological characteristics and are of varying aptitudes and abilities. We find that there are some who, for their intellectual penetration, creative genius, or nobility of heart, tower above their fellows. A rough hierarchy can be discerned of qualities and virtues – although it is not always easy, or even fruitful, to place anyone in their particular degree. Moreover, many of the great figures of human history, though they may have been born with uncommon gifts, have gone to considerable lengths to cultivate those talents and to improve themselves. They have, in Goethe's words, made something of themselves. Whatever excellence they have had in particular areas, beyond the rest of men, they owe to their own efforts – over and above the advantages conferred on them by nature or society. They could be said to have undertaken their own evolution beyond the stage of ordinary man. Could they point the way to the next phase of evolution?

Man appears as a kind of watershed in the evolutionary process; we are the product of biological evolution both in the sense of having a body that has evolved from lower life-forms over billions of years and in that it has, in its growth from zygote to mature adult, mirrored that evolution. Biological evolution, by whatever mechanism, can bring us thus far without any conscious intervention on our part. But, from this point on, we must make ourselves. This lower, purely biological, evolution prepares the basis for a development of a more qualitative nature; one that is not solely the development of more complex biological forms, but the development of higher and higher levels of consciousness.

The lower evolution consists in the elaboration of sense consciousness. From the rudimentary sentience of the most primitive single-celled organism up to the sophisticated sensory awareness of the higher animals, there is a change of degree only, not of kind. The world is perceived in greater depth and detail the higher up the evolutionary ladder we climb. But there are no persons or individuals to whom the perceptions belong or to whom they are attached. Perception is, as it were, part of the undifferentiated consciousness of nature; the individual organism has, as yet, no self-identity.

But, probably from the higher animals upwards, a new kind of consciousness gradually emerges: reflexive or self-consciousness – a consciousness that has the possibility of completion in man. The undifferentiated, primitive harmony of sense consciousness has been broken. These possessors of consciousness have now identified themselves; they are aware of their own awareness. As self-awareness matures, the individual – for such there now is – makes a fundamental split in experience, between what is himself or herself and what is other. From now on, the basic structure of perception is the differentiation of those elements of experience that belong to the individual and those that do not. Consciousness is polarized into self and other.

With this split, a whole new range of possibilities opens up: self-consciousness makes possible the infinite ascent of a higher evolution than the purely biological – and is also the progenitor of cruelty and greed unknown in nature. With this development we are barred from the perfect (albeit entirely without reflexive awareness) balance of nature, yet we are given the possibility of a new and far higher harmony in the full flowering of consciousness. It is, perhaps, the fruit of the Tree of the Knowledge of Good and Evil that Adam and Eve were forbidden to eat. It was for their disobedience and the ending of their primal innocence that they were banished from Eden. Buddhists, however, are strongly encouraged to eat of the fruit of the Tree and to go forth from Eden of their own agency without the need of angels with flaming swords. They are urged to take upon themselves their human destiny by following through to the full the implications of self-consciousness.

Self-consciousness has a number of different aspects. Memory is perhaps the most important, for to be self-conscious is to have a sense of an identity continuing from the past. From this awareness of ourself as having a history is derived an awareness of the relationship between actions and effects, of oneself as author of one's actions, and thus of responsibility for their consequences. Out of self-consciousness, there emerges our moral sense.

Imagination, too, is a part of self-consciousness. Imagination frees us from our immediate situation and allows us to rove unfettered through the many possibilities of existence. As memory gives us a past so imagination gives us a future. Not only do we remember but we can anticipate. We can set ourselves goals and aims, we can see ourselves other than we now are. In a sense, self-consciousness is itself an act of imagination because self-consciousness consists in being an object of one's own awareness, and yet we cannot literally perceive ourselves as an object.

Imagination is double-edged. As we will see in the following chapters, it gives rise to distortions and perversions of self-consciousness that lead up grotesque and terrifying evolutionary culs-de-sac. Yet it is through imagination that we can envision high ideals and soar to new heights of being. Imagination is the source of creativity and reveals to us the Spiral of higher evolution. When functioning in its purest form, imagination is the faculty whereby we apprehend spiritual truth.

Imagination allows us to enter into sympathetic communication with others. Having identified ourselves as centres of action and experience, we can now see that others also have selves. We are able to enter imaginatively into their lives and thus to understand and talk with them. This capacity for mutual understanding means that self-conscious beings may co-operate together both in the business of physical survival and, more especially, in the task of further, higher evolution. Mutual co-operation and communication are, indeed, among the hallmarks of a mature individuality.

With self-consciousness, then, comes individuality, self as distinct from other, subject from object. Up to that point, evolution has been a blind, unconscious process. It is whole groups and classes of living beings that evolve together, not particular individuals. With the dawning of individuality, evolution must be consciously undertaken. As individuals we become responsible for our own future growth and, without our own consistent effort, no natural forces will sweep us forward. No one can force us to evolve from this point, or do our growing for us, though others may be crucial guides and companions on the Path; as the Buddhist texts say, 'The Buddhas do but show the way.' No saviour can do one's growing for one. No guru, incarnation of God though he claims to be, can give one knowledge. It must be won by our own efforts with the inspiration and advice of those who have trodden the Path before us.

The full emergence and acceptance of our individuality is the first step in the development of our consciousness. To begin with, our sense of ourselves is often sketchy and incomplete. We are, as it were, amphibious, spending much of our time in the vast oceans of lower evolution and making a few, usually intellectual, forays on to the dry land of higher evolution. It is this transition that we must complete by drawing ourselves fully up on to the solid ground of self-awareness. What is involved is the fulfilling of our self-consciousness, bringing all aspects of being into awareness: physical, emotional, and intellectual.

The distinction between self and other, subject and object, has first to be firmly established. Then it must be transcended. The ascent of the Spiral Path draws the two poles of experience closer and closer together. For instance, our awareness of the beauty of an object draws us beyond the tight limits of our own selfhood in a kind of communion with the beautiful object. In profound thought – not compulsive intellection but 'man in his wholeness wholly attending' – we penetrate to a level of understanding deeper than our normal perception of the duality of subject and object. In meditation, our purified and sharpened concentration gives us access to dimensions in which consciousness is increasingly unified. In friendship, when

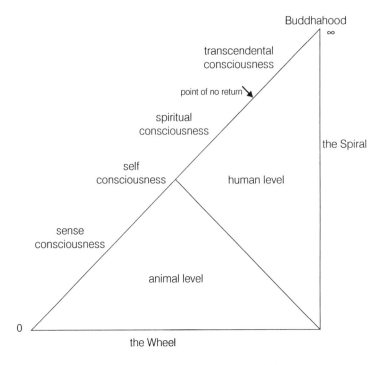

FIG 1. THE TRIANGLE OF THE EVOLUTION OF CONSCIOUSNESS

co-operating with others, working for them, communicating intensely with them, we forget ourselves in our concern for them and
gain access to a wider awareness.

The drawing together in our experience of subject and object and
the relaxing of the tension between them belongs to a new kind of
awareness: what might be termed spiritual consciousness. Level
upon level of ever more beautiful, joyous, and satisfying states of
mind rise up one above the other. But, though the tension between
self and other is being eased as they are drawn into greater harmony,
there is still that same fundamental split in the structure of our
perception. Spiritual consciousness must give way to something
more, something we could call transcendental consciousness, in
which the distinction between subject and object is finally dissolved.
At this level, consciousness is experienced in its wholeness as a total,
absolute awareness, completely free and unobstructed, luminous
and all-pervading.

It is hard for us to gain any understanding of what this state must be like. It is to be without a self as we ordinarily understand it but not to be immersed in the unconscious pre-selfhood of nature. Many interpreters of Buddhism have fallen into the trap of considering this transcendental consciousness to be a kind of ultimate blank – hardly a desirable goal for the whole of evolution. It is perhaps best – although, in a way, false or rather inadequate – to consider that, with transcendental consciousness, there is still, in some sense, a continuation of the Spiral Path but functioning in a way that for the present we cannot comprehend. All things are seen, as they are, in all their unique detail and all are pervaded by an overwhelming love and compassion. This Buddha-consciousness is freed from all suffering and knows only the 'Great Bliss' which, needless to say, in comparison makes our everyday happiness look like misery.

The process of evolution begins in the unconscious wholeness of nature that is broken by the dawning of self-awareness. The split is finally healed in the transcendental awareness of Buddhahood. As human beings we stand at the mid-point of the great evolutionary drama that begins with the single-celled organism and ends with the Buddha. We cannot go back into the innocent darkness of natural ignorance, and to remain suspended where we are is to experience alienation and frustration. We must push on, by our own individual efforts, with the help and guidance of friends and teachers, towards that goal of Buddhahood.

3

The Wheel and the Way

The Origins of the Wheel of Life

The origins of the Wheel of Life as a symbol of the Buddhist vision of mundane existence are to be found in the earliest phase of Indian Buddhism. One text, belonging to the important Sarvastivada School, gives an account of the Buddha himself instructing that the Wheel be painted at the gateway of every monastery, and detailing how it should be done.*

According to this text, Maudgalyayana, one of the Buddha's two foremost disciples, occasionally visited beings in all the different realms of existence. All the Buddhist traditions attest to his mastery of psychic powers, and this was but one of those abilities. He could see the beings in hell-like states or in heavenly worlds, and in all other possible phases of being. He could see what had brought them to that condition, what the imperfections and sufferings of each state might be, and where they led. He had, it seems, an extraordinary capacity to empathize with others, to see into their minds and their hearts, to feel their sufferings or joys, and to understand how they had come to be as they were.

With this ability to enter deeply into the lives of others, it is perhaps not surprising that Maudgalyayana was also able to communicate very effectively. The same text tells us that if any senior monk was having trouble with a disciple who was losing his inspiration he

---

* *Sahasodgata Avadana*, Divyavadana 21

would send him to Maudgalyayana who would 'exhort and teach him well' to such good effect that 'such dissatisfied monks would again lead the spiritual life with keen ardour, even distinguishing themselves with the higher attainments'. It seems that he had the power to reinvigorate flagging zeal by sharing his own deep insight into all the various conditions of existence.

So much in demand was he that he seemed to live surrounded by monks and nuns, laymen and laywomen. The Buddha, noticing this, commented that there were not enough people like Maudgalyayana to teach all those who needed him. He therefore proposed that a picture should be created to represent Maudgalyayana's teaching, and he instructed his followers to paint the Wheel of Life, depicting the different realms of existence and the processes that underlie them, at the entrance to every monastery, where a monk would be deputed to explain the imagery to visitors and novices.

This story is interesting from a number of points of view, not least because it shows the use of visual arts as a medium for teaching the Dharma in the very early years of Buddhism. (The source is a text thought to have been compiled some time in the first century BCE and almost certainly enshrining much earlier traditions.) Its chief interest lies in its spiritual message, however. Some may not find it easy to take literally the 'miraculous' element in the story. (Buddhism has always maintained that there is nothing miraculous about such matters, in the sense of a disruption of the laws of nature by a higher power. It considers, rather, that our faculties and powers are restricted by our limited point of view and that, if we expand our minds, we may be able to do things that now seem impossible.) Even if one cannot accept that Maudgalyayana literally visited those other dimensions of being by the exercise of his psychic powers, it is possible to see that he had some sort of visionary insight into other people's states of mind and the way they experience things, and that his vision was no mere theory. He knew these states for what they were, by his own immediate perception. The basis of this symbolic representation, the Wheel of Life, is direct experience. The image attempts to convey that insight in visual terms. We should always bear this in mind and try to stretch beyond the confines of the structure of the symbol to the transcendental vision that underlies it.

The other point of immediate interest in the story is the effect Maudgalyayana had on the dissatisfied disciples. Few who make some effort to tread the Path do not know moments when they feel no inspiration for any of the practices that will help them to grow. In those moments, in fact, they will probably feel little interest in the very idea of growth. It can all seem too much effort and struggle for little tangible result. At such moments, although we may be able to give a perfect account of Buddhist teaching and may be in full intellectual agreement with its conclusions, yet we have no zest for it. Emotional engagement is lacking and we feel little or no enthusiasm for the spiritual path. The world has become flat and two-dimensional and it is only in the little gratifications of everyday life that we can see any hope of happiness. Somehow, Maudgalyayana could rekindle the fires of inspiration in such cold ashes as these. Even from the scanty information in the story it is clear that he did not do so by giving a lucid, rational description of reality. Such a description might have roused the intellectual curiosity of some but it would hardly cause them to 'lead again the spiritual life with keen ardour' and even to distinguish themselves by the excellence of their attainments. He touched them in such a way that not only were their understandings deepened, but their hearts were moved. He appealed, in other words, to their imagination.

The Imaginal Faculty

The faculty of imagination accompanies the emergence of self-consciousness. At its most general, it is simply the capacity to bring to mind images of what is not actually present to the senses. This general definition covers anything from fantasies about food or sex through dreams of world domination to the sublime vision of the artist or mystic. Clearly, this imaginative capacity can be used mechanically to produce images in which we picture our egoistical desires in fantasy or what Freud termed 'hallucinatory wish-fulfilment'. Anyone who has tried to meditate will know how much of our mental activity is taken up with this kind of imagination, for one often experiences in learning to meditate a constant stream of fantasies before one can settle the mind to concentration. This kind of imaginative activity belongs to the reactive mind, to the Wheel.

Imagination, however, can also go way beyond this mechanical function; it also has a creative aspect through which we can unfold higher potentialities from within ourselves. The images perceived by this faculty, coming from our own depths, are projections of levels of consciousness beyond those we ordinarily experience. From another point of view, the creative imagination is the faculty with which we respond to a higher level of reality, to spiritual vision and truth. True works of art can have the effect of stirring our imaginations in this way. In this sense, the creative imagination is not dissimilar to the faculty of 'Imagination' referred to in the literary criticism of the English Romantics, especially Coleridge. The Imagination or the 'imaginal faculty' as a creative power of the human mind must be clearly distinguished from imagination as reactive fantasy.

Reason and Emotion Transcended

The imaginal faculty unites and transcends both thinking and feeling. In contrast, the psyche of many, if not most, people in modern, industrialized societies is deeply divided. Our intellectual faculties today in the West are to some extent differentiated and developed through education – although not necessarily to a very high degree at all. Our emotions are, however, woefully immature. It is as if modern man has two personalities: one on the surface that is capable of reason and fairly sophisticated intellectual comprehension, and the other a semiconscious or subconscious personality, consisting of immature, even infantile, emotions. A degree of alienation has developed between the two which usually leaves them, at some level within us, in conflict with each other. Because of this split, we have little conception of a process of understanding that is full of feeling, or of emotion that is suffused with intelligence. But the imaginal faculty is of this kind. It is a function of the whole, integrated personality. When the Imagination is alive in us, we are whole individuals, reaching beyond ourselves to fresh heights of consciousness. Sadly, we have no ready language with which to refer to such a capacity – and, lacking the words, it is hard for us to experience it. But the imaginal faculty is latent within us, as an ability to apprehend and appreciate higher dimensions of reality. Without such a faculty there could be no art, no true creativity, and certainly no Spiral Path. It is to this faculty that Maudgalyayana appealed, and it is because he did so that he had such success with those weary disciples.

The imaginal faculty, then, unites and transcends both emotion and thought. It unites them in so far as they no longer operate as autonomous sub-personalities within the overall person. They are but two aspects of one whole. They are transcended in that they are no longer 'thought' and 'emotion' as we normally know them. Thought as a component of the imaginal faculty is not merely the capacity to infer valid conclusions from given premises. It is the penetration and cognition of truth at higher levels. Emotion no longer consists of those crude and coarse outbursts and longings, often blind and impulsive, that characterize much of our emotional life. It is not negative and self-centred but positive and expansive, opening out beyond the tight confines of self-interest. It is the kind of inspired, uplifted, even exalted emotion that is part of aesthetic experience, as when we are deeply absorbed in music or wonder at the flaming tints of the setting sun. And, since it is united with understanding, it is suffused with sensitivity, awareness, and clarity.

Poetry can offer a clear example of this kind of integration. Schoolchildren are often asked to give a gloss on the meaning of a poem, but the best poems will never entirely reduce to conceptual analysis of this kind. There are levels and shades of meaning that are lost in translation to such reasoned prose. Yet something in us, at our best, understands what the poem says even if we cannot ever adequately expound or explain it. In these cases, the poet has managed to distil into lines of verse a perception of a higher level of truth than ordinary language can convey. If the poetry speaks to the imaginal faculty within us, which responds to beauty and to truth, our apprehension of its meaning is not one-sidedly cognitive. The sensuous qualities of the poem, the power of the images, flow of words, rhythm and rhyme, speak to our emotions. The meaning of the words and the symbolism of the images they conjure up appeal to our intellect. Here, in the imaginal faculty, thought and emotion are united and transcended.

At this point, it should be stressed that Buddhism does not undervalue reason, which is an essential attribute of human life and an indispensable tool of human growth. We need to be able to think clearly in ordering our worldly affairs, otherwise our decisions and predictions can only be based on guesswork and so-called intuition – often a very doubtful process amounting to little more than subjective prejudice. We need to be able to gather and examine evidence in order to draw reasonable conclusions from what we know. More than this, reason is essential to clarify the tangle of confused ideas that so often chokes our minds; those views, opinions, assumptions, and prejudices that we saw in Chapter 1 can have such a disastrous effect upon our lives. Much of our confusion arises because we have never examined the mass of our assumptions in the light of reason, away from inherited prejudices and emotional rationalizations. Through reason we can get a preliminary grasp of the Buddhist vision as it is conceptually formulated and we can investigate it to see whether it makes sense. Again, until we can establish a deeper contact with other people, reason is the common ground on the basis of which we can relate to one another. The person who is incapable of reason is still immersed in the half-light of instinctual feeling – reason, as has been said, distinguishes man from the animals.

Yet despite all this, the sphere of reason is strictly limited. Reason, as I am using the term here, is the faculty by which we order concepts and perceptions so that we can arrive at conclusions about our world. It is a function of our self-consciousness. Having split the world into what is self and what is other, we then divide what we regard as other into smaller and ever smaller units to which we can attach useful word labels, such as stone, tree, horse, etc.

These words allow us to hold in our minds, and to consider, the various objects to which they refer and to think about the constituents of our world and their interrelationships. We break up what is outside us into objects, and in doing so we unconsciously follow a set of rules that determine *how* we break it up. For instance, if a portion of what we perceive consistently exhibits the same characteristics over a period of time, we will automatically interpret it to be one object that is different from all others.

These rules are basic assumptions that we are not usually conscious of applying because they are buried deep in our language, in our culture, and in the very structure of our minds. Needless to say, we do not each of us determine for ourselves how we are going to see the world. We drink it in with our mother's milk. Reason, then, is part of the way in which we see the world. In Buddhist terms it is a function of a subject–object-dominated perception, or dividing the world into self and other, and is oriented to the material world.

The fact that reason rests upon such assumptions does not mean that it is an illusion. Within their own sphere these assumptions will yield valid conclusions that will enable us to function effectively in the world. Most of us would do well to *develop* this rational faculty further and to apply it more consistently and thoroughly. Problems arise only when we try to apply reason outside its own limits. Reason cannot comprehend the fundamental nature of things because reality lies beyond the framework of subject and object that, as the basis from which reason operates, we impose upon it. To be able to reason about our world we must reduce it to manageable order, but in reducing and simplifying we lose the indescribable complexity of things, their full richness and wonder. The ultimate nature of things is beyond the reach of reason.

The Role of Imagination

I have already suggested that ordinary reason cannot provide us with an understanding of an inspired poem, although it may give us a basis of understanding from which our Imagination can take flight. In the same way, a symbol or myth cannot be understood in its fullness by the use of the rational faculty, for a symbol may be at the same time one thing and its opposite – defying the law of non-contradiction! Reason can do no more than give us a working model of the world, effective for most practical purposes as long as it is not taken too literally. But a model is not the reality, and to get closer to reality we need to use another mode of cognition – found in the imaginal faculty.

The Imagination can express itself through, and respond to, concepts when these concepts are inspired or illumined by vision. Some Buddhist philosophy is of this kind. The system may be rationally articulated – yet it is not just a speculative construct, erected purely on the basis of reason. It is the attempt to convey the insights perceived by the Imagination using concepts, but concepts as metaphors for a truth that lies beyond reason. On encountering a philosophy of this kind, one's own imaginal faculty may be stirred to life. There are dangers, though. This sort of philosophical expression can degenerate, all too rapidly, into a rationalistic dogma as successive generations read it more and more literalistically and fail to raise themselves beyond the level of words to the vision that the words are meant to convey. This process of decay is certainly evident in some Buddhist schools. For this reason other schools have preferred to baffle the intellect with paradoxes and negations so that the rational mind is unable to fasten on to any concepts and solidify them into a fixed model. *Perhaps the main point is that the student of the Dharma should never mistake an understanding of the words used for an insight into truth.* We should always be striving for our own direct experience of the meaning behind the words.

It is in the arts that we are probably most accustomed to witness the functioning of the imaginal faculty. Art that is anything more than decorative, merely interesting, or clumsily didactic, can draw us up to a new level of awareness that we share for a while with the artist. If we are moved in this manner, the way in which we perceive the world is affected and we may feel a new sense of wholeness and purpose. Images, symbols, myths, whether in art or our own dreams and visions, are the common language of the Imagination, able as they are to communicate many levels of meaning and, at the same time, call up a powerful emotional response.

The imaginal faculty, finally, may go beyond images, however refined and subtle. Images, too, are a refraction of reality, not reality itself. The Imagination can rise to burst through all that veils us from the Truth. When it does so it is Insight, the direct perception of the nature of things in perfect, non-dual awareness. It is the dawning of this Insight that makes one a Stream Entrant and Enlightenment is the bright light of day by which we can fully see reality.

Images are the common language of the faculty of Imagination, and that faculty, as we have seen, has the power to move the heart as well as to illumine the mind. It is for these reasons that the Buddha caused Maudgalyayana's vision to be translated into the visual image of the Wheel of Life. For these same reasons the Wheel of Life and other symbols have been chosen as the framework for this exposition of the Dharma. To some extent, the images speak for themselves to that faculty of Imagination within every one of us. Perhaps all analysis should be abandoned and the different elements of the symbolism described and left to convey their own message. But that task requires a Buddhist Dante or Milton and awaits another pen. In the remainder of this chapter, we will briefly describe the Wheel, the Spiral, and the Mandala of the Five Buddhas, which, in the chapters that follow, we will examine for their various meanings. Throughout, we should not forget the purported origins of the Wheel as the Buddha's depiction of Maudgalyayana's insight. It is with inspired vision that we are dealing and we must open our Imaginations to the images as they are presented.

A Brief Description of the Wheel and the Way

We have seen one version of the origin of the Wheel in the story of Maudgalyayana's journeyings in other realms of existence. Other sources tell a different story. Most of what we know about the Wheel comes from Tibetan Buddhism. Apart from one solitary example in the ancient cave temples of Ajanta, not a single picture of the Wheel has survived in India, so complete has been the Muslim and Brahminical extirpation of Buddhism in the land of its origin. But in Tibet, which inherited the rich traditions of Indian Buddhism, it is used to this day as an edifying image painted in the vestibule of many temples. A Tibetan legend attributes its origin to the Buddha once more, but pictures him outlining the Wheel for his followers in grains of rice in a paddy field. The details of the Wheel have, to some extent, been supplemented in Tibet, and it is on one type of Tibetan Wheel of Life that this account is based.

The Wheel consists of four concentric circles. In the central circle or hub are three animals: a cock, a snake, and a pig, each of which bites the tail of the one before it so that they are linked together in a circular chain. The next circle forms a thin band around the hub and is divided vertically into two segments, the left coloured white and the right, black. In the black half, naked beings tumble downwards, harried by demons, their faces contorted in agony and their arms flailing helplessly to prevent their fall. In the white section, beings are performing all kinds of meritorious actions: meditating, distributing money, venerating the Buddha. They rise upwards with joyous faces.

The next circle is placed close to the rim so that the third area occupies almost half the Wheel. It is divided into six equal segments. In the bottom segment is shown the realm of hell, containing all the tortures conventional in depictions from medieval Christendom: beings are roasted, boiled, flayed, crushed, and dissected by the pitiless demons who preside over this world of horror. The intense heat of ever-burning fire fills the hell realm, apart from the deepest section where there is an absolute cold as in Dante's Inferno. At the centre of hell stands an enormous figure with massive limbs, glaring wrathful face, and a halo of flickering flame. This is Yama, the judge of the dead; he holds in his hand a mirror wherein are shown the deeds of those who come before him.

FIG 2. THE WHEEL OF LIFE

In the right lower segment is the realm of the hungry ghosts. Smoke-coloured and insubstantial, these creatures have large bellies and pinhole mouths. Whatever they drink turns to fire, and whatever they eat turns to swords in their stomachs. In the corresponding section on the left is the world of the animals. Birds and beasts graze, and hunt, to be preyed upon in their turn by man.

The upper left segment shows the human realm in which men and women go about their daily business. On the right are the titans, or jealous gods – fierce, ugly, powerfully-built creatures for whom life is permanent warfare, they struggle against the gods who occupy the top realm for possession of the wish-fulfilling tree that grants all desires. The gods themselves live in a world of great beauty and happiness wherein all their wants are instantly satisfied.

In each of the six realms there appears a Buddha, each a different colour, holding an implement. In the hells, a dark blue Buddha carries a pot of ointment; in the hungry ghost realm, a red Buddha holds a jar of nectar; a light blue Buddha, holding a book, appears to the animals; a yellow Buddha, dressed in an orange robe and holding the staff and begging bowl of a wandering monk, comes to the human world; a green Buddha (sometimes in full armour) carrying a flaming sword ministers to the titans; and a white Buddha plays to the gods upon a lute.

The outer ring of the Wheel is divided into twelve segments that represent the twelve links in the cyclic chain of conditioned co-production as revealed in the process of human birth and death. In each segment is an image representing a stage in that flow of conditioned factors. At the top, a blind man staggers forward, feeling his way with a stick. Then, in clockwise direction, are depicted a potter making pots at a wheel; a monkey leaping from branch to branch in a tree; four people in a boat, one of whom is steering; a house with a door and five windows; a couple embracing; a man with an arrow in his eye; a woman offering a drink to a seated man; a woman plucking fruit from a tree; a couple in the act of sexual intercourse; a woman giving birth; and a dead body being carried to a funeral pyre. With the next link, the Wheel has turned full circle to the blind man with a stick once more.

Above the rim of the Wheel appears a ferocious face with three fiercely glaring red eyes and a crown of skulls. This is the monster of

FIG 3. THE WHEEL, THE SPIRAL, AND THE MANDALA

impermanence, who allows nothing conditioned to stand still. He devours the Wheel with his fangs and tears at it with strong talons.

Taken by itself, this is but one side of reality: the cyclic kind of conditionality. The other side, the process of moving from conditioned existence towards Enlightenment, can be symbolised by the spiral. This process is more often traditionally represented as a path, but the image of a spiral conveys how the practitioner can pass round and round the same mental states, at successively higher levels. In the Wheel, the Spiral is represented by the Buddhas appearing in each realm, but this is not really an adequate apportioning of emphasis. Although it is certainly important, as it were, to know the enemy and to know the worst about our situation, we also need a strong feeling for the positive possibilities of human life if we are to have a full vision of reality. In many versions of the Tibetan Wheel of Life, there also appears a Buddha above the Wheel to the right, pointing the way to Enlightenment.

If we imagine the Wheel laid flat upon the ground, spinning so fast in the claws of the monster of impermanence that its details are lost and we see but a blur of confusion, then we can picture the Spiral rising from its outer edge and circling round at higher and higher levels above it. The Spiral is divided into two parts at the point of Stream Entry. Below that point we see godlike beings of ever-increasing beauty and radiance ascending the Path. Above, the beings grow in intensity of beauty, but now wisdom too shines in their eyes.

Finally, the Spiral merges into the Mandala, a vast symmetrically ordered circle, which we shall explore in Chapter 11. Here sit five radiant figures representing the culmination of the Path in one sense (for at this level, the Wheel has been completely transcended); but the spiral process still unfolds. The figures glow and pulsate with energy, sending out dazzling beams of light. They begin to manifest from within themselves more and more figures and forms in a process of infinite creative unfoldment. Perfection improves upon perfection, without end.

4

The Roots of Evil

At the Hub of the Wheel

The motive force that drives a wheel is at its hub. At the hub of the Wheel of Life are the cock, the snake, and the pig, representing the forces that keep it turning. They are known as the 'three unwholesome roots' because from them grow all life's evils, or as the 'three poisons' because they corrupt us from within. The cock represents greed, the snake hatred, and the pig ignorance, and it is these three that underlie all human bondage and misery.

It is appropriate that these forces are depicted as animals, since they represent primitive urges beneath the supposedly civilized exterior of many men. Yet we do injustice to animals in using them as symbols of greed and hatred because animals rarely display these emotions, which are all too common among humans. They certainly experience hunger and desire but they rarely indulge in overeating or other neurotic behaviour – unless they have been in close contact with humans. Men, however, can carry deep and deadly hatreds that lead them to destroy other human beings, even those close to them in affection and kinship. These hatreds lead sometimes, as we know, to human destructiveness on an immense scale. Man is capable too of intense longings, longings that may lead to a whole life given over to heaping up wealth or power despite terrible suffering caused to others. Human greed and hatred are of a quite different order from the hunger and aggression of the animal. They are specifically human failings, and to understand their nature we must look more closely at human consciousness.

The human being is self-aware. Out of the womb of nature has emerged a separate identity, differentiated from the world around it. Initially, that differentiated selfhood is very fragile and is maintained only with some difficulty. It is crude and rigid, closely identified with the physical body, material possessions, relationships with other people, and a fixed world-view. This insubstantial self is constantly washed away from within by the preconscious forces that swell beneath the surface of self-awareness. It is also threatened from without by the continual decay and death of the objects and people in its world. Everything from which the sense of identity is at first derived is subject to the law of impermanence and consistently fails to provide a lasting and reliable source of security. A sense of insecurity is an inevitable accompaniment of enlarging self-consciousness as it is buffeted, again and again, by the transitory processes of life.

The immature self or ego tries to make itself secure by using the same instincts as those by which the animal preserves itself. Just as the animal hunts for the food that will nourish its organism, so the ego tries to possess those things it considers as securing its identity. And as the animal will often attack and destroy whatever threatens its survival, so the ego seeks to destroy whatever undermines its integrity. Aided and amplified by the human power of imagination, these reactions can reach the monstrous proportions of ruthless empire-building and of mass destruction through war. Although greed and hatred are fundamentally defensive reactions, they do not always appear so. They may be the timorous and desperate impulses of those who feel they are finally cornered by life, but greed and hatred may also manifest themselves with all the panache and vigour of those who believe they are successful in the bid to secure their identity.

Greed

The strutting cock with his bright plumage represents greed. No doubt his proverbial vanity and lust make the poor bird an appropriate symbol for this most human failing. The word 'greed' does not really do full justice to the emotion symbolized by the cock, which includes the whole spectrum of unwholesome desire, from vague hankerings to intense longings that allow nothing to stand in the way of their fulfilment. 'Neurotic craving' it might better be called, suggesting both its potential power and the delusion and sickness that underlie it. Neurotic craving is the longing to possess things so that one can make them part of oneself in the belief that they will help to secure one's identity. It may be *objects* that we covet in this way; for instance, when we lose something and experience not merely regret or irritation at no longer being able to enjoy it but a deeper sense of loss, even a kind of panic. It is as if we have lost not merely the object but part of ourselves. It may be *ideas* to which we cling, building our security upon them. This is revealed if we feel personally undermined when those ideas are attacked or questioned. But it is other *people* who provide the principal objects of our craving: themselves. We crave their love and approval, their admiration, or just their presence, as stable factors in our universe. When this craving is connected with biological and social needs, such as sex or the support of the family, particularly unpleasant and painful situations can develop.

Craving should be distinguished from healthy desire. Hunger, for instance, is not neurotic craving. One can experience an empty stomach and the desire for food in a quite straightforward way so that when one eats, hunger is satisfied. No emotional disturbance or feeling of insecurity arises out of healthy hunger. Food only becomes an object of neurotic craving when the otherwise healthy desire is entrapped in a personality dominated by insecurity. Craving is to be eradicated by spiritual practice, healthy desires are not. To differentiate the one from the other we must question whether the desire has an emotionally disruptive effect and whether the satisfaction of the desire leads to its termination. Not only are there physical desires that are healthy and that should be satisfied so long as no harm comes to oneself or others, but there are desires that should be actively cultivated. There is the desire for friendship, for beauty, and for other ideal qualities, and there is the desire to develop as an individual. These should be strengthened as much as possible, and much Buddhist practice is directed to this end. The cock represents only neurotic craving, not healthy desire or aspiration towards an ideal.

Hatred

The snake is chosen to represent hatred because of its cold blood and its poisonous bite. With its icy glance and scaly skin, rearing up, its forked tongue flashing, it seems the archetype of malevolence. Yet most snakes won't attack another animal except to eat it or to defend themselves against what they consider a physical threat. Human hatred, however, can lead to acts of senseless cruelty against completely innocent people. At the other end of the scale, it may amount to no more than a mild dislike and a frosty manner. Whatever the degree of intensity, we hate what we feel threatens or undermines our sense of self. The animal instinct of self-preservation is now usurped to defend the weak ego. Although it may be vented on inanimate objects, hatred is nearly always directed at people. Whether they are, objectively speaking, working against us or not, we can feel that other people's very existence threatens ours and we want them removed so that they can no longer harm us. If the threat they pose to our self-identity is deep enough we may feel that the only way we can gain security is to destroy them utterly.

Ignorance

There is a third way in which the immature ego tries to stabilize itself. At the centre of the Wheel is a fat black hog, rooting around in the muck with its snout, its ears falling over its eyes so that it sees nothing but the patch of dirt before it. In the West the pig is usually considered the epitome of gluttony, but here it becomes a symbol for delusion or ignorance. Blinkered by its ears, the pig is conscious only of what its snout is sticking into. In the same way, the deluded person is limited in his or her perspective on life. The limitation is not the result of plain lack of information; it is a defensive stratagem. When we are deluded, we refuse to see anything that might threaten our identity. Security is sought in blindness. The ostrich with its head buried in the sand to avoid detection might be a better image for the ignorant person! In our delusion, we take refuge in a narrow world and ignore everything outside it. We will not look at the basic facts of life: that everything in our world must decay and that we will, ourselves, inevitably die.

We can sometimes catch ourselves using ignorance as a defence. A friend may draw our attention to unpleasant truths, perhaps about our own motives or behaviour. We comprehend what is being said but then, at the same moment, turn our mind away from it. This self-distraction is deliberate and is a manifestation of delusion. It also displays itself in the fixed view of life adopted by many who refuse to examine or acknowledge anything that lies outside the confines of what they presently think they know.

Ignorance does not always show itself in overtly stupid or unintelligent behaviour. It can be highly sophisticated and give rise, for instance, to very complex systems of thought; for ignorance is the basic poison, the root of roots, and it is present up to the moment of Enlightenment – it is nothing less than our refusal to open ourselves to a wider sphere of reality. Whether or not we are entirely happy in our presently achieved level of consciousness, we at least have a relatively stable sense of ourselves, fragile as it may be. We know who we are, or we think we do. To move beyond ourselves as we now are to a wider dimension of consciousness is to step into the unknown and to leave behind the self as we presently know it. This is a kind of death and it is deeply threatening to the ego. So we turn away, refusing to recognize the truth that was always there but that is now forcing itself upon our attention. Sometimes, people learning to meditate will observe this reaction in themselves as they begin to touch upon a higher level of consciousness. However happy and clear that state may be, it is unfamiliar and it offers nothing through which one can identify oneself. Panicking, one seeks the safe ground of ordinary consciousness. The ignorant person is like the prisoner who prefers the confinement, which is at least known, to the mysterious possibilities of freedom. Until we are Enlightened, we are all ignorant.

Our lives are dominated essentially by two contradictory forces: the evolutionary urge within us that drives us to achieve new levels of consciousness, and the dead weight of our ignorance that pulls us back to more limited horizons. Our task, in taking up the spiritual path, is consciously to allow the force of evolution to carry us upward and to prevent ignorance from binding us down.

We are, as it were, strung between two great heavenly bodies, the Wheel and Buddhahood, each of which exercises its own gravitational pull. The spiritual path leads from the one to the other. In the earlier part of our spiritual career we are working all the time against the force of ignorance, which is the gravitational pull of the Wheel. The pull of Buddhahood, which is the evolutionary urge, is there within us all, but it is heavily outweighed by ignorance. For any progress to take place we must make a constant effort to overcome the pull of ignorance that binds us to lower stages of being. At a certain point the two gravitational forces are evenly matched between the Wheel and Buddhahood. Once past this point, the evolutionary force is stronger than the pull of ignorance, and we enter the stream that leads to Buddhahood. The spiral trend works so strongly in Stream Entrants that, although there is still ignorance, they continuously transcend whatever limitations they encounter at each new level and they cannot fall back. Up to that point of no return, we need to strive unceasingly to overcome our own tendency to contraction and stagnation, symbolized by the pig of ignorance.

Recognizing the Three Poisons Within

The cock, the snake, and the pig circle round together, each biting the tail of the one before it. This illustrates the way in which craving, hatred, and delusion are inextricably tangled together. Delusion underlies the other two and is present, to some degree, in all states short of Enlightenment. It is even found in some highly positive states in which there is neither greed nor hatred. Greed, if it is thwarted, quickly turns to hatred and most hatred contains an element of frustrated desire. Most negative mental states are made up of complex mixtures of all three. And so the three animals writhe and twist, spinning the Wheel of Life.

We seldom encounter greed, hatred, and delusion in their raw forms. Such naked egoism is usually disguised and refined by conventions of social life that cushion us against the three animals within. A polite veneer hides them from others and it may be that we are not conscious of them in ourselves. This can be observed in people talking in a polite and friendly way, while the set of their faces and the way they hold their bodies reveal an underlying hostility or fear of which they are not themselves fully aware. Often, if our contacts with others threaten to bring such fundamental negative feelings into the open, we break them off. In some people, however, the tight knot of defensive ego is relatively near the surface and it does not take much to precipitate quite extreme reactions. In healthier and more confident personalities that knot is far more deeply buried, seldom showing its naked face since the person is socially so well adapted. None the less, the three animals remain the driving force. Often it is in the closer relationships of life that the cushioning breaks down. In romance and family life, tensions and rows, impossible expectations, and their inevitable disappointments, the fragile ego and its desperate attempts to secure itself are revealed.

It is of great importance that we learn to recognize the cock, snake, and pig within us, for by bringing them into consciousness we can stop them dominating our lives and we can eventually eliminate them altogether. We must look with great honesty at our actions and admit what really motivates us beneath our rationalizations and social face. Being with other people often helps us to do this, for people are the primary targets of our emotions, and close contact with them will tend to bring us up against our raw feelings. If they are not themselves trying to cultivate greater honesty, however, we may simply get very tangled with them. If they are seriously concerned to know what is in their own hearts and are trying to evolve along the Spiral, then our own efforts will be greatly enhanced. With our friends we can openly acknowledge what is going on in our minds. They will be able to give us advice and encouragement or simply listen to us.

Openly communicating our thoughts and feelings to those we trust not only gives emotional relief but also helps us to perceive more clearly what we ourselves think and feel. For such trust to exist, we must feel confident that our friends share our basic desire to grow. In the end, this form of openness can only exist between two people who are both committed to the spiritual path and who are therefore members of the spiritual community in its only meaningful sense. One of the primary characteristics of a true sangha, or spiritual community, is the frankness that exists between its members. At their best, members of a sangha can admit freely to each other whatever their thoughts and emotions may be, and no one pretends to be other than they are, whether from guilt or to gain advantage over others. At the same time, since such openness takes place against the background of a higher ideal, it never becomes a mere indulgence in moods and tantrums. No one inflicts their states upon others. Everyone tries to know what is in their own mind, for better or worse, and is prepared to reveal themselves to their friends. In the true sangha, everyone is prepared to listen to the comments and views of those they have opened themselves to and is, of course, ready to listen when others reveal themselves.

Most people will find that all three animals are within them. One of them is, however, likely to predominate and, according to an early Buddhist system, human beings can be classified on the basis of which poison most commonly determines their behaviour. Finding out whether one is a greed type, a hate type, or a delusion type can help in getting to know oneself, highly generalized though these categories may be. It is said that people of each type betray their character in their every action:

> The stance of one of greedy temperament is confident and graceful. That of one of hating temperament is rigid. That of one of deluded temperament is muddled. Likewise in sitting. And one of greedy temperament spreads his bed unhurriedly, lies down slowly, composing his limbs, and he sleeps in a confident manner. When woken, instead of getting up quickly, he gives his answer slowly as though doubtful. One of hating temperament spreads his bed hastily anyhow; with his body flung down he sleeps with a scowl. When woken, he gets up quickly and answers as though annoyed. One of deluded temperament spreads his bed all awry and sleeps mostly face downwards with his body sprawling. When woken, he gets up slowly, saying 'Hum'.*

So says Buddhaghosa, the great fifth-century Indian Buddhist scholar, in his *Path of Purification*, and he goes on to give the characteristics of each type in working, eating, dressing, and other everyday actions. He also describes the positive counterparts of greed, hatred, and delusion types.

Greed types are probably the easiest to get on with, since their basic purpose is to find objects that give them pleasure. They enjoy life and form strong attachments to people. Hate types, on the other hand, are always critical. They see the unpleasant side of everything and it is the avoidance of pain that primarily concerns them. Delusion types are neither one nor the other. Shambling, distracted, and bewildered, they live in a grey fog and cannot make up their minds about anything. They suffer from chronic vagueness but will not clarify their thoughts. Most people do not fall neatly into any one of these three categories; rather, each of us combines all three in his own personal mixture of poisons.

Whether one finds this particular method useful or not, it is important that one gets to know oneself. This is not easy to do and it necessarily takes many years to discover what are our real motives

---

* *Visuddhimagga* iii.89 (*The Path of Purification*, p.105)

and inclinations, vices and virtues. Greed, hatred, and delusion are not the only possible motivational forces, and the corresponding types are, therefore, not the only possible ones. With work that is directed to some positive end, and friends who are also committed to self-knowledge and who have our best interests at heart, we can slowly come to understand ourselves as we are and as we could be.

The Healthy Individual

The three poisons are essentially the defence mechanisms of an immature ego. Although some residue of greed and hatred remains until very high levels of development have been attained, and ignorance is present until Enlightenment itself, a sense of personal identity can be achieved which is far more stable and mature. Attaining this healthier individuality is an important step towards making spiritual progress. On the basis of a balanced and healthy individuality one can develop all the spiritual qualities, and eventually attain transcendental insight.

The embryonic ego, in the initial stages of its emergence from the sleep of nature, is very weak and feels its own vulnerability. Not only is it fragile but it is crude: it sees the whole world as existing for itself and tries to impose its demands upon its surroundings. This tyrannical project is, except in the rarest cases, quickly thwarted by resistance from the environment. Things never do quite bend to one's will or completely conform to one's desires. One is often in direct conflict with life itself. Other people are particularly intractable to our wills, for they have wills of their own. In order to deal with this basic tension in life we must either erect a superstructure of personality adapted to the chances and disappointments of human life yet fundamentally rooted in greed, hatred, and delusion, or we must evolve a more mature sense of selfhood.

The ego matures by developing genuine confidence in its own identity. Less and less is the sense of selfhood dependent on objects and people outside, and more and more is it to be found within. This more mature ego is what might be called healthy individuality for, up to this point, individuality has been only partly achieved. Maturation is largely the result of personal effort but it is also aided by a secure and encouraging background that imparts a sense of well-being without restricting or smothering the emergent self. Parents, teachers, and friends provide support and sympathetic guidance while acknowledging and accepting the crystallizing individuality. People who have matured in this way have a natural and easy self-confidence. They can appreciate and care for themselves, love themselves and wish themselves well. I am not talking here of a narcissistic self-obsession or egoistical self-assertion, which is merely a manifestation of the immature ego, but of a healthy self-esteem that does not begrudge others valuing themselves. Many Westerners do not find it easy to love themselves since the effect of our Christian culture has, in all too many cases, left people scarred with irrational guilt and self-hatred and with the view that they are sinful and unworthy. Self-love is indispensable for further evolution, for otherwise our attempts to grow are manifestations only of self-punishment and repression. Growth can only come out of health, out of a desire to see oneself in a happier and more fulfilled state.

Self-confident, mature people are relaxed and open to new experience since their sense of themselves is less easily threatened and undermined. Such people are, in particular, more open to others, who no longer appear as dangers to their identity or as possible objects of neurotic craving. The healthy individual will therefore see other people as people. At this crucial juncture, one is no longer a 'self' in a world that is 'other', but a self interacting with other selves. By realizing that others feel in the same way that we do, we can enter sympathetically into their lives and wish them well just as we wish ourselves well. Thus, on the basis of self-love, we can recognize that others are selves and feel a disinterested love for them.

Besides being confident, the healthy individual is independent and self-reliant, finding security and self-assurance within. This is not, however, the shallow self-confidence of the stereotyped pseudo-hero who arrogantly claims that 'I did it my way', and only enters into human relationships on his own egoistical terms – effectively denying the selfhood of others. Such behaviour characterizes not the individual but what can be termed the individualist. The healthy individual can relate to others in friendship and cooperation, and can learn from them and accept their lead, if appropriate, without losing self-esteem. Greed, hatred, and delusion are replaced by generosity, friendliness, and awareness. As the cock, snake, and pig are the motive force of the Wheel, so generosity, friendliness, and awareness lift one up the Spiral Path, transforming healthy individuality into something altogether finer and more in accordance with the reality of things, and which might therefore be called real, or true, individuality.

From Greed to Generosity

Greed is displaced by generosity. Greed is the desire to possess and appropriate because of a belief that by doing so one can fortify one's crumbling ego. Individuality, as it flowers, needs no such buttress since such individuals find their security within themselves. As well as this self-confidence, they have an inner wealth that overflows to others. In contrast to the selfish, grasping attitude of the greedy they are open-handed and freely giving. This is a giving that is not limited to material charity, the sharing of a portion of one's goods with those in need. It is a whole attitude and approach to life. True individuals are not only generous with their goods but also with their time and energy, their assessment of others, and their willingness to forgive those who have wronged them. Above all, it is themselves that they give, since they have finally transcended all self-attachment.

This level of giving is not done in order to get something back or to place the recipient in debt. Those who give at this level give simply out of their own inner fullness. At the same time, they do not exhaust themselves through their generosity – that would come only from self-hatred. It is the superabundance of their self-regard that enables them to see the needs of others. Their generosity enables them to enter into co-operative relations with others and to work with them in friendly association, balancing their own needs and those of others. They are not competitive and neither mind following the advice and guidance of others nor get neurotic satisfaction from giving it. Their desire is simply to share whatever they have with their companions. Whatever they possess flows out to others.

Because it represents such a radical shift from the Wheel to the Spiral, the practice of generosity has assumed a special place in Buddhism. Everyone can give something, and it is the minimum spiritual activity that all Buddhists can engage in. The attitude of generosity, as outlined above, must be assiduously cultivated, for, like all the positive qualities, it rarely springs up of its own accord. In order to move towards true generosity, we should develop the habit of helping others and of giving to them, whether we whole-heartedly feel like it or not. Our actions help to form our minds, and by giving consistently we cultivate the desire to give. Whenever we feel any stirring of an impulse of generosity we should follow it through, even when sober reflection later counsels against it. In this way we will gradually wean ourselves away from tight-fistedness and develop the genuine spirit of generosity, and so move nearer to becoming true individuals.

Our friends and families, workmates, and acquaintances should all be the recipients of our generosity, as well as those in need whom we do not know. It is also important that we show our gratitude and generosity to those who are further along the spiritual path than we are and who are wholeheartedly devoted to the practice of the Dharma. They are our own teachers and guides upon the path and if we do not give to them then we have not really appreciated their worth and we cannot benefit from them. In our gratitude for the help we have ourselves received we will also want to help spread the Dharma, whether directly or indirectly. Even though generosity has to be cultivated by conscious effort, however, we should never forget that it is a generous spirit or feeling that we are trying to achieve and not a forced giving with a reluctant heart. We are endeavouring to call up in ourselves the natural generosity of the true individual who gives out of his own inner richness.

From Hatred to Love

Love replaces hatred as the inspiring force of the Spiral Path. The English word 'love' is too ambiguous to convey with any precision the emotion in question, since it commonly connotes anything from a keen interest or desire for something to romantic attachment. 'Friendliness' lacks strength in modern usage as does 'loving-kindness', which also has a somewhat sentimental ring. It is probably best to use a word from the canonical Buddhist languages and to incorporate it into English untranslated. The word most commonly used is *metta* in the Pali language, which is *maitri* in Sanskrit. Metta is a strong, even intense, desire for the welfare of others that expresses itself in action. It is impartial and is felt regardless of whether it is returned or whether there is anything to be gained from the other person – it is no 'cupboard love'. When it is reciprocated it flowers as friendship. Like generosity, metta is based on inner fullness. One feels such a wealth of self-metta that one can empathize with the selfhood of others and wish them the same welfare that one desires for oneself.

Metta must be carefully distinguished from other emotions that may seem to share some of its characteristics. It is said to have both a 'far enemy' and a 'near enemy'. Hatred, being the direct opposite of metta, is the far enemy. The near enemy is a love that is really self-interested. One appears to be very concerned for the welfare of the other person but one's affection is really dependent on what one can get from him in return. In reality one is demanding a contract or bargain and has little genuine appreciation of the other's individuality. The relationship rests, in the end, upon craving, for one wants something from the other person – acceptance, affection, approval – that will help to secure one's identity. Such need-based relationships are often connected with the biological ties of kinship and sex. Families are often bound together in this sort of mutual craving and it is very common in sexual relationships. Romantic love is of this kind. What starts out as that highly idealized fascination that goes by the name of love is very often revealed as neurotic craving. All that is called love is by no means metta.

Just as generosity must be actively cultivated, so must metta. We have seen that one of the two principal meditation practices of most Buddhist schools is the 'development of loving-kindness' or 'development of metta' – in Pali its full name is *metta bhavana*. This practice consists in sitting down quietly in seclusion and systematically trying to bring the feeling of metta into being. The beginner will do this perhaps once every day or two for a period of about half an hour, and the more advanced may meditate several times a day for periods of an hour or more.

We begin by trying to feel metta for ourselves – for we cannot love others unless we love ourselves – by repeating over and over to ourselves, 'May I be well, may I be happy, may I be free from suffering, may I progress.' At first, these words may be more or less empty but, after a while, the feeling of metta will begin to flow. In this way we connect with, intensify, and refine the self-love that we naturally feel, so that we can identify with others and thereby love them too. We let the feeling of good will for ourselves accumulate and then, in the second stage, allow it to spill over towards a near and dear friend, someone for whom we already feel some genuine affection. To avoid other feelings confusing the practice, it is recommended that the friend should be someone still living, of approximately the same age as us, and to whom we are not sexually attracted. Again, one repeats the phrases of well-wishing. We then move on to more difficult subjects: a mere acquaintance towards whom we feel neutral; and then an enemy – someone with whom we have some definite difficulty and towards whom we may be actively antagonistic. In the fifth and final stage we take all four persons together – self, friend, neutral person, and enemy – and try to feel metta for all equally. This overcomes any tendency to prefer one person to another, and therefore eliminates any hint of craving that may infect one's metta. Metta is then extended out from the spot where we are meditating to include an ever wider circle of people, until the whole world is encompassed. It is then extended to embrace not merely humans but all living creatures – the whole of evolution, we might say. From the beings on this planet metta is radiated towards all sentient creatures of whatsoever kind, wherever they may be in the entire universe. Buddhist cosmology has always envisaged that, in the infinity of space, there are many other world-systems. Within each, there are many levels and dimensions in which consciousness manifests itself. The *metta bhavana* meditation culminates with one's metta pervading all these worlds and dimensions. If it is practised regularly it will noticeably improve one's attitude both to oneself and to others. Indeed, it can have the remarkable effect of dissolving old enmities as one comes to see one's adversary in the new light of one's metta.

Basic though the *metta bhavana* is, it is not the only means to develop metta. We can systematically work upon our relationships with others in all the various situations of life. The more those with whom we are in regular contact also try to do the same, the more success we are likely to have. Some people choose, for this reason, to live and work with others who share their desire to develop, and Buddhists have established residential communities and working situations for this purpose, both in traditionally Buddhist countries and in the West. If the people one is in close contact with have no interest in working upon themselves in this way there is no sure basis for resolving the difficulties that inevitably arise in any relationship. If, on the other hand, all are committed to ascending the Spiral Path, genuine friendships can more readily grow that transcend the overlapping of likes and dislikes in a deep sense of mutual appreciation and concern. Friends of this kind are not tied together in bonds of exclusivity as is often the case with romantic love. One's care for the welfare of one's friend does not diminish one's concern for others and there is certainly no question of jealousy ever arising. Indeed, real friendship is not possible until there is this kind of maturity, for such friendship can only develop to the extent that there is no neurotic need or exclusivity. The companionships of the less mature are not based on metta but more on the coincidence of self-interest and need. The capacity for disinterested friendship, one of the chief joys of the Spiral Path, is the mark of mature individuality.

From Delusion to Awareness

Delusion is replaced by awareness. No longer is there that ignorant recoil into a narrower sphere of understanding. Now the healthy individual reaches out to embrace a new and more expansive vision. The true individuals who gradually emerge from this effort are aware, in the first place, of themselves in their various aspects. They are, as it were, in full possession of their own bodies: they know what their posture is, what they are doing, and the direction and purpose of their movements. They are careful and dignified, never clumsy or forgetful, and are likely to enjoy good health since they will be aware of their physical needs and will see that they are catered for in a healthy way. Their awareness extends to their emotions: they know whether they feel greed, hatred, or delusion, or metta, generosity, and clarity. They know what they think: what thoughts and images are passing through their minds. And they know where those thoughts have come from. Awareness brings the ability to distinguish what in their minds is simply the product of past conditioning and what is genuinely creative. Thinking for themselves, they apply their minds to disentangling the various difficulties and problems that life presents to them. They use their minds creatively, and can rise to challenges with imagination and resourcefulness. Their minds are not passive and dull but bright and alert, interested in life, and ready to read its diverse lessons and draw conclusions from it.

Beyond themselves, this level of awareness includes an awareness of surroundings, both the natural environment and human culture. The eye of aesthetic appreciation replaces that of egoistical appropriation. Those possessing this awareness can be profoundly moved by beauty in nature and in art. They are aware of other people as selves separate from them with their own individuality and do not project on to others their own subjective desires. They are aware of others' needs and can balance them objectively with their own. We have seen that individuals feel metta and friendship for people and have a natural sensitivity to what hurts or helps them. Above all, they have developed the imaginal faculty and can see that there are higher dimensions to reality. They are aware that the meaning of life is to surpass one's present limits and that the Path spirals ever upward from where they themselves now stand.

The Transition from the Wheel to the Spiral

Once these three forces of generosity, metta, and awareness have become the dominant motives for action, the true individual has emerged. From the first dawning of self-consciousness to this point is a long dawn dominated still by greed, hatred, and delusion. In this half-light the proto-individual with his or her rudimentary self-consciousness functions as a member of a group. Each is scarcely differentiated from any of the other members, and all simply derive their values and opinions from the group to which they belong. The family, the hunting band, the tribe, the clan, the city state, are the earliest forms of the group whose modern manifestations are the nation, religious sect, political party, social class, and so forth. Group members have limited separate identity apart from their group. Some may appear to function free of the group, but they are simply its most powerful members, equally dependent upon the group for their psychological security although they are strong enough within it to follow their own fancies, even at the expense of other group members. Another type of pseudo-individual is the one who has become culturally alienated, cut off prematurely from the necessary nurturance of his group. Taking refuge in brittle self-assertion, this type remains stridently unreceptive to all influence or co-operation.

The true individual, having differentiated himself or herself from the group, is no longer subject to its pressures. Those who are individuals will feel no need to belong because they find their security within themselves and they therefore do not have to buy acceptance with conformity to the group's beliefs. But at the same time these individuals are not hostile to the group. They appreciate the need of many people for its support and, since they will not themselves be susceptible to its influence, do not feel threatened by it. The group, however, may all too often be the enemy of the individual and even try to destroy him or her to enforce its supremacy.

Finally, individuals have accepted responsibility for themselves and for their actions. They no longer leave their fate in the hands of fortune and do not blame others for setbacks in their own lives. They take the initiative both as regards their own development and in the situations they encounter. They know that life is their own for the making and they commit themselves irrevocably to the task of the spiritual life.

The transition from greed, hatred, and delusion to love, generosity, and awareness is the transition from the Wheel to the Spiral, from the group to the individual. It is also the transition from what has been called the 'power mode' to the 'love mode'. Those whose ego is immature see the whole world solely in terms of their own needs. They try to dominate and impose themselves, whether directly or by cunning, manipulating others to their own ends. They function in terms of power, seeing everything, other people included, as objects for their own gratification. This is the power mode of operation. The love mode, conversely, consists in seeing others as independent selves and treating them with metta. It is on the basis of the love mode that the spiritual community exists. Its members do not come together to exploit or manipulate each other nor to gain the support and solidarity of a group. They try to relate as one individual to another, in awareness of the ideals to which all are committed, and to encourage and inspire each other's efforts. So the transition from the power mode to the love mode can be seen in the transition from the group to the spiritual community.

True individuality, however, contains one more decisive element. In the healthy individual, greed and hatred have less and less control over the mind, and the grosser forms of delusion are purged away. A basic delusion, however, still remains; experience is still limited by the polarization of consciousness into subject and object. The two sides of the duality are now in more harmonious dialogue and the object is no longer considered by the subject as a threat or a source of permanence. It is viewed appreciatively and, when the object is another person, communication and metta flow towards it. None the less, to see things in terms of a subject and object is, from an ultimate point of view, a constriction of the perfect non-dual awareness of reality. In the end, the division into subject and object is only the way we structure our experience; it does not correspond to reality itself. Gradually, the love mode needs to be intensified, metta and generosity to radiate more and more powerfully; there must be a deeper and deeper awareness, individuality has to become stronger, and the spiritual community needs to be experienced more vividly. The more one can feel metta for others, the more that tension between self and other is lessened. Yet still one's metta is based upon love of oneself, highly refined as that may become. At a certain point, however, metta breaks through the barrier of self and other and one feels no essential difference between oneself and the other. One identifies equally both with what used to appear as the self and with what used to appear as the other. Consciousness is freed from the limitation that duality imposes and a perfectly equal metta pervades all, and, with the end of self-identification, generosity becomes the outpouring of compassion. The healthy individual becomes the true individual at this point of Stream Entry, and, though the Wheel and the Spiral still coexist even at this transcendental level, the Wheel can never again be the deciding influence. Greed and hatred may sprout from time to time and a refined delusion may still persist, but love, generosity, and awareness are now suffused by insight into the true nature of things. Slowly the three poisons are worn away until, with full Enlightenment, the last trace of ignorance disappears.

5

To Be Born Again

Conditionality

To the Enlightened mind the whole of reality is a process of becoming. So intricate is that process, so interwoven is each aspect with every other, that it can never be adequately described or explained in words. Whatever we say, we can never do justice to the full complexity of things.

However, in order to understand life and thereby learn how to shape our own actions we have to simplify that process by breaking it down into smaller systems – about which we can make generalizations and formulate laws. But in simplifying in this way we inevitably falsify. This procedure of simplifying is very necessary to our survival, however, and it only gives rise to problems when we think that, having comprehended the generalizations and laws with which we pattern our experience, we have understood reality. An intellectual grasp of the conditioned process can help us to orientate our lives. However, real understanding, according to Buddhism, can only come about through the direct experience called Insight which transcends the intellect.

We have seen that the most basic formulation of the Buddha's Insight is stated in this way:

> This being, that becomes; from the arising of this, that arises; this
> not being, that does not become; from the ceasing of this, that
> ceases.

Every element of reality depends upon conditions – without which it cannot occur. This principle governs all phenomena. We make generalizations and formulate laws in order to explain the relationship between specific conditions and their effects. The whole conditioned process can be broken down into the different levels of evolutionary development we have looked at in previous chapters. At each level a new set of laws applies.

One school of Buddhist philosophy distinguishes five levels or orders of conditionality. There is, first of all, the physical-inorganic order whose laws are, more or less, those of physics and chemistry. Secondly, the organic order is similarly the concern of biology. Thirdly comes the lower mental order, which involves mental functions of a non-volitional kind, such as perception. Fourthly, the higher mental order, which is the karmic order – the volitional level. The fifth is the Dharmic or transcendental level.

These laws can be related to the different levels of evolutionary development. Inanimate objects are subject to the laws of the physical order. Simple organisms are subject to both the physical and organic orders. These two orders, together with the non-volitional mental level, govern organisms with developed sense faculties. Moving up the evolutionary scale, human beings are subject to these three lowest orders together with the karmic level, and they may be subject, as they make spiritual progress, to the Dharmic order as well.

These orders may also be correlated with our previously established hierarchy of the evolution of consciousness. The physical and organic orders correspond to the non-conscious, the organic to the lowest level of primitive sense consciousness, the non-volitional mental order to sense consciousness, the karmic order to self- and spiritual consciousness, and the Dharmic to transcendental consciousness. The higher levels of consciousness, as we will see later, are not always associated with the lowest orders of conditionality according to tradition: self-consciousness is not always associated with the physical and organic levels, for instance; that is, it is not always connected with a material body. Self-consciousness in the human being, however, encompasses the first four levels up to and including the karmic order and moreover has the capacity to unfold the highest level, that of the Dharmic order, from within itself. It can form a bridge, in other words, stretching from the non-conscious to the superconscious.

This is an inspiring picture of the human place in evolution, but it also makes clear that any analysis of human behaviour according to these orders of conditionality is very difficult. Each of these orders, which together govern human functioning, is a complex of laws. Furthermore, each order is interwoven with all the others, acting and being acted upon by them. A human being is a nexus of all these orders and, because of this, we cannot, or should not, arrive at easy generalizations and rapid judgements about people, even ourselves. Not only do we need a deep understanding of human nature in general but also a thorough acquaintance with the person in question to disentangle all the different conditioned processes on all the different levels.

I hope it is now clear that the karmic order, with which we are concerned in this chapter, is but one level of conditionality within the very subtle mingling of processes that is the human being. We need to beware of interpreting it too rigidly, as some modern exponents of Buddhism have done, and we should not forget that we are dealing with that elusive quantity, the human heart, and not with a mechanical robot.

The Principle of Karma

The second circle of the Wheel of Life illustrates the workings of the principle of karma. It is divided into two segments, one black and one white. In the black half, tormented beings tumble downwards, naked, hounded by fierce demons. In the white half, smiling men and women wearing bright garments wind upwards, performing meritorious actions. The message of the image is that we inevitably reap the appropriate fruit of our karma.

Karma is a Sanskrit word (in Pali it is *kamma*) that means 'willed action'. It is therefore applicable to the level of self-consciousness and applies to the deliberate actions of individuals, however partial or distorted their self-awareness may be and however sketchy their individuality. The law that governs the functioning of the karmic order is that *every willed action produces an effect that is, eventually, experienced by the agent, the nature of the effect being determined by the intention with which the action is performed.*

A willed or intentional action is one consciously undertaken by an individual to bring about a desired end – to be distinguished from involuntary behaviour such as blinking, falling over when pushed, or inadvertently knocking over a cup when reaching for the teapot. The *degree* of consciousness involved in a deliberate action may, however, be relatively low. We often act in a divided state, giving only part of our attention to what we do. This may be the consequence of a habitual distractedness very common amidst the many stimuli of modern life, or it may come out of an unwillingness to recognize fully what we are doing, which may stem from a variety of reasons. This can result in the sort of behaviour often labelled 'Freudian': we have a desire for something but we also have a strong feeling that we should not want that thing. So we set about expressing the desire in whatever way we can whilst, at the same time, not fully acknowledging, even to ourselves, that it is what we want. We banish the desire to the very fringes of consciousness so that we can effectively pretend that we do not feel it. Though complex, actions performed under the influence of such unwanted desires are none the less intentional, however peripheral to our consciousness the wish may be. The terms 'subconscious' or 'unconscious' motivation are misleading in this case, for where there is motivation there is some degree of consciousness. Willed actions, then, range from those directed to an objective that is very clearly formulated and whole-heartedly longed for to the kind of cloudy, vague, or incidental behaviour in which we do not allow ourselves to be clear about what we are doing.

Intentional action is not only bodily action. The principle of karma includes both speech and thought as actions that also produce their effects upon the agent. It is the intention, the act of wanting something and forming the decision to get it, which establishes the karmic conditions. A strong intention that is thwarted by circumstances produces much the same karmic consequences as the same degree of intentionality that fulfils its objective. From the point of view of the karmic principle, consciousness or intention is primary – and the karmic status of acts of body or speech is determined by the state of mind that lies behind them.

The Effects of Karma

Intentional actions, then, produce effects that are experienced by the agent. The law of karma therefore governs the relationship between the self-conscious subject and the world which is objective to him or her. The self is, as it were, in dialectical interplay with the other. One way to look at this is to see the karmic order as a kind of 'feedback system' incorporating the subject and the object. Every time the subject acts, the whole system is affected. The actions of the subject modify the object – that is the world of the subject – which then adjusts itself in order to absorb the modification. This, in turn, feeds back an effect upon the subject. The kind of adjustment needed depends upon the nature of the initial action and so the effects that feed back to the agent depend upon the intention with which he or she acted.

The effects of karma are experienced both subjectively and objectively. What we think, do, or say reinforces certain trends within our own mental life and, to that extent, modifies our own consciousness. The mental images and memories that occur to us, the moods that overcome us, are shaped by what we have thought, said, and done in the past. This is the subjective effect. Objectively, the effect of our past actions is to be seen in the situations we find ourselves in and the experiences that come to us. Since the karmic order is not based upon a simple mechanical causation, it is very hard to discern the way in which our past actions condition our present objective experience. What draws consciousness and experience together is a type of affinity. 'Like attracts like,' the intentions we form attract to us the appropriate experiences. To give a simple example: when I first became interested in Buddhism, I suddenly noticed Buddhism all around me. Newspaper headlines made reference to it; Buddhist book titles jumped out at me in shop windows; I would meet people who would tell me anecdotes about Buddhism. Whether or not such phenomena were there before, my consciousness now had some connection with them and seemed almost to attract them to itself.

If the nature of the effect is determined by the nature of the intention with which the action is performed, it is important to be aware of one's motivation. Intentions can be analysed into those based on greed, hatred, and delusion and those based on metta, generosity, and awareness. Actions performed with the unwholesome motivations of greed, hatred, and delusion are often described as 'unskilful' and those based on metta, generosity, and awareness as 'skilful'. These are the basic terms of Buddhist ethics. Put simply, under the principle of karma, skilful actions produce pleasant effects and unskilful actions produce unpleasant effects. The consequence of acting from unwholesome motivations is that, in the end, we suffer. When we act from a positive state of mind we are building up happiness for ourselves.

The Complexity of Karma

The basic principles of the law of karma may be stated simply, but it is seldom possible, with any certainty, to ascribe a particular experience to the workings of karmic conditionality. It is even more difficult to connect any particular volitional action with any particular effect. In the first place, the karmic order is only one of five orders of conditionality and it may be possible to explain an effect satisfactorily within any or all of the orders. To quote a classic example: a fever might be the consequence of a sudden change in temperature and, therefore, belong to the physical order of conditionality; it might be caused by a viral infection, operating under the biological order; mental strain may have brought it on, under the lower mental order; some past unskilful action may be its cause, under the karmic order; or else it may be due to the restructuring of the whole system of body and mind as a result of Insight, under the transcendental order. The only way in which one can tell whether an experience is the result of past karma is by eliminating all other possible explanations. If none of them adequately accounts for the phenomenon in question, then karmic forces may be at work, although there can be no certainty. So, in the case of a fever, one would try to cure it by using remedies appropriate to each order of causation; only if these failed might one tentatively conclude that past actions were the cause.

The fact that there are many levels of conditionality at work in our lives makes it hard to discern when karma is operating. The complexity of our human motivation further obscures the picture, for we are thinking, speaking, and acting all the time, setting up trends with each intentional act that modify our experience both directly through the mind and indirectly through the environment. It is very difficult to isolate particular acts from this great current of willing. Karmic conditionality is, rather, a matter of broad tendencies and trends. All our different acts of intention mingle together, some setting up dominant themes, some merely reinforcing established patterns, some diluting the effects of others, and some cancelling others out. Different intentions are not all of the same strength and the degree of unwholesomeness and wholesomeness varies from action to action. Some karmas are said to be 'weighty', such as murder on the one hand and the experience of higher states of consciousness on the other. These have a very powerful influence on the overall pattern of karmic activity. Some actions are habitual and shape our future by inertia, for the more frequently we behave in certain ways the more they become a permanent part of our character. Some karmas simply have a cumulative effect in conjunction with others. The 'weight' of a particular action and its relationship to the overall stream of willing determines how long it takes to mature in an effect or, indeed, whether it matures at all. We cannot, therefore, very readily ascribe a particular effect to a particular past action. The karmic level within us is like a mighty current of energy that is fed by each single thought, word, and deed. It is the total momentum of this current that shapes our minds and the world in which we live. By our own actions, we constantly recreate ourselves.

The Natural Law of Karma
The operation of karma is entirely natural and in no way depends upon some superior, divine power. No external authority metes out suffering or happiness to us. Our own actions determine whether we have pleasure or pain, for we attract suffering or joy by the way in which we live our lives. The momentum generated by our actions leads to suffering or pleasure under the karmic law just as a stone falls to the ground when it is released under the law of gravity of the physical order.

The Buddhist teaching on karma is in no way fatalistic. It does not teach that everything that happens to us is the result of karma, as there are all the other orders of conditionality to be taken into account. So even though all intentional acts have effects for the agent, it is not the case that all the effects one experiences are the consequence of past actions. Moreover, even when weighty unskilful karma has been performed, it is possible to counteract it with skilful actions, although they will have to be of corresponding, or even greater, intensity. Nor does the fact that our past actions have, even in a general way, shaped our present experience mean that we must passively accept the situation. We should do whatever we can to remove the pain and suffering that is the consequence of the other orders of conditionality, as well as try to establish a more skilful pattern of behaviour that will override any negative effects of our own past deeds. Buddhists should work strenuously to remove suffering wherever they find it, whether in themselves or in others. Poverty, cultural deprivation, and crippling diseases may or may not be the result of karma but, in all cases, every effort should be made to relieve them. The charge of passivity sometimes brought against Buddhism has no basis in its doctrines for, above all, the Dharma stresses personal responsibility and effort as the prerequisites for any further development.

One final, minor point of possible misunderstanding needs clarification. At the outset of this discussion on karma, we saw that involuntary actions were not the subject of karmic conditionality and the example of knocking over a cup while reaching for the teapot was given. Now, one did not intend to knock over the cup and could not be accused of doing so with 'malice aforethought'. But one can be blamed for having carried out one's intention to pick up the teapot carelessly and without due mindfulness. To take a well-known and less trivial example, a certain monk of the Buddha's time went to visit some householders. Finding them to be out, he went into the house and seated himself on what he thought was a bench covered with a cloth. It was actually a crib containing a baby that was smothered and killed when he sat on it. The Buddha was asked if the monk had committed murder and he replied that he had not since it was not his intention to kill. He was, however, guilty of an act of gross carelessness from which he would suffer a karmic consequence. Inadvertence springs from an unwholesome mental state.

This, then, is the second circle of the Wheel of Life that shows the operation of the karmic principle. In the black half, under the influence of unwholesome mental states, beings perform unskilful actions and suffer the painful consequences as they spin upon the Wheel. In the white half, under the influence of wholesome mental states, beings perform skilful actions and experience happiness and pleasure as they ascend the Spiral. This Spiral eventually leads beyond the Wheel. Once the state of Enlightenment has been reached, no more karma is produced. Even though he acts, and acts with very great and subtle effectiveness, the Buddha's actions have no consequences for him. Dwelling as he does in non-dual awareness, there is, as it were, no feedback system for him to set off – one might say he has become the total system. The Buddha moves in perfect harmony with all things, unrestricted by any conditions.

An understanding and appreciation of this principle of karmic conditionality – since it underpins the ethical and spiritual life – is vitally important. If there were no such principle the consequences of skilful and unskilful actions would be unpredictable and unrelated to the intentions with which they were performed. It would not matter how we acted because pleasant and painful experiences would come to us in a quite arbitrary way without any meaning or discernible pattern. Sustained effort at any spiritual practice such as meditation would be worthless because we could not be certain of its positive effects. In the same way as the other orders, the karmic order is subject to stable laws by which effect follows cause. The law of karma guarantees that our actions will have appropriate consequences and therefore that we can grow. Scepticism on this point, from the Buddhist perspective, is fatal, for one would be doubting that personal effort has any effect and, therefore, that there can be any spiritual progress at all. Human beings would be merely the helpless victims of an inscrutable fate without any logic or coherence. Confirmed rejection of this principle is itself a weighty unskilful action since it negates both morality and the Spiral Path.

It is not hard, in a general way, to see that actions have consequences in accordance with the law of karma, yet there are some things that happen to us that seem to frustrate all our efforts, for which no cause in our past actions can be readily discerned. Some of what happens to us seems quite arbitrary. Furthermore, each of us is born with certain advantages or disabilities. How can we bear karmic responsibility for our birth? Buddhism asserts that the law of karma does not operate within one lifetime alone because we are, in accordance with our karma, born again and again.

Many Lives

Before we can explore more fully the Buddhist doctrine of rebirth, we need to build some picture of the cosmological background against which our many lives are lived. The Buddha denied that the cosmos was created, teaching that the cyclic process has no discernible beginning or end. Within the limitless dimensions of space, the ageless play of conditions throws up from time to time innumerable world-systems that come into being and pass away in the course of immeasurable aeons. In some of these world-systems conditions are established that can support life and so the long march of the lower evolution begins.

At the same time, streams of self-consciousness, under the force of their past volitions, take embodiment again and again within these various world-systems. This process, too, has no beginning. It will end only if spiritual progress is made and Buddhahood is reached, at which point consciousness passes beyond our comprehension and there is no further rebirth within the mundane.

We have, then, these two parallel processes at work in multitudinous world-systems: the evolution of lower life-forms and the wanderings of streams of self-consciousness from birth to birth. These streams of self-consciousness intersect the lower, biological evolution at the point where it has evolved organisms that are capable of expressing self-consciousness. Rebirth continues to take place within the different spheres and levels of the world-systems until Enlightenment is reached.

Each time death occurs, the continuum of consciousness forms a new body for itself in dependence on its own past actions, for it is our own intentions and volitions that are the force that assembles, out of the raw material of the physical, biological, and mental orders, a body and a personality. The kind of body we have and the kind of world we inhabit are appropriate to our own state of consciousness, which fashions them in its own likeness. This stream of volitional energy, modified with each new act of body, speech, or mind, is what we fundamentally are, and it moulds life, again and again, to suit its own changes. This we have been doing since beginningless time and we will continue to be reborn in this way unless we choose to evolve to a higher level.

Not only are there innumerable world-systems capable of supporting life, but each such system, according to Buddhist cosmology, contains many dimensions. Each world consists of stratified planes, paralleling the evolutionary hierarchy. The lowest group of planes is termed the sphere of sensuous desire. It is made up, first of all, of the four unpleasant and painful places of rebirth: the hell, hungry ghost, animal, and titan realms. The human world and the lower heavens complete the sensuous sphere that corresponds to the Wheel, and to sense and self-consciousness. The next two spheres, those of archetypal form and of no form, contain the heavens of the higher gods and correspond to what we have called spiritual and transcendental consciousness and to the Spiral up to the point of Buddhahood. The realm of the Buddhas is outside the world-systems altogether and corresponds to the dawning of Absolute Consciousness.

Within the mundane spheres – of sensuous desire, archetypal form, and no form – with their many subplanes, the drama of rebirth takes place. Unskilful actions, performed with unwholesome volitions, tend to direct consciousness towards the lower, painful realms of the sensuous sphere. Skilful deeds lead to all the other realms of the sensuous and to the spheres of form and no-form. Insight into reality, alone, leads to the highest sphere of all, the transcendental. Until that point of Insight, one can pass up and down, around and around, within all the different worlds, in accordance with one's state of mind. No world is permanent, there is no eternal damnation or salvation. One remains in any particular state only so long as the momentum from one's previous intentions is sufficiently strong to keep one connected with that world and no counteracting tendency has been established.

The concepts of rebirth and of a multi-layered universe are both, perhaps, unfamiliar to most people today. We will examine the Buddhist teaching of multiple worlds and the mechanics of rebirth in later chapters, but first we will give some attention to the basis for the Buddhist belief in the doctrine of rebirth.

In the West, the two most commonly held views regarding death are that it is the absolute termination of consciousness or that it is succeeded by a state of eternal bliss in heaven or suffering in hell (though many may hold this view in a less categorical form). The materialist position that human consciousness is obliterated at death is more and more commonly considered the most reasonable alternative. It has no greater claims, however, to probability than any of the other three possible beliefs about birth and death. Indeed, it may be the least supportable of the four beliefs that are logically possible. It must be the case that there is either no life before birth nor after death, or life before birth but not after death, or after death but not before birth, or both before birth and after death (this latter includes the Buddhist doctrine of rebirth). If one approaches these four positions with an open mind, as it were for the first time, there is no immediate reason to adopt any one of them, for each of them is *logically* consistent. As Voltaire has said, 'To be born many times is no more miraculous than to be born once'! Materialists claim that their view is the most reasonable because there is no evidence for any other. There is no conclusive evidence, however, that there is *no* life before birth or after death. How can there be? There can only be the negative evidence of no evidence. One who believes firmly in the materialist view holds to it through faith no less than he considers his opponents cling to their beliefs. If there was, indeed, no evidence, then, in reason, one could only be cautiously agnostic, declaring that *in the present state of knowledge* there is nothing to suggest that life extends beyond birth and death, and remaining open-minded about whatever new evidence might appear.

I know of no one who believes that there is life before birth but not after death – although, in itself, it is no more or less absurd than to assert that there is life after death but not before birth. Both these positions generate problems in positing an entity with an eternal beginning and a finite end in the one case and a finite beginning and an eternal end in the other. It seems, on the face of it, far more likely that if existence succeeds death it also precedes birth and vice versa. Certainly, those who hold either of these views will not find it hard to consider the possibility of rebirth in the Buddhist sense.

Evidence for Rebirth

If, then, there were no evidence for rebirth we would have to remain agnostic. There is, however, quite a lot of evidence, and there are other supporting reasons for accepting at least a provisional belief in rebirth. None of this evidence or these reasons amount to full proof because, on this particular topic, conclusive proof is very difficult since many of the phenomena offered as evidence may be explained in other ways. Taken together, however, all the different facts build a strong case for the doctrine.

It should give us pause to think, in the first place, that belief in rebirth has been widespread in human history. It is by no means a peculiarity of the great religions of India: Buddhism, Hinduism, and Jainism. Many tribal peoples the world over, such as some North American Indians, Polynesians, and African tribesmen, have such a belief. It has even had a distinguished history in our own Western culture. According to Greek accounts, the ancient Egyptians believed in rebirth – although this has been disputed by modern scholars. Before they were Christianized, the Celtic peoples considered that each man lived many times. Among the Greeks, the doctrine was taught by the mystery schools of Orphism and inherited by the Pythagoreans. It is probably from them that Plato derives the famous Myth of Ur in *The Republic*, which gives an account of the experiences after death leading to rebirth. Many Gnostics and Neoplatonists believed in reincarnation and, most astonishing of all, among early Christians the belief was not uncommon. Two prominent Church Fathers, Origen and Justin Martyr, are known to have taught the pre-existence of souls. Origen's doctrine of metempsychosis was not finally declared anathema until the sixth century. In the twelfth and thirteenth centuries the Cathars of southern France and Italy held reincarnation as one of their main tenets. It was to eradicate this 'heretical sect' that the first European crusade was launched and the 'Holy Office' or Inquisition established. The belief continued to recur in Europe despite strong opposition from the Church, which enforced orthodoxy with violence if necessary. In this connection, it is interesting to consider that, though Buddhists have hardly ever persecuted those who disagree with them, no one has seriously challenged the teaching of rebirth from within the Buddhist tradition while many Christians have been prepared to die for this belief. More recently, various individuals – Voltaire, Benjamin Franklin, Napoleon, Henry Ford, to name a few of the more prominent – have, quite independently, declared their belief that they have lived before. This fact of widespread and recurrent belief does not, of course, prove the truth of rebirth. However, many independent versions of the belief in reincarnation display strong similarities.

More concrete evidence can be found in reports by people who claim to have been reborn. In many traditions, people have recounted what they supposed were memories of past lives. The Buddha himself is said to have had the capacity to remember many previous lives and to have recounted them to his followers. In the Tibetan Buddhist tradition there is a detailed teaching contained in the so-called *Tibetan Book of the Dead* about the process of death and rebirth, and this is said to derive from direct experience.

Historical accounts of this kind are not susceptible to any form of verification. Closer to home, however, some children claim that they can remember having lived before. In the West, these are usually dismissed as fantasies or worse but, in the East, where rebirth is accepted belief, they are taken more seriously. Some modern academic researchers have carried out detailed enquiries into cases of this sort, both in the East and in the West. Their findings have been quite remarkable. Children have claimed to remember a past existence in a place that they have never visited in this life. They have given details of a past life that no one around them could have known and which, when checked, have been found to be extraordinarily accurate. Although the various cases come from very different cultures and backgrounds, there is, again, considerable concurrence in the broad details of the stories and certain themes are seen to recur. Much more research needs to be carried out but already the evidence is mounting that some children, at least, have lived before. Absolute proof is impossible in this field since, in the nature of things, one cannot set up an environment so rigidly controlled as to rule out all other potential sources of the information that presents itself as memories of a past life. These stories are sometimes explained away as collusion or trickery, unconscious influence from forgotten experiences, or as instances of telepathy. They do, however, constitute further suggestive evidence.

Similar cases were known in Tibet before the Chinese invasion. It was widely held that those who had developed far on the Path could choose where and when they would be reborn. Some lamas – Tibetan spiritual teachers – would give indications on their deathbeds of the time and place of their next birth and a watch would then be maintained for the fulfilment of those predictions. Children born under the appropriate circumstances would be very carefully examined to see whether they gave any signs that might suggest they were the reincarnated lama. Usually, neither the parents nor the child would be told what was happening at this stage so that no collusion could take place. Finally, once a child had been selected as the most likely candidate, he would be shown various articles that had belonged to the dead lama, mixed with similar items. In many cases, it appears, the child would not only select the lama's belongings but would show signs of recognizing his former friends and associates and some would even have strong memories of their former lives. Once a child had been acknowledged as an incarnation, he would be trained to continue his previous life's work. Sometimes, of course, this procedure was abused for the sake of the power and prestige that recognition could bring to the child's family and sometimes, no doubt, it was carried out in a naïve and superstitious manner. It is very unlikely that all or perhaps most of those considered to be the incarnation of former teachers were really so. None the less, some of these 'tulkus' – incarnate lamas – were very remarkable men and their selection seems to have taken place under what amounted to something like scientific control.

Further supportive evidence for rebirth is to be found in certain cases of hypnosis and of anaesthesia. Some practitioners of hypnotherapy have been able to take their patients back to their own birth and then back to what presented themselves as previous lives. Sometimes, it is claimed, this has yielded details about the past that have later been independently verified and that the subjects were unlikely to have known in their present life. Under anaesthetic, many people have reported looking down at their own bodies from a point several feet away: in itself, this suggests that consciousness can exist independently of the body. There are cases of people who have been clinically dead but have then come back to life again. Their hearts have stopped beating and their respiration has ceased temporarily during an operation. They, too, have reported experiences of being out of the body but they have also related stranger experiences, very similar to those recounted by people who claim to remember what happened to them after their death in a previous life.

The doctrine that we are born many times may help to explain a number of difficult questions. For instance, some of the phenomena of spiritualism seem to be authentic and may be accounted for in these terms. A newborn child, under this belief, is shaped not only by heredity and environment but by the momentum of consciousness carried over from a previous life. Infant prodigies can best be explained in this way. The great musical geniuses – the youthful Mozart, Beethoven, and Handel – are well known, and there are, in other fields, many examples of knowledge and talent manifesting at a very early age. Buddhist tradition argues that these talents have already been acquired and developed in a previous life.

Buddhism and Rebirth

For the Buddhist, the truth of the teaching of rebirth does not rest upon scientific evidence. Such evidence is, of course, interesting in itself and may dispose others to give more favourable attention to the Dharma. Ultimately, the truth of the doctrine lies in experience. In the first place, it is said to be possible to remember past lives and it is a mark of the attainment of higher levels of development that one can do this. Some meditation practices are even specifically directed to developing this ability – although they are probably rarely used. One establishes, to begin with, a very powerful state of tranquillity and concentration and then systematically takes oneself back in memory from the moment one started meditating, recalling everything that happened until one remembers the moment of birth and then, before that, the previous life. For the Buddha, however, memory of past lives is not merely a feat of prodigious concentration, but derives from the very nature of his Enlightened mind. He has realized an awareness beyond duality and beyond time, and he has, thus, access to any point in time. One way to look at this is that it is not so much that he remembers his past existences but that he directly surveys them from a point outside time.

The truth of the doctrine of rebirth is also to be found in the higher state of meditation. Consciousness is there experienced in a far purer form that transcends physical existence. It becomes clear that the body depends upon consciousness, not consciousness on the body. One realizes that consciousness cannot be destroyed and that it is a powerful stream of energy that cannot be contained within one life.

Many Buddhists, however, have neither the ability to remember their past lives nor the experience of those higher states where consciousness is seen to transcend the body. Their belief in rebirth rests not on their own direct evidence but, for the time being, on their respect for others. They have faith in the Buddha, in the Buddhist tradition, and in their own spiritual teachers and friends. Just as we believe in the existence of countries that we have never visited on the basis of what we are told by those we have found to be reliable in other instances, so we place our reasoned faith in those whom we find to be spiritually trustworthy. It is by no means a blind or superstitious or unquestioning faith and it can only be provisional until further experience confirms or denies it.

Although some modern, rationalizing Buddhists have tried to explain away the Buddha's teaching of rebirth so that they can make the Dharma fit in with modern 'scientific' views, it is an integral part of Buddhism. It is open to doubt whether anyone actively disbelieving in rebirth can be a Buddhist – though many Buddhists, especially in the West, are agnostic on the subject. One cannot really be a Buddhist unless one does have faith in it. This does not mean that those who find themselves unable to give it credence cannot develop as individuals or cannot make good use of Buddhist teaching and practice. Since their perspective on existence, however, will be limited to the period between a single birth and death and since their conception of consciousness will be essentially materialistic, from a Buddhist point of view their development will be restricted. None the less, any development is better than none and, so long as a person retains an open mind, experience of higher levels of awareness is likely to convince them that consciousness does transcend the physical body and therefore that it may be reborn. A scepticism that arises from an honest intellect is certainly no barrier to growth. It is only rigid dogmatism and stubborn closed-mindedness that can be a permanent barrier to truth.

The principle of rebirth has application outside the round of birth and death. Coming into being and passing away is the destiny of all conditioned things. The passing of each phenomenon gives rise to a new one in dependence upon it. This is as true on the psychological plane as on the natural. Just as flowers, trees, and our own bodies die in order to be reborn in new substances and organisms, so our thoughts and feelings rise and fall in an endless sequence. We are, in this sense, reborn moment by moment, recreated by our own past. Those who cannot provisionally accept the teaching of rebirth as applied to human life can see it symbolically as an underlying principle in all phenomena. And, as my own teacher has pointed out to sceptics, those who call themselves Buddhists but who do not believe they will be reborn will have to make sure they gain Enlightenment in this life!

Limitless time and immeasurable space are the background to the Buddhist vision of human existence. Self-consciousness flows in a powerful stream of volition, building for itself bodies and worlds that most appropriately express its own nature. If it is unwholesome in character it forms lives of pain and frustration. If it is wholesome it will make progress on the spiritual path. It may traverse the Path in the course of countless aeons, rising slowly, life by life, or it may, with exceptional gifts and prodigious effort, pass from self-consciousness to transcendental consciousness in a single lifetime.

Ethics

It is against these vast perspectives that we now consider Buddhist ethics, for it is whether we act skilfully or unskilfully that determines our future rebirths – in dependence on the law of karma. As our self-consciousness grows, so too does our sense of what we should and should not do, connected with our realization that our actions have an effect – both upon ourselves and upon others. We begin to realize their effect upon ourselves, through the operation of the law of karma, when we see that our unwholesome states of mind produce further unpleasantness for us. When we indulge in negative states we feel worse and we seem to draw upon ourselves more and more difficulties and obstacles. Conversely, when we act from positive, wholesome states, we find that we feel lighter and happier, and life flows more smoothly. The more healthy-minded we are, the happier we become.

To begin with, it is seldom as straightforward as this since we may have bad karmic influences from the past still playing themselves out in our lives, so that it is not so easy to see the equation between our actions and their consequences upon us. For many people, the earlier stages of their spiritual life may be a process of purgation of habits and mental currents from the past that continue to affect them even though they are no longer behaving in those old ways. Present, more wholesomely motivated activity can help to counteract those past tendencies, but it may be some time before the direct benefits are reaped. In some cases it may even be that, if the process of purification is not carried through deeply enough, previous, very unskilful volitions do not allow present actions to come to fruition in this life. Our skilful activity is said to 'make merit'. It stores up for us a stock of good karmic potential that we will experience in the future, even in a future rebirth. In making merit, one gathers to oneself the conditions that will assist future growth: health, well-being, and good fortune.

Our first concern with ethics is likely to be self-interested, but there is more to Buddhist ethics than intelligent selfishness. As we develop, a natural sensitivity to others should begin to guide our actions. The mature individual empathizes with the selfhood of others and feels metta and concern for them. When they suffer, he or she feels compassion and does whatever can be done to alleviate their pain. When they are happy he or she rejoices with them. In this way, rising above the extended self-interest of family, nation, or social group and feeling disinterestedly for other beings, his or her actions are wholesomely motivated by metta and generosity. The individual cannot do what would harm another being and always tries, as much as possible, to help others. The ethical life, then, can be said to be based upon the love mode.

Our ethical life may start as a conscious attempt to cultivate better states of mind for ourselves, but it should blossom into a natural sense of what is skilful and unskilful on the basis of our empathy with others. This natural ethical sense is what might be called conscience. It is not, however, a superego or internalized authority, ordering one what to do or not do. Rather it is the promptings of awareness and metta, a resonance with all that lives.

Buddhist morality is not at all authoritarian. No God ordains on tablets of stone what should and should not be done. Morality is not conceived of in terms of law. True ethics cannot be reduced to a system of rules, for it is not what an action is that determines its ethical status but the intention that underlies it. As we have seen, those actions performed on the basis of unwholesome volitions, rooted in greed, hatred, and delusion, are termed unskilful and those that spring from the wholesome states of generosity, love, and awareness are called skilful. That an act is said to have been done skilfully implies that it is done with intelligence and care, with a kind of practical ethical ability equivalent to the practised skill of a craftsman. To act skilfully, it is not enough blindly to follow a set of rules. We need a mature sensitivity to, and feeling for, others, as well as an awareness of what the consequences of any action are likely to be. It is only then that we can be in a position to act skilfully for the benefit both of ourselves and of others.

The Precepts

While we are still learning to act skilfully it is hard to maintain sufficient mindfulness so that, at all times, we consider the consequences of every deed and take into account the feelings and needs of others. We need some sort of guideline against which we can measure our own behaviour. This is provided by the precepts, which outline the kind of behaviour that one who has developed a natural and spontaneous ethical sense does not engage in or even contemplate – because no trace of animosity or egoism mars his or her perfect sympathy with all life. It is only the Enlightened whose actions are completely skilful because all trace of the Wheel has been eradicated from their minds. The precepts outline what the Enlightened do not do and they are for us a standard or ideal with which we can compare our own behaviour. We are still motivated to act in ways that are unskilful but we want to develop skilfulness. The precepts act as a check on our own deeds and a reminder of what skilfulness really is. We undertake the precepts as a way of training ourselves in ethics:

I undertake the training principle of abstaining from harming
living beings.
I undertake the training principle of abstaining from taking
the not-given.
I undertake the training principle of abstaining from sexual
misconduct.
I undertake the training principle of abstaining from false speech.
I undertake the training principle of abstaining from intoxicants
that lead to heedlessness.

The five precepts, though negative in character, embody the positive virtues of loving-kindness, generosity, contentment, honesty, and mindfulness. My own teacher has formulated these as a set of five positive precepts, corresponding to the traditional ones.

With deeds of loving-kindness I purify my body.
With open-handed generosity I purify my body.
With stillness, simplicity, and contentment, I purify my body.
With truthful communication I purify my speech.
With mindfulness clear and radiant I purify my mind.

The first precept enjoins non-harm to living beings and advocates metta. This is the basis for all the other precepts since the ethical life is the life based on the love mode of operating. It is far-reaching in its implications, ruling out all forms of violence, coercion, manipulation, or exploitation. It calls for a vegetarian diet, and it certainly makes careers that involve the killing or ill-treatment of animals, let alone human beings, impossible. If one accepts this precept in its full depth it means the complete eradication of the power mode of operating – the complete antithesis of the love mode – and the uprooting of greed, hatred, and delusion. It means living in harmony with all beings. In the end, it means going beyond oneself altogether.

The remaining precepts work out in greater detail the implications of living by the love mode. To take from others what they do not give, to exploit them sexually, or to lie to them is to deny their selfhood and to act violently towards them. The last precept is more specific and cautions against a loss of mindfulness through intoxication for, in getting drunk, we revert to a lower level of consciousness and are likely to lose awareness of what we are doing so that we may fall from the love mode.

The precepts are an aid to the cultivation of a natural moral sense. The most effective means of developing more skilful behaviour is to associate with people whose actions and way of life are already skilful. In fellowship with them, we will imbibe morality. When we feel respect and genuine friendship for such people, they will be guides to what is skilful until our own conscience matures. We will naturally feel that we do not want to let them down by acting badly – not because of fear of being punished by them but because such is our respect for them that we do not wish to belittle ourselves in their eyes. They have become, as it were, the guardians of our nascent conscience and idealism and our sense of personal dignity will not allow us to act unworthily.

This second circle of the Wheel of Life shows us how ethics determine our future experience under the law of karma. The essential principles of the Dharma are here conceived in terms of morality. In a sense, all we really need to know is here: that we must develop wholesome mental states so that we will rise higher and higher on the Spiral and away from the Wheel altogether.

6

The Endless Round

The Twelve Links of the Endless Round

Out of the all-pervading gloom, we discern a tottering shape, unsteadily groping towards us. It is an old man, bent with his years but not with their wisdom. His eyes gaze before him in the vacant stare of total blindness, yet his face expresses a kind of stupid hopefulness. He thinks he has been this way before, he seems to picture to himself the landscape around him, and he moves forward eagerly. But, alas, he has never come this way before and the scene he imagines is quite different from the reality. Over and over again, he staggers and falls. But each time he drags himself to his feet with renewed hope. Now, he thinks, I remember the route. And he stumbles, on and on.

Next, we see a potter turning lumps of clay on a wheel and, with deft hands, shaping vases and bowls, pots and dishes. If we look closely, we will see that many different moods flit across the potter's face: sadness, anger, joy, guilt, conceit pursue each other, one by one. And each emotion leaves its mark; rage leaves the pot hard and awkward in shape, and the desires of craving too are mirrored in the resulting creation.

A young monkey frisks in a tree, leaping from branch to branch, never still for a moment. It sees, at the top of the tree, the glint of ripe fruit and up it leaps, hands and feet clasping the trunk, long tail curled and waving. It seizes the fruit, plucks it, and takes an enormous bite. Its mouthful still unchewed, another fruit catches its eye, further down this time. It drops, without noticing, the fruit it has just picked, swallows whole what is in its mouth, and dashes off, down towards the new enticement. Soon, the foot of the tree is heaped with half-chewed fruit.

Four people are seated in a rowing boat. One of them has the oars and another is steering. One is the lookout and shouts out excitedly, from time to time, reporting the vague shapes seen on the horizon. The fourth maintains a running commentary on where they are going, gives advice on how he thinks the others should be doing their jobs, and states his own preferences as to their destination. Occasionally, they quarrel and accuse each other of failing in their tasks. None of them really knows where they are going so they turn this way and that, following the whim of the moment. They do not realize that terrible dangers surround them: storms, rocks, and sea monsters. They do not know that their boat is leaking and is badly in need of repair.

A man sits within a house which has five windows and a door. Through these apertures he watches the world. A great concourse passes in and out at the door, consisting of many people, each dressed in their own way, carrying shopping or their lunch, work tools or sports gear, some happy and smiling, some with evil intent. The man watches these many sights very carefully.

A man and a woman gaze at each other, passionately. At last, they are alone together. Their hands entwine and pull each towards the other. Clasping each other close, they kiss and lock in embrace, straining to press their two bodies into one.

A howl of pain shatters the silence and a man falls to his knees, groaning, his hands pressed to his face. At the centre of his right eye, embedded deeply in it, is an arrow.

The day has been hot and dusty and a man has been working hard in the fields. He is seated, waiting. He is tired and dirty and, above all, thirsty, for he has not had anything to drink for some time. His mouth is dry and his tongue feels thick and heavy. A woman slowly and gracefully brings a glass of cool water to him. He calls her to him, angrily, with desperate impatience.

A woman is walking in the countryside. She has not eaten for many hours and her stomach gripes with hunger. She sees apples growing in an orchard and hurries over to them. Stretching on tiptoe, she grasps a fruit and pulls it from the branch.

Lost to all but their own urgent desire, the couple melt together in the act of love. Tumbling rapturously to their release, they do not know that a new life will soon begin in the woman's womb.

Beads of sweat cover the woman's face and her mind is swallowed in pain. Between her wide-open legs, with careful hands, a midwife gently eases the new being into the world.

A man has died and his corpse is being carried to the cremation ground, where a pyre will be built and the dead body consumed by fire.

These twelve scenes present themselves to us like tableaux on a revolving stage, each giving way to the next in an endless round. At each turn of the Wheel, the postures are slightly different, the figures are dressed in different ways and have new features, but the twelve scenes are always the same and always will be until we move from the Wheel to the Spiral.

Conditionality

Words can never capture the full richness of life. They can only be pointers or guides that we use to leap in imagination to the reality that they attempt to express. Often we become tangled with our own language and our words enmesh us in simplistic understandings that we cannot see since they are embedded in everyday speech. Because we label objects in the world with nouns we come to think of them as unchanging entities – isolated, coming into contact with each other only by a system of mechanical exchanges. We even think of ourselves in this same way. When we seek the origins of particular events, we tend to look for single causes, as if reality were a gigantic engine made up of levers and pulleys. We search for causes that have brought about the most subtle events, just as the unwinding spring turns a clockwork motor. While such a simplified view is perfectly adequate for ordinary practical purposes, it overlooks the inexpressibly complex interlinking of all elements of our universe. Objects are not opaque and solitary units but processes woven in with all the other processes that make up reality. It could even be said that each single event is the product of the entire cosmos.

These processes are not only interwoven in space and time; they are also, as we have seen, arranged into five orders, each level having its own laws of functioning, each affecting and being affected by the other orders. It is this dizzying dance of forces that our flat words try to convey. We need to make this attempt to describe the indescribable because words help us to reduce this cosmic complexity to a workable simplicity for the purposes of everyday functioning. With care, we may also find that words can lead us beyond themselves to an experience of the ineffable richness of existence. We will only succeed in achieving this transcendent realization if we use words not as mathematical signs but as poetry to carry us to new levels of direct understanding. This is how the Buddha used language in trying to communicate his own vision of the nature of reality.

In his famous formula of conditioned co-production, the Buddha showed that each thing, person, or event arises out of a field of conditions without which it passes away. It *arises in dependence on* these conditions. Each single event arises in dependence on a vast network of conditions that ultimately embraces the entire universe. Buddhist philosophers have distinguished a number of different kinds of conditioned relationship; not every condition has the same power of determination or is of the same importance as a conditioning factor. Some conditions are, in Western terms, efficient causes, some provide the supportive environment in which an event can take place, some are catalysts, and others again arise simultaneously with the object they condition. We do not have space here to go into the details of these and other kinds of conditions. The important point is that the Buddha did not see the world as a mechanical model: A causing B like billiard balls knocking one into the other. He gave expression to his vision in terms of a very complex set of conditioned relationships between ever-changing processes. It is, as it were, an ecological view of causality rather than one based on simple mechanics. In this way, far greater justice is done to the total complexity of things and it is a shorter step from words to direct experience.

All phenomena are subject to the principle of conditionality. Whether it be a rock or a passing bad mood, each can be shown to be one link in a vast chain of conditions. We have now to explore the application of the principle of conditionality to the phenomena of human birth and death. We move to the rim of the Wheel of Life since, for purposes of exposition, it is best to deal with this outer circle before we examine the six realms. Twelve scenes are arranged around the rim, each representing one 'link' in the 'chain' of conditionality that is human life.

According to early accounts, the Buddha, sitting beneath the tree of Enlightenment, with his new-found Insight systematically stripped back the layers of conditions within human existence. He was not seeking a first cause in the metaphysical sense. Buddhism teaches that there is no discernible beginning to the conditioned process and that, therefore, there was no act of creation from which everything unrolled. Whatever condition we come to, we can always seek the conditions in dependence upon which it arose. The round of conditions wheels on endlessly and always has done. What the Buddha revealed was that the chain of conditions that makes up human life is circular, without beginning or end. That chain consists of twelve links, although that number is, in a sense, arbitrary and the process could be analysed into more or fewer factors. Any link can be taken as the starting point and all the others will follow from it.

The Buddha's enquiry led him through different levels of conditions which, in the twelve links, are spread out over three lives (although the twelve links can also be seen moment by moment in our lives). Each condition is not necessarily of the same kind as the one that it precedes, so some factors turn up more than once during the chain. It is by no means a simple series of causes chasing the origin of any event back through time, from cause to cause – that could only lead to an infinite regress. But, despite its apparent complexity, the basic message of the teaching of the twelve links of the chain of conditioned co-production should become clear as we examine each link in detail. The chain is usually begun at ignorance, for this is the condition of greatest generality that underlies all the others. Ignorance, too, arises in dependence on causes, and even death gives rise to new phenomena, but we have to break into this vicious circle somewhere and ignorance is, methodologically speaking, the best place.

Ignorance

This link is illustrated by the image of a blind man who blunders forward, unable to see where he is going. So ignorance is blindness, a not seeing. It is lack of insight into the reality of things, lack of imagination, lack, even, of Enlightenment. Ignorance does not, however, consist merely in the fact that we do not see but that we think we do: we are ignorant of the real nature of things but we think we know.

All our actions and thoughts are based on assumptions about the meaning and purpose of life, albeit unconscious and unsystematized.

A course of radical self-questioning quickly reveals our ignorance. If we start to examine what is in our minds, trying to see how we came by what we take to be our knowledge, and questioning our own underlying assumptions, we realize that there is very little that we really know in any strict sense. As we have already seen in the opening chapter, most of what passes for our knowledge is derived from other sources. The views of those around us we absorb by a kind of osmosis – we want to belong, to be part of a wider group, and so we accept the prevailing view. What the group takes to be knowledge, that we know. The facts or views held by the group may well be correct but our basis for holding them is not our own individual assessment but our primitive desire to belong. Not only does the group form our opinions, but our own desires determine what we believe. To a large extent, we believe what we want to believe and we see what we want to see. Our 'knowledge' then is rationalization, the intellectual crystallization of our basic attitudes. Our perception of the world is riddled with our subjective reactions.

Even when we begin to think a little for ourselves, leaving behind the shallow opinions of hearsay, we are only too ready to arrive at final judgements on matters about which we have little, if any, information. To give an example from my own experience, it is surprising how swiftly intelligent and well-respected people can dismiss Buddhism as cold and nihilistic. Perhaps they have been misled by poor translations of Buddhist texts. But, as reasonable people, they should have examined the source of the evidence they were accepting to see whether the testimony was sound. Again and again, in many fields of experience, we assume knowledge prematurely. We think that we understand other people's motives. We assume we comprehend the complex manoeuvrings of international politics. We confidently predict the outcome of events in our own lives. Having very little experience of the phenomena in question does not seem to stop us from coming to our conclusions. Even if we had information from sources we considered reliable, we could not be sure of our conclusions, we could still only arrive at an inference. We do not have certainty. This is not to argue that we shouldn't use inductive inference to make predictions and generalizations about what we do not know using whatever evidence we may possess. But we should reason soundly in drawing our conclusions and be aware of the worth of our evidence, and, above all, we should not forget that our judgements are inferences and not certain knowledge. The fact that we do not work in this way shows how the element of egoistical desire swamps our reason.

So, lost in our own ignorance, we formulate views based for the most part on shallow evidence and our own desires. Views surround us on all sides, thrust at us by the entire culture in which we grow up and live. It is almost impossible not to be influenced unless we are exceptionally strong-minded and awake. So hemmed in are we by opinion that it is hard to discriminate between what is wholesome and what is harmful. Wrong views, in the Buddhist sense, flourish in our immature minds. These views cover a vast range of attitudes from the most trivial to the most fundamental. Two examples may help illustrate this: the unthinking quasi-egalitarian view many people hold, and the materialist outlook on life.

The quasi-egalitarian has not only rejected outmoded social distinction based upon birth but has gone on to reject the very idea that some people are more developed than others, considering this also to be 'elitist' or 'undemocratic'. The attitude behind this view might be expressed as 'I am as good as anyone else and no one is better than me.' Such people will find great difficulty learning anything of importance from others and they certainly consider that looking up to them is a sign of weakness. Muddled egalitarianism of this type is very widespread in the West and gives rise to an outlook which is without any vertical dimension. All is flat and mediocre and real excellence is denied. Social hierarchy based on privilege of birth rather than individual merit needs to be clearly distinguished from a spiritual hierarchy based on individual attainment of higher levels of consciousness. Unless we acknowledge such a spiritual hierarchy we cannot develop through its various levels. If we feel no respect for those who have gone further than ourselves, we will be unable to learn from them. This hierarchy does not need to be formalized into grades and ranks (our own experience will teach us whom to respect if we are sincere), but our perspective must include that vertical dimension if we are to grow.

While confused quasi-egalitarianism flattens everything down to the level of the 'ordinary' man, materialism effectively restricts human life to the gratification of material needs. If we believe that all phenomena, ourselves included, are but arrangements of matter and that consciousness is annihilated at death, we can place little value on the development of the mind. Philosophy, aesthetic appreciation, culture in general, become at best mere pastimes to beguile us on the way to the grave. Morality – if it survives at all – is only a means of arranging our lives at least inconvenience to each other. Few values or ideals can survive in such a view of the world. It leaves the world meaningless and dull, and productive of only a few years of purely sensuous pleasure, if we are fortunate. Many people who hold this view believe it is 'scientific'. Yet, other more philosophical questions aside, before the materialistic outlook can be said to be scientifically proven, all the phenomena of mind must be satisfactorily explained in terms of physical laws, which is far from being the case at present. Materialism, then, is another belief, adhered to on grounds other than rational. Held firmly, this view leads to a shallow and egoistical hedonism and is characterized by a crushing drabness of outlook.

There are many views endemic in society at large, infecting those who are not immunized by awareness. Honest investigation may lead us to conclude that most of our mental contents are of this kind. There are views that cloud and confuse us about all aspects of life. According to Buddhist teaching, all these wrong views ultimately rest upon one of two fundamental views, eternalism or nihilism. Eternalism, put briefly, is the belief that behind all the phenomena of experience is an Absolute Being or God. The eternalist, therefore, thinks of life as an effort to liberate the ultimate in us, the soul, from the enslavement of the senses right up to union with that Absolute Being. A stern, even authoritarian, ethic and a wilful asceticism can stem from this way of seeing things. The eternalist lives removed from life, seeing the experiences it brings as illusory distractions from the God who lies behind them. Nihilism, on the other hand, is, according to Buddhism, the belief that death is the final end of life and that there is no reality beyond what we experience with our senses. Before the darkness swallows us up, all we can do is enjoy sensual pleasures, albeit quite refined ones. In one form or another, our lives are founded upon either of these two basic attitudes or else we oscillate from one to the other.

Both these views rest upon the distinction between subject and object. Eternalism is belief in an ultimate subject existing without any object, and nihilism is belief that the object alone has any reality. Caught in the split in our consciousness, we can only think of what is ultimate by eliminating one side of the split and absolutizing the other. At less rarefied, metaphysical levels, we either overemphasize our subjective life at the expense of the world around us or we devalue our consciousness by overvaluing the sensuous world. These distinctions are not only of philosophical interest, they have psychological and ethical ramifications for everyone. Eternalists, it is traditionally said, retreat from life, repressing the instinctual within them, and are preoccupied with their own subjective experience. Nihilists grab at the gratification of the senses and place no importance on the cultivation of higher faculties, except as a means to more refined sensuality.

Eternalism and nihilism underlie behaviour that is both very crude and greatly refined. Most of the great world religions are eternalist, although they have followers who are highly intelligent and sensitive. In the end, both are wrong views and lead only to distortion and cramping, for they rest upon that split in consciousness which is, from a Buddhist point of view, only a stage in evolution. As self-consciousness differentiates itself out of the mass of simple sense awareness, one aspect is identified as the subject of experience and the remainder is perceived as the object. Gradually, the literalness and rigidity of the boundary between the two is relaxed and they begin to intermingle and merge as consciousness is raised. In the end, the barrier between subject and object is removed altogether and a state of mind is experienced which is beyond duality and in which reality is seen as an endless play of conditions of inexpressible creative potentiality. There is no eternalism because within the play of conditions is to be found nothing permanent or fixed and no being that is absolute. There is no nihilism because the individual is just such a flow of states, one arising in dependence on the other, and death is merely a point of transition from one stage to another.

While there remains within us yet one hair's breadth between subject and object, we are ignorant and we do not see things fully as they are – that is, as part of the vast network of processes, all interwoven and interpenetrating, all arising in dependence on conditions. For Buddhism this is knowledge. When one has a direct experience of reality as the rise and fall of conditioned processes then there is certainty. And knowledge, here, is one and the same as compassion, for every element of reality is loved as if it were oneself – indeed, since no distinction now exists between self and other, it could be said that one is identical with the whole of reality.

Ignorance is our basic condition and we should face up to it. We need to accept that even our mundane knowledge is intelligent guesswork. All we can be certain of, at this moment, is that we are having certain experiences whose exact nature eludes us for the present. Everything else is assumption and estimate. Such honest scepticism is the beginning of knowledge. This point was made by Socrates when, on being pronounced the wisest man in Greece by the Delphic oracle, he declared that if he was wisest it was because he alone knew that he knew nothing whereas other men claimed to know. Once we are aware of our ignorance, we can begin systematically to cultivate wisdom.

Until ignorance has been replaced by wisdom, we need some intellectual guidelines. It is not enough to eradicate wrong views; we must cultivate right views. Right views are intellectual understandings that help us to grow. They are the basis on which vision and wisdom can arise. Fundamentally, right view consists in seeing that between eternalism and nihilism is a 'middle way' which is the perception of things as arising in dependence on conditions. Right view is this same conditioned co-production that we are now studying. It reveals, above all, a Path that we can follow, eventually crowning our efforts with wisdom.

While we are ignorant, however, we cannot help but act in an ignorant way. So, in dependence on ignorance, there arises volitional activity.

Volitional Activities

The next image, moving in a clockwise direction round the rim of the Wheel, is a potter shaping pots on a wheel. How each pot turns out depends upon the potter. What the pot is to be used for, the skill and experience and aesthetic sense brought to bear, even the potter's mood at the time of creation, all these determine what shape the lump of clay will become. The volitional activities are the formative forces which, like the potter and the pot, shape our own future. They are the sum total of all our willing, whether the intentions manifest themselves in overt action or in speech or remain as desires in our hearts. Although some volitions may be very powerful and have a dominant influence, it is the accumulated momentum of all our wishes that determines the flow of our lives. As a rope is plaited from many tiny fibres, no one of which reaches more than a fraction of its full length, so the direction and tendency of our being is shaped by the countless acts of volition that we make in the course of every day of our existence.

Our volitions are formative forces. Not only do they form our words and deeds but they imprint themselves directly on the world around us. Thought, desire, and consciousness are energies just as radiation or electricity are within the physical order. A thought has a direction, an inherent momentum that discharges itself upon the world. With every mental image, every longing, every coherent idea, we are radiating a very subtle, but extremely powerful, field of energy that influences our environment. When our thoughts are concentrated and intense enough, that influence may even be measurable. The phenomena of parapsychology – telepathy, clairaudience, psychokinesis, etc. – are all examples of the direct action of the mind. According to Buddhist tradition, such powers can either be systematically cultivated – although this is considered to be something of a sidetrack – or they arise spontaneously as one cultivates higher stages of consciousness. As one's mind becomes more and more unified and powerful, so the field of its influence becomes stronger. Sometimes, such powers arise as 'gifts' in people who have no apparent spiritual commitment. This is often explained as the consequence of actions performed in past lives.

The volitional activities are a kind of blueprint that acts on the level of the karmic order, moulding the mental, biological, and physical orders, and expressing its character through them. The impulses that move us manifest themselves concretely, not only in our actions but in our bodies and the worlds we inhabit. This is, in essence, what our lives are: the embodiment of our volitions in a world of experience.

The blueprint is a very complex one. It encodes all the greed, hatred, and delusion whereby we seek to build a false security for our fragile egos, but it also contains the outline of far deeper and more creative urges. Consciousness, at whatever stage, contains within it a momentum to attain higher levels. The pull of Buddhahood is present in the most egoistical and twisted personality. Just as the seed contains the flower and unfolds from within itself, so even rudimentary sense consciousness contains the full flower of transcendental consciousness and rises up towards it. We have the power to continue evolution by actively co-operating with the force of our own unfolding consciousness. Impulses expressive both of this urge to grow and develop and of our ignorance are part of the blueprint of our volitional activities. We are made up of these conflicting tendencies and our lives give full expression to them. Which one predominates is a matter for each of us to determine.

It is this formative blueprint of the volitional activities that carries over from the past life to shape the new one, forming matter into a body. Many traditions and the evidence available from modern research suggest there is an interval between one life and the next, known as the 'intermediate state'. According to the *Bardo Thödol*, the so-called *Tibetan Book of the Dead*, which gives a detailed account of the experiences of death and rebirth, the intermediate state lasts for forty-nine days – but this is probably symbolic. The length of time probably varies, depending on the volitional activities of the person who has died.

As death approaches, says the *Tibetan Book of the Dead*, consciousness gradually recedes from the physical body. This is spoken of as the dissolution of one element into another: earth dissolves into water, water into fire, etc. Just as when we go to sleep our hold on the world around us slips away bit by bit, so the physical world slowly recedes from us as we die. Each of the senses becomes weaker and weaker until we are left in a state of pure consciousness without any objective grounding. Nothing remains whereby we can identify ourselves, and so we experience our egohood being swallowed up in the undifferentiated infinitude of pure consciousness. Without the bases upon which we usually ground ourselves, we are brought face to face with reality. With nothing to limit or restrict it, the pure, non-dual awareness inherent within our self-consciousness is released.

The moment the experience of the 'clear light of reality' dawns upon us we recoil from it and scramble for the sure ground of ego-identity. Consciousness is still connected, though more and more loosely, with the body even after the heart has stopped beating. So, recoiling from the overwhelming vastness of pure awareness, we find ourselves again at the scene of our death. But we can no longer communicate with those around us. Consciousness is not situated in the body any more, and we find that we are witnessing our own funeral from within a 'mind-made' body. This body, although it has the appearance of a physical body to us, does not interact with the old world except in so far as we perceive, very vividly, what is happening there. Since it is, as it were, the direct emanation of our volitional activities, it moves as swiftly as our thoughts. As soon as some place comes to mind, we are there; as soon as we remember old friends, we stand before them.

So we find that we can no longer connect with our old life and that none of the people we spent our time with are even aware that we are still in their midst. Unable to ground ourselves in the old life, we continually oscillate between the experience of reality latent within our minds and the pull towards egohood. We cannot bear the brilliance of pure consciousness and yet the intermediate state offers us nothing firm upon which we can build an identity. We are lost in a storm of visions that are the productions of our own volitional activities. Now the visions unfold the deepest potential within us, now they represent to us our own greed, hatred, and delusion. In this intermediate state, we live out all the tendencies within us. Gradually, the fluctuations stabilize and the overall drift of our character asserts itself. We long to possess a body again that will crystallize our identity and we are drawn to a world that matches our own volitional blueprint.

According to the Tibetan tradition, death offers a unique opportunity to gain liberation or, at least, to attain a deeper understanding, for with the safe and familiar removed from consciousness we are faced directly with reality. Even if we cannot come to terms with this experience, we have the chance to see our own motivations and functioning more clearly, no longer hidden by the comfort of familiarity. We have the opportunity to make major changes in our consciousness since the fixed, habitual routine of our world has gone. Although death is the greatest of such periods of transition, it is not the only one. At death, we are removed from our old lives quite literally, but experiences of failure or loss of loved ones or extreme disruption through war or disaster are smaller deaths within life in which 'the bottom drops out of our world' and we are left 'floating in a vacuum'. Often these are times of mingled hope and anguish. The pain of loss and insecurity can be accompanied by an awareness of new horizons opening up and of freedom from old, restricting routines. Usually, of course, we settle back into our old ways but sometimes major breakthroughs can be made after such experiences.

Meditation, too, is an intermediate state since we are deliberately withdrawn from the sure ground of the senses. Dreams, even life itself, are considered to be intermediate states, for – all phenomena being impermanent – we can rely on no conditioned state for security.

From the *Tibetan Book of the Dead* it is clear that contact can be maintained with the dead person up to the time when they are conceived. They, at least, can hear us even if we cannot hear them. It is said that we can help them considerably by directing positive feelings towards them and even, if they are Buddhists, by reading to them from the *Tibetan Book of the Dead*, which guides the dead person through the different experiences between death and rebirth and teaches how to deal with them. The art of helping people to die in such a way that they enter the intermediate state in a clear and confident condition is well studied in the Tibetan tradition of Buddhism. Our attitude and behaviour can have a strong influence upon our dead friends and can help them to face the bewildering experiences of death with courage and awareness. This will, in its turn, enable them to be reborn under circumstances favourable to their future development.

It is the volitional activities that drive us through the intermediate state, determining the sequence and intensity of the visions and the world into which we will be reborn. By the process of attraction of a mental state for a like experience, which is the mechanism of the karmic order, the pattern of volitional activities leads consciousness to the appropriate world where rebirth is to take place. As we will see in detail in the following chapters, the human world is not the only one in which rebirth may take place. In some worlds, rebirth is by parturition as among humans, but in others it is apparitional – one appears, instantaneously, as a fully mature inhabitant of that realm.

If we are to be reborn into the human world we find ourselves wandering over the earth, seeking a body. We will be attracted to a particular couple who suit our karmic propensities. It seems that rebirth very often takes place within the same locality as previously inhabited and even in the same family, since the consciousness seeks the familiar, and the bonds of strong feeling, whether of craving or hatred, bind it to well-remembered places and faces. We see then the chosen couple in the act of copulation and, if we are to be reborn as a man, feel a strong attraction for the woman, and for the man if our karmic tendencies will find best expression as a woman. We try to take the place of the future parent of the same sex towards whom we, apparently, feel intense jealousy. At the moment when sperm and ovum meet, the full force of volitional energy concentrates upon that point of fusion and a living cell comes into being. So great is the shock of the condensing of our volitions upon one tiny cell that, at that moment, we faint away. Some highly developed beings can maintain consciousness as they enter the womb, some can even leave the womb fully mindful, but for most the moment of conjunction of sperm, ovum, and volitional activities is the moment when we are dipped in the waters of Lethe and memory of everything that went before is lost.

When that junction of the father's sperm, the mother's ovum, and the consciousness to be reborn takes place, there arises, in dependence on the volitional activities, sentience, the first tiny flash of consciousness in the single cell of the embryo.

Sentience

The third link is represented by a monkey in a tree, restlessly jumping from branch to branch as his eye is caught now by one fruit, now by another. The monkey represents the very primitive spark of sense consciousness which is the first moment in the mental life of the new being. Traditional expositions of the twelve links are at pains to insist that there is, in fact, nothing that is reborn. There is no soul that drops the shell of one body and takes on a new one, like a hand taking off one glove and putting on another. This would be eternalism. At the same time, the new life is not completely different from the old one. We would not be able to speak of rebirth at all if that were the case – this view would be nihilism. The new life is said to be 'neither the same as nor different from' the old one. This is not nearly as mysterious as it seems. The two lives are two different phases of one continuous process consisting of a flow of conditions. The old life establishes the conditions in dependence on which the new one arises. When a wave passes across the sea, there is no single drop of water that travels along with it from start to finish – the water particles do not move along but only around in circles. None the less, we speak of one wave, for there is a continuity of causation between the wave at its origin and at the point where it breaks upon the shore. In fact, everything conditioned is like that: a process consisting of conditions arising in dependence one upon the other. Thus sentience arises in dependence on the volitional activities established in the previous life.

Conception is the point at which biological evolution is intersected by the continuum of self-consciousness. The father's sperm and the mother's ovum contribute the material base, but this is not sufficient for life to start. There must be the blueprint generated in a previous life which can manifest itself through that particular genetic combination, a pattern of volitional activities which, suiting that particular sperm and ovum, can unfold itself through the developing embryo. Without both the genetic and the karmic factors, then, according to tradition, no conception can take place.

This first flash of sentience, though rudimentary, contains, in condensed form, the entire momentum from the past existence. Just as the first single cell of the embryo contains the genetic code in its DNA that will determine the general characteristics of the mature body, so the preliminary consciousness carries the seed of the adult personality. Sentience is the point at which the volitional activities begin to ground themselves in a new identity. In studies of rebirth, some physical characteristics and deformities seem to be the consequence of actions performed in the past life. It is traditionally held that karma determines whether one is good-looking or ugly, strong or weak, and the like. Human motivation is complex, however, and we have seen that it is hard to discern the workings of karmic conditionality, so we should beware of ascribing every physical infirmity to past actions. Yet the physical form is strongly influenced by the pattern encoded in sentience. The energies latent in acts of volition begin to discharge themselves by moulding the physical body. They have, as it were, seized upon a material configuration that corresponds to them and this they begin to shape. This is the karmic order of conditionality patterning the physical, biological, and mental orders – without in any way disrupting their laws.

Though the link of memory between one life and the next is usually lost, the broad characteristics of personality pass over – for personality is the general outline of our volitions. Carried in that seed of consciousness are the reactions of greed, hatred, and delusion and whatever there might be of love, generosity, and awareness. The embryo is no *tabula rasa*, a blank sheet formed simply from its environment. We come into life with dispositions and tendencies that emerge more clearly as we mature. So we see children displaying marked preferences and repulsions that they have not, apparently, learned from their parents. Indeed, it has often been remarked how quickly a little personality appears in an infant, well before it has had time to be shaped by its surroundings. Exceptional talent and genius, even, when displayed very young, is to be explained as the continuation of trends established in the past. Our attitudes and responses go very deep in us. We can never fully disentangle all the factors that have made us what we are since some of them go back over many lives. A certain amount of self-analysis may help us to understand what we feel more clearly but we cannot always determine why we feel it. We carry with us into life a residue of hatred and craving and of love and generosity. These will assert themselves no matter what our upbringing is in the present life. Neither our parents nor our social environment can be made to bear more than a part of the blame for how we are. Most of it we must shoulder for ourselves.

Life begins at the point when sperm, ovum, and volitional activities merge. It follows, then, that any termination of an embryo's development destroys life. When this is done intentionally, it is killing and therefore unskilful from a Buddhist point of view. Since self-consciousness does not begin to emerge or, rather, re-emerge – until the first years of a baby's life – it is not, perhaps, so obvious that abortion is murder. Yet Buddhism teaches that the harming of any living being, at whatever stage of evolution it may be, is unskilful and should be avoided. Since the sentience in the womb will, in the normal course of development, become the full self-consciousness of a human being, the unskilfulness is all the greater. From the point of view of the teaching of rebirth, one must also take into account the disruption to the being whose life would be cut short. Having just experienced the trauma of death and the terrifying uncertainty of the intermediate state, at last they have found a point upon which their energies can focus. When the consciousness is abruptly cut loose again, the effect may well be to accentuate feelings of fear and insecurity. All this needs to be taken into account when considering whether or not to have an abortion, in addition to the effects upon the woman herself, who may suffer deep feelings of guilt and regret persisting for many years. There may well be other karmic consequences resulting from such an act.

Considered in this light, it is clear that abortion should be avoided. Most contraception, however, does not interrupt a life-continuum since sentience does not arise until sperm and ovum actually meet. It is not, therefore, in itself unskilful.

The Psychophysical Organism

Sentience is the germ in dependence on which the whole psychophysical organism unfolds. This link is depicted by four people sitting in a boat that one of them is steering. This image represents all the different bodily and mental processes of a mature human. The psychophysical organism is, traditionally, divided into five 'heaps' or categories of interrelated functions – hence the four men plus the boat. Every element of our being, Buddhist teaching says, can be assigned to one or other of these heaps of form, feeling, recognition, motivation, and consciousness. It is probably more helpful to see this classification not so much as a philosophical analysis of human personality, but more as a kind of meditation upon everything that makes up our experience. Every aspect of our experience can be assigned to one or other of form, feeling, recognition, motivation, and consciousness, which we shall look at in a bit more detail below.

If we first break our experience, both inner and outer, into its constituent elements in this way, we can then examine each part more closely. What we will find is that every one of them is transient. Every aspect of us is a process arising in dependence on conditions and we are the sum total of all of them, woven together into a dynamic and complex whole. We realize that we cannot identify ourselves in a rigid way with the body, personality, or any particular state of being. This, in its turn, helps us to see that we can develop. Every one of these processes can be made to function at higher levels.

Our analysis begins with *form*. This is a difficult concept in Buddhist thought, quite different from our ordinary understanding of matter. Buddhism does not accept uncritically the 'common-sense' view of matter as something solid, 'out there', independent of human perception. As in everything else, it requires us to come back to what we really know. All that we can with any certainty claim to know is that we are having certain experiences. We seem to occupy a world of objects which we perceive through the senses, but in reality we do not experience objects or a world – we experience sensations. The assembling of those sensations into the world we perceive is an addition to our basic experience. Something of this distinction can be seen if we analyse a situation such as sitting in front of a fire. We feel the heat on our legs, hear the crackling in our ears, see the flickering with our eyes, and smell the pungent fumes with our nose. All these sensations present themselves to us as the coordinated perception of sitting in front of a fire. If we deliberately let go of the assembled picture we can feel each of these impressions as raw sensation, playing upon its own sense organ, independent of the others. This is our basic experience and it is all that is given to us. Everything else we add on.

Buddhism's approach, here, is strictly empirical. It invites us to strip away the layers of our ignorant assumptions by becoming aware of what our immediate experience is before we work it up into objects. What we are left with is the experience of different kinds of sensation, as if of resistance. When we touch something hard, we have the experience of being resisted, pushed back at. This sensation of resistance is a manifestation of form. Such resistance is of four different kinds, referred to as earth, water, fire, and air. These are, however, not physical elements; the terms are symbolic. Earth is what gives rise to the sensation of a solid impediment to our senses, water is everything that gives the sensation of pliability with cohesion, fire is the experience of radiance and heat, and air is that which moves freely, barely resisting our senses at all. These four elements are the bases of all our perception and it is from this raw data that we derive the objective world as we perceive it. Form, then, does not correspond to matter at all. In the basic experience of sensation there is no reference to an external object, since form is just these elementary resistances from which the physical world and our own bodies are made up. At every moment, they pass across our minds in very complex patterns, an endless flow of sensations each of which arises and passes away, instant by instant.

Form is the objective element in our experience that is illuminated by *consciousness*. There is a seeming difficulty in considering consciousness as part of the fourth link which arises in dependence on the spark of consciousness which is the third. The fourth link, however, represents the fully developed psychophysical system that evolves out of the seminal flash of sentience which is the third link. Consciousness means, in this context, the faculty of discriminative awareness. The sensations of resistance called form are distinguished and attended to in an act of awareness. Consciousness is never still, constantly changing with the ever-flowing stimuli. We must not allow our words to mislead us into thinking of consciousness as a single, substantial entity, for it is like everything else, a process whose different phases arise in dependence on conditions and pass away again.

Our consciousness compares the sensations that present themselves with past sensory data and fits it into a pattern of perception – and so we form 'our world'. *Recognition* is the process of assimilating sensations and recognizing them as particular objects with certain properties and relations. One can observe this process in action when, for instance, there is an object in the distance that one cannot properly make out. It may be a goat, grazing among the trees, or it may be a rock, or perhaps it is something else again. While one looks, trying to see what it is, it actually is a goat for a while, then it is a rock, as one interprets the sensations now this way, now that. Recognition is the point in the perceptual process where we split our experience into a subject and an object, an inner personal world of mind and an outer objective world of things. Both subject and object are interpretation, neither being given in the raw data of our experience. Our perception is composed of a never-ending series of such judgements, each of which is an interpretation of our sensation in the light of our own past perception, experience, and view of life. We are constantly readjusting our picture of life as we try to fit new data into our overall view of ourselves and the world.

Having assembled various sensations into one object and having assigned that object a place in our scheme of things, we have certain hedonic *feelings* about it. These may be direct physical pleasures or pains or they may be of a more mental kind based upon anticipation or memory. Some objects, of course, barely arouse our feelings at all and have little or no hedonic tone. All the time, we are making evaluations as new experiences come to us and as our own inner states shift and change.

Finally, *motivation* is our active response to things. After we have evaluated our experiences, volitions arise. We want to possess those things we judge pleasant and to reject or destroy those that we see as painful. Motivation includes the whole complex world of our emotions which are as much ever-changing processes as any of the constituents of the other heaps.

If we examine carefully the different phenomena of our experience we find them all to be conditioned processes. Most cells in our bodies are completely renewed at least every seven years and our mental states are far more fleeting. It is this complex of bodily and mental processes that now unfolds in dependence on the third link, that potent seed of primary consciousness. The pattern of the five heaps of form, consciousness, recognition, feeling, and motivation contained in the blueprint of sentience gradually unfolds itself in the womb.

The psychophysical organism is, at this point in the chain, considered as a potentiality, but it begins to function actively, opening up to the world around it. In dependence on the psychophysical organism, the six senses arise.

The Six Senses

This link is represented by a house with five windows and a door. The senses are the 'portals' through which we gain our impressions of the world. Each of the senses is the manifestation of our desire to experience things in that particular way.

The six sense organs are the five outer organs of eye, ear, nose, tongue, and body (here considered the organ of touch), together with the mind. Just as the eye takes in sights and the tongue tastes flavours, so the mind has its own data. Memories, anticipations, fantasies, thoughts, are all objects of the mind considered as a sense. It is both imagination as the mere capacity to produce images, and the imaginal faculty, able to perceive higher dimensions of reality. The worlds to which the physical senses give us access are, as we will see, the lowest. It is through the door of the mind that we have access to the higher worlds which are no less real than the physical. If we want to perceive higher 'worlds', we will do so as our organs of mental perception become more acute.

All the links we have seen up to this stage in the cycle of conditionality are the passive resultants of previous volitional activity. The body and the senses are the inevitable consequence of what we have done in the past. This means that they are not themselves volitional and, therefore, that no ethical evaluation applies to them. The body and the senses are innocent and cannot be considered either skilful or unskilful. Simply to see things, of whatever kind, cannot be wrong. Problems arise only when we start to react mentally to what we perceive. It is because of these mental reactions that we need to be very much aware of what we take in through the senses. In the traditional phrase, we must 'guard the doors of the senses'. We need to try to prevent ourselves from attaching unwholesome volitions to whatever we let into the mind through the senses. This may mean restricting ourselves from experiencing those sensations that are likely to trigger reactions that we cannot control, at least until we are strong enough to perceive them without generating negative volitions.

The senses are the apertures through which the external world is perceived and so, in dependence on them, arises sensuous impression or contact.

Sensuous Impression

A couple embracing depicts the contact of the sense organs with their objects. With this link, the psychophysical organism begins to interact with the world.

When we were examining the five heaps that make up human experience, we saw that form does not correspond to matter in the ordinary sense. Form is the sensation of resistance, whether earth, water, fire, or air. By interpreting these sensations we arrive at our picture of the world. What then are we contacting with our sense organs? Let us be wary of the fascinations of philosophical speculation on this and stick to the empirical traditions of Buddhism.

We can only remain agnostic about what it is that our senses contact. What we call the contact of our senses with an object is no more than the experience of resistance. The concept of resistance, of course, implies something that resists and something that is resisted. There is no way in which we can express that experience without implicit reference to a subject and an object, but the basic data yield us only the one fact, that there is resistance, without reference to resister or resisted. Perhaps, since we are constrained both by our language and by our own level of consciousness to think that there is something independent of our perception that we are contacting, it is best to imagine that the four elements that resist our senses are actually more like spirits than matter. The world that we are in contact with is not made up of dead atomic building blocks but of a living energy that animates every object. This is how our ancestors saw the world when they imagined tree sprites and river gods, spirits that inhabited every part of nature. We cannot recapture the innocence of that perception but we can learn to see things as vital, animated by forces that mirror the quickness in our own consciousness. We can free ourselves of the sterile materialistic view of nature and recapture the experience of its wonder and power.

Our particular experiences of resistance come to us as the consequence of our volitional activity. Just as our psychophysical organism arises, by way of the initial sentience, from our past volitions, so the kind of sensations we feel are determined by the kind of body and senses we have. From this point of view it can be said that not only do we create ourselves, but we create our world.

All we really know, at this stage, is that we have certain sensations and that we work up from the raw data of these sensations an image of the world – which is actually mostly assumption. By and large our world picture holds true for operational purposes: it usually allows us to operate effectively – although we do make terrible mistakes from time to time. If we accept it as a kind of working diagram that we adjust and improve as our understanding increases, then no difficulties arise. But if we forget the raw data of our senses and become attached to our own mental constructions we run into problems, for we then see things very rigidly and mistake our mental picture for reality itself. We are therefore closed to other worlds of experience and to the possibility of seeing things as they really are.

We have our sensations which we interpret and place within our total view of things. This then gives rise to our evaluation of our perceptions and so, in dependence on sensuous impression, arises feeling.

Feeling

To illustrate this link, a man is shown with an arrow sunk deep in his eye. The arrow represents sense data impinging upon the sense organs, in this case, the eye. In a very vivid way, the image suggests the strong feelings that our sensory experience evokes – although the illustration is one of painful feeling, both painful and pleasant are intended. We are not like television cameras, impartially scanning the environment, for what we perceive has an effect upon us and gives rise to very strong feelings.

Feelings are either pleasant or painful or are so low in hedonic tone as to be neutral. Pleasure and pain are experienced on a number of different levels ranging from direct physical sensations to the loftiest bliss of liberation from the Wheel. According to Buddhist psychology, the experience of direct pain is confined to a relatively small area of the total possibilities of conscious experience. These are, however, the areas in which we habitually dwell!

At the lowest level, feeling is a response to the five physical senses. At a very basic level of feeling, pleasure is a release of built-up instinctual tension, and the frustration of physical energies or the damaging of the body is experienced as pain. We experience a more refined form of sensuous feeling in our enjoyment of beauty and dislike of ugliness. Many of our evaluations are not directly sensuous but psychological in character; they include feelings of insecurity and security, of triumph and failure, feelings deriving from our expectation of pleasure or pain to come, or from the reliving of past experiences. Feeling includes more generalized moods of well-being and elation, of depression and hopelessness and other such responses to our total experience. Our immediate likes or dislikes of other people are also aspects of feeling.

So far, all the kinds of feeling mentioned are based upon the physical senses, whether directly through the five senses or through the mind. They therefore belong to the sphere of sensuous desire, the lowest of the three mundane levels of existence. In the higher spheres, there is no pain at all of the sensuous or mental kinds. Pain is restricted entirely to the sensuous sphere. In the sphere of archetypal form, there is a subtle experience unmediated by the five senses. There is very great beauty, but beauty no longer limited by the imperfections of the physical form. It is an ideal beauty but not an abstract beauty, for it is vividly envisaged by the imagination and arouses intense feelings of pleasure, far greater than any earthly rapture. In the higher sphere of formlessness, we go still further to contact, not the outward form of beauty, however refined and exalted, but Beauty herself. It is a world of pure qualities whose essences are conveyed directly to the sublimated Imagination. Here there is a delight of an even more powerful kind, surpassing the ecstasy of the visionary dimension.

Yet all the way from gross physical feeling through to the heights of pleasure in the formless sphere, there is a basic underlying tension: the tension between subject and object. As we burst through boundary after boundary, the tension diminishes and we experience the increasing harmony of self and other as a growing pleasure. But the tension remains, however subtle. There is a final pain and a final pleasure: the pain of consciousness divided and the bliss that comes from breaking, totally and for ever, the distinction between subject and object and experiencing the non-dual awareness of Enlightenment. This is what could be called 'absolute pleasure' and is the perpetual experience of the Buddhas.

It should by now be clear that Buddhism does not condemn pleasure. Progress on the spiritual path is accompanied by ever-increasing happiness and joy. A certain amount of pleasurable experience seems to be essential to human well-being, otherwise all but the strongest lose heart and their vitality drains away. Persistent pain tends to colour one's whole mental outlook, causing a mood of depression and hopelessness unless some deeper sense of meaning has been contacted. A moderate amount of pleasure stimulates and helps to create a mood of confidence and well-being that is an essential basis for further growth. In this respect, we probably do not appreciate the extent to which our surroundings influence us. Every sensory impression leaves some mark upon us, whether pleasant or painful, unless we have the indifference of the bored, the withdrawn, or the saturated. The ugliness, dirt, and noise of many parts of big cities must powerfully affect people. Often, as a desperate substitute for the simple pleasures of natural surroundings, modern man seeks very strong sensations in loud music, garish colours, highly flavoured foods, and intoxicating substances. It is as if only these can reach jaded feelings, worn down by ugliness and deadened with overstimulation. A beautiful and harmonious environment can, in itself, have a tonic effect upon a weary mind.

Pleasure and pain only become a problem if we relate to them neurotically, and make the pursuit of pleasure and the avoidance of pain our only guiding principles. Sensuous pleasure and pain arise in dependence on our sense organs and their contact with the world. They are, as it were, by-products of our lives; and pleasure cannot be healthily taken as an end in itself. If it is, we simply become entrapped once more in the turnings of the Wheel. While we live our lives, pleasure may come to us and we can accept it and enjoy it to the full, relinquishing it without regret when it passes. In addition, as far as possible, we can open ourselves to the enjoyment of the more refined pleasures, since these will lift our consciousness. Pain indicates that there is something wrong either with our bodies or in our attitude to life. We should do whatever we can to remove the cause of pain in either case. If it cannot be alleviated, we need patient forbearance. We need to work to ensure that neither pleasure nor pain overwhelm us so that we lose our awareness and become lost in a new cycle of reaction.

This link of feeling marks a crucial transition in the whole chain of conditionality. It is a point to which we will be returning in a later chapter of this book, for it is after feeling that volition once more enters the picture. Once the volitional activities in the past life have been set up, they form sentience, the psychophysical organism, the six senses, sensuous impression, and feeling, none of which have volition attached to them. The body, the senses, the objects we perceive, and the feelings they give rise to, are all the passive resultants of our past intentions. But then a new phase of willing in the present life begins. That volitional activity may be skilful or it may be unskilful, and so this transition between feeling and the next link is the point at which we either renew the cyclic motion of the Wheel or begin the steady ascent of the Spiral. It is the Wheel with which we are concerned, for the time being, and so we must spin on through its remaining links. Later, we will return and commence the ascent of the Path.

If we react to feeling, we long to continue the pleasurable experiences and we reject the painful. With no regard to the overall direction or purpose of our lives and with no thought for anything but immediate gratification, we crave and we hate. So, in dependence on feeling, there arises craving.

Craving
This next link is illustrated by a seated man being offered a drink by a woman who stands before him. The word here translated as 'craving' literally means 'thirst'. Of course, thirst is just a physical sensation arising out of the body's need for water – it is not craving at all but a healthy need. The image of thirst is used because it suggests the immediacy and strength of neurotic craving. The fact that it is a woman offering a drink to a man may be intended also to bring to mind the intensity of sexual desire.

We have already seen that craving is the longing to enjoy things, events, or people because we believe that their possession will make our egos more secure. More particularly, we want those things that we think will give us pleasure and therefore affirm and strengthen our sense of self, and we want to be rid of those things that we judge will cause us pain, checking and crushing us. So we crave and hate in dependence on feeling.

There are said to be three basic forms of craving. Firstly, and most simply, there is *craving for sense objects*. Any of the sense faculties, the five physical senses or the mind, can provide objects for our neurotic longing. *Craving for existence* is the deep-seated urge to exist in a fixed state of being, particularly in one of the worlds of heavenly delight, and it is connected with the wrong view of eternalism: that there is a soul within us which is eternal and that there is an absolute being or God. It is our desire to maintain our ego-identity and it is the basic force that keeps most of us alive – the will to live, as it has been called. *Craving for non-existence* is connected with the wrong view of nihilism that considers that there is no consciousness after death. One who craves non-existence longs to pass into the complete oblivion that is believed to follow death. In its absolute form, this is perhaps a very rare condition which results from craving that is so severely frustrated that one cannot believe there is any possibility of satisfaction. Human hope has its limits and a point is reached where one just gives up the will to live, whether in this life or any other. Although craving of this type is seldom encountered in such an extreme form, it is an element in many people's make-up where it may manifest as the lassitude of despair, the desire for a quiet life, or a longing for narcosis or anaesthesia. It may lie behind some forms of drug addiction. It is the unwillingness to face up to the responsibility of being an individual, and an attempt to find refuge in the group or in unconsciousness or in any state of existence in which no demands are made upon one as an individual. Each of these three kinds of craving – for sensuous objects, for existence, and for non-existence – arises out of feeling and, together, they are the basic force that propels us through life, around and around the Wheel. Hatred is not mentioned here, since craving is treated as the primary unwholesome volition and hatred is considered as frustrated craving.

Craving is no purely mental phenomenon, of course. We act upon it, seizing the objects of our desires. Thus, in dependence upon craving, arises grasping.

Grasping

A woman plucking fruit from a tree is the image for this link. Craving has taken effect in concrete action. The objects that we grasp are said to be of four kinds. First of all, we grasp after sense pleasures. Our longing for them turns into attachment and we live our lives for their sake. But it is not only objects of sensuous experience to which we become attached; we are also bound to our *views and opinions*. The way we look at the world, our beliefs and prejudices, are objects to which we cling, making them part of our identity. This is why people are seldom able to hold a friendly conversation on matters about which they disagree. To question or deny someone's views is to question or deny their being. Religious or political dogmas in particular are often the objects of such attachment and have sparked off persecution and 'holy war'. All our wrong views are rationalizations of basic attitudes we hold and are manifestations of the ignorance that underlies the whole cyclic chain of conditionality. We compound our ignorance by grasping after more ignorance.

The remaining two forms of grasping are also connected with views – illustrating the importance of thoughts on our lives. The first is attachment to *external observances and ethical rules (as ends in themselves)*. When we assume that merely to do something without the corresponding mental attitude is sufficient to gain the benefits we expect and desire, we are attached to external observances. For instance, we may know that the regular practice of meditation helps us to gain higher states of consciousness. But we will not experience those benefits if all we do is sit down for a period every day in the correct posture for meditation. We must be making an active attempt to concentrate and refine our minds. Again, merely to 'obey' the precepts, as if they were commandments, will not help us to develop the natural ethical sense that is the mark of a healthy individual. People tend to cling to routines and patterns of behaviour, little personal rituals that are familiar and therefore seem to provide comfort and security. Even what we consider to be our spiritual life and practice can all too easily become an empty habit that we perform with faithful regularity but without any real effort or meaning. Worse still, we come to think that just to do the practice, to perform the ritual, to keep the rules, itself guarantees us, almost magically, spiritual progress or at least material well-being. This is the world of superstition and hypocrisy into which religious observance often deteriorates. This is not to say, of course, that regular spiritual practice, a skilful routine, and ethical observance are not all essential in following the Path. They only constitute objects of grasping if we treat them superficially and use them not to bring about changes in our consciousness but as talismans to bring us good luck.

Lastly, there is attachment to *belief in a permanent, unchanging self.* The ultimate objective of the immature ego is to stabilize itself eternally. It comes to believe that this is possible, that beneath the ever-changing circumstances of life there is a core that remains untouched. It is clinging to this idea of an 'absolute ego' that gets in the way, in the first place, of our developing our consciousness and, further down the Path, from leaving the ego behind altogether.

By clinging to sense pleasures, opinions, rules and routines, and ego identity, we condemn ourselves to the Wheel and a new round of birth and death. So in dependence upon grasping, arises becoming.

Becoming

The image for becoming is a man and a woman performing the sexual act, initiating a new life. This link sums up the whole Wheel of Life, for the Wheel is one continuous process of becoming. The word here translated as 'becoming' is the same word in Pali and Sanskrit as is translated as 'life' in 'the Wheel of Life'.

Becoming has two aspects: one the active and volitional part, the other the passive result of the active phase. The Wheel moves from volition to its consequences as the potential energy of volition fulfils itself in states of being and concrete experiences. With this link, we rise to the most general view of the conditioned process. Set up by our clinging and grasping in this life, we establish tendencies that lead to our rebirth in a new life – on the plane of existence that corresponds to our volitions. Thus, in dependence on becoming, arises birth.

Birth

This link is represented by the very explicit image of a woman giving birth to a child. Once more the momentum of our volitions has resulted in a new life in whichever of the many planes of existence corresponds to our pattern of willing. This new life is, itself, the very condition that leads to death and decay.

Death and Decay

The final link is portrayed by a corpse being carried towards the cremation pyre. Whatever is born is bound to experience the attacks of sickness, the waning of physical powers in old age, the pain of separation and loss, and finally death. Once birth has taken place a process has been set in motion that must end in death, for birth and death are two sides of one process of becoming. The inherent decay in all conditioned things leads to 'sorrow, lamentation, pain, grief and despair, in short, this whole mass of suffering', as the early texts have it, which is the lot of those who cling to the Wheel. We are born because we cling, but from what we cling to we must be parted.

The Message of the Wheel

The twelve links in the chain of cyclic conditionality show how the ignorance that lies in the depths of our hearts guides all our actions; how the total pattern of our mental volitions forms for us a mind and body in a new life that is in contact with its appropriate world; how that contact gives rise to our pleasure and pain, likes and dislikes. We see, at this point, that we have a choice: whether to continue to spin on the Wheel or to start to ascend the Spiral. If we merely crave the pleasurable and hate the painful, we form for ourselves the volitional momentum that carries us again into a new birth with its own share of pain and its inevitable death. It is indeed a vicious circle, without end. Whatever pain we feel, whatever frustration or imperfection we see in life, it is our own desires that have in the final analysis created them.

The message of the chain is simple; however, its exposition is very subtle and complex. The whole chain is spread over three lives: ignorance and the volitional activities belong to the past life; sentience, the psychophysical organism, the six senses, sensuous impression, feeling, craving, grasping, and becoming, all belong to the present life; birth and death and decay belong to the life to come. The twelve links can also be analysed into those that are active volitional forces that have a formative effect and those that are passive resultants, following inevitably from volitional activities. All conditioned processes can be divided in this way into a causal phase, during which the conditions are established, and a resultant phase when the effects of the conditions come to fruition – although, of course, since we experience the effects of our previous actions at the

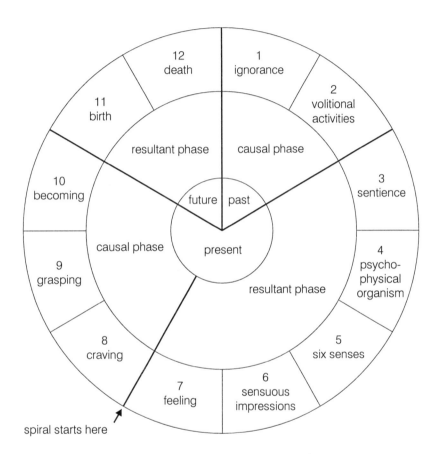

FIG. 4. THE TWELVE LINKS

same time as exercising our volitions, causal and resultant phases are happening simultaneously. Within the karmic order, it is volitions that establish the causal phase. So ignorance and volitional activities are the causal phase in the past life; sentience, the psychophysical organism, the six senses, sensuous impression, and feeling are the resultant phase in the present life; craving, grasping, and becoming are the causal phase in the present life; and birth and death and decay are the resultant phase in the life to come. All these divisions are shown in fig.4.

When we look closely we will find that the causal phases in the past life and in the present are the same process but looked at from slightly different points of view. In the past life it is seen at its most general: as a formative force. In the present life, we are shown in greater detail how that pattern of volitional energy comes into being. Similarly, the resultant phase in the present life is the same as that in the life to come but is examined in much closer detail. The same movement from resultant phase to causal phase is present in each life and each life can be considered as, itself, either a past, present, or future life since they are part of an endless chain. So each life contains both the causal phase of the past and of the present and the resultant phase of the present and of the future. Each life can, therefore, be considered as containing thirty-six links. The links can also be seen as all being present at every moment of our lives as we create our own future out of our acts of will, again and again. Each link can be seen as acting simultaneously with all the others. The chain is a very subtle, dynamic process, not a rigid mechanical routine.

We should not allow ourselves to become lost in the complexity of the chain but try to feel and picture the forces that the links represent: the forces of human desire based upon ignorance forging for us, again and again, worlds of inevitable decay that restrict and confine our consciousness. We then react to the worlds we have ourselves constructed and the chain turns once more. It is this process that has brought about the life we live at this very moment.

Perhaps more dangerous than to become swamped in the complexities of the chain is to think too readily that we understand it. On a well-known occasion, the Buddha's friend and personal attendant, Ananda, commented to him on the straightforwardness and

clarity of the teaching and the ease with which it could be comprehended. The Buddha rebuked him, saying:

> Say not so, Ananda! Say not so! Deep indeed is this Causal Law,
> and deep it appears to be. It is by not knowing, by not
> understanding, by not penetrating this doctrine, that this world of
> men has become entangled like a ball of twine, become covered
> with mildew, become like munja grass and rushes, and unable to
> pass beyond the doom of the Waste, the Way of Woe, the Fall and
> Ceaseless Round [of rebirth].*

In the end, the teaching points to an experience beyond intellectual
apprehension. It is meant to turn us away from our craving, to lead
us onto the Spiral Path, and to induce in us that vision of reality as
a network of conditions, a vast nexus of interpenetrating forces of
infinite creative potentiality.

* *Samyutta Nikaya* xii.6.6o

7

Worlds of Woe

The Six Realms

The third circle of the Wheel of Life, between that of karma and that of the twelve links, shows the six realms of conditioned existence. The lower five realms – those of the hell-beings, hungry ghosts, animals, titans, and humans – are all contained in the sphere of sensuous desire. The sixth, the realm of the gods, is stratified into many layers that extend from the peak of the sensuous sphere through the sphere of archetypal form and culminate in the formless, each of these three spheres in addition containing a number of sub-spheres. Existence as a whole is therefore made up of many different worlds of which the six realms are the generic types. These worlds are found here, in our world – although countless world-systems other than our own are said to exist in all the regions of space (a world-system is a kind of 'island universe' made up of all the different planes and subplanes from the hells to the highest heaven). It is not possible to reach the other planes within our own world-system by spacecraft, however sophisticated, for these worlds exist in different dimensions. We can only reach them by changing our consciousness.

A world is the objective counterpart of the self. As our individuality crystallizes, we divide what is self from what is other. The other is the world. The world is what is experienced and the self is what experiences. The world is everything 'out there', the self is everything 'in here'. The nature of the perceiving subject determines the nature of the perceived object. As we have already seen, our perception comes, in the first place, from our interpretation of the raw data of sensuous impressions. We sense shapes and colours and these we assemble into visible objects – on the basis of our past experiences of similar kinds and of what we have learned from the culture in which we have been raised. Not only is what we make of our sense experience determined by the kind of consciousness we have but so are the impressions themselves. Our own past volitional activities establish the type of experiences we will encounter. Our karmic pattern attracts to itself matching impressions just as our own character leads us to be reborn in a world that corresponds to it.

This concept of reality as having many dimensions to which varying states of consciousness give access may be unfamiliar, yet it is a commonplace insight that there are great differences in the way in which people perceive the world. Climate and geography, political and economic structures, history, culture, and language, even genetic factors perhaps affect the outlooks of various nations and peoples to such an extent that they effectively live in different worlds. Even within a single country we speak of worlds: the underworld, the theatre world, the world of high finance. People from these separate worlds can sometimes barely comprehend each other at all. Again, people have very dissimilar temperaments and dispositions and see the same surroundings in quite different ways. In this sense every one of us is unique, each with our own experiences, history, and viewpoint. So, to an extent, each of us has our own world, though there may be considerable overlap between our separate worlds.

Even within the life of a single individual, mental states may be experienced that are so unlike each other that they amount to different worlds. Fluctuations of mood can alter the appearance of things to a very great extent, even though a sufficiently strong common thread may run through them all for us not to think of them as different worlds. Yet in moments of very intense experience, as for instance under poetic inspiration or deeply moved by art, nature, or our human communication, we speak of being transported, uplifted, taken out of ourselves, and we see the world transfigured or as if renewed. Sometimes, so great can be the difference between such moments and normal consciousness that people talk of dwelling for a while in another world. At the other end of the scale, moments of depression and despair can be equally transporting, although it is to hell that one may then be taken. Some people have greater fluidity of consciousness than others and are gifted (sometimes perhaps cursed) with the facility of slipping into quite different visionary or prophetic worlds. Drug-induced experiences, harmful as they may often be, are a further illustration of consciousness gaining access to radically different ways of seeing things. Experiences of any of these kinds – ecstatic, prophetic, or psychedelic – are not uncommon, and many people will acknowledge, by their own witness or by acquaintance with others, that the range of possible states of mind is far wider than we usually allow.

Most people are not perhaps familiar with visionary or inspired states in any depth. There is, however, a state in which everyone dwells quite regularly and which carries them to other worlds: dreaming. Although dreams are usually, if not always, assembled from the data of waking life, the dream world obeys its own dream logic. We often dismiss dreams as irrelevant, as a kind of mental filing system best left to itself, or else we consider them as providing important messages about our unconscious functioning which, should we decode them, will benefit us in everyday life. We identify almost entirely with the waking state and place value on dreams, if we value them at all, only in relation to it. While it is undoubtedly true that dreams have the function of sorting out daytime experience and that they may help us to understand ourselves better, we are severely undervaluing dreams if that is all we make of them. The dream world is no less a reality than the waking state and should be enjoyed and valued as such. The worlds to which we are carried in sleep can appear as much 'out there' as the world that surrounds us now – even though they may change within an instant or be two contradictory things at the same time. On those occasions when we are aware within a dream that we are dreaming, all our impressions can be as cogent and convincing as waking sensations. From the point of view of our actual experience within each world, we cannot say that one or the other is more real. We are usually totally convinced by the dream world while we are in it, and it is only later, from the prejudiced viewpoint of the waking state, that we relegate dreams to the status of psychological by-products.

From this we can more easily understand, perhaps, Buddhism's contention that modifications in our consciousness give us access to different worlds of which there are as many as there are possibilities of consciousness. Some of them differ far more radically from normal human consciousness than do either the worlds of inspiration or depression or those of dreams. All of them are, none the less, objective realities, experienced as 'out there', for a world is simply whatever we experience: each world is equally real to those who inhabit it. The worlds are ordered hierarchically in accordance with the refinement of the consciousness that they reflect. The higher the state of consciousness, the more pure and beautiful will be the world. In so far as the higher worlds are more subtle refractions of the subject–object dichotomy, they are closer to the ultimate nature of things.

These many worlds are inhabited by those whose volitional patterns correspond to them. The higher godlike realms of the spheres of archetypal form and formlessness may also be visited by those who practise meditation at all deeply because the states of consciousness enjoyed in meditation correspond to these worlds. Until physical death, however, the meditator always returns to the human state. Certain highly gifted individuals, like Maudgalyayana whom we have already encountered, have access to all the different planes and can visit any of the worlds at will.

Not all worlds function according to the same laws. In dreams, for instance, what we perceive is far more malleable and the environment and the sequence of events may change with extreme rapidity. Similarly, we saw earlier that in the mind-made body between death and rebirth what one experiences changes with the speed of thought. In other worlds, like our own, there is greater stability in what we perceive and the core of experience persists despite our own mental fluctuations. We could say that some worlds have a more stable objective content and that other worlds are perceived as more immediately influenced by subjective factors. Thus, according to Buddhist tradition, birth takes place by parturition in some worlds, whilst in others we appear instantaneously, fully mature, by a process known as 'apparitional birth', in the same way as we simply find ourselves within a dream. Whether the worlds appear to have more cohesive and stable processes or whether they are closely influenced by alterations in subjective mood and outlook, they are all worlds.

So my world is the field of my experience – but it contains other beings who have their own subjective experience. These are worlds of common experience inhabited by those who share similar patterns of volition. The personal worlds of each are never identical (as identity of the object would entail identity of the subject) but they overlap to a greater or lesser extent. Perhaps this provides us with our most useful definition of the word 'world': a world is where the experience of two or more perceiving subjects coincides. To the extent that we share with others a world in which our personal experience overlaps with theirs, we can relate to them. The fact that there are other beings within our world with whom we can interact helps to reinforce the solidity of our world. We are educated into seeing things in a particular way when we communicate with them. The inhabitants of each world have bodies that are the appropriate manifestation of their consciousness. In some, the bodies are solid and heavy, as stable as the objects around them. In others, again according to tradition, they are not made of solid matter at all but consist of a subtle, luminous substance. In the hells, the body is indestructible until the full force of the karmic pattern that keeps it in being is spent, even though these bodies are subject to continuous dismemberment and destruction.

This Buddhist vision of a multi-layered universe is not one that fits well with most modern opinions, although many other cultures have traditions concerning non-human beings, often with quite elaborate systems of classification. If one accepts that consciousness survives after death and that the world is the counterpart of consciousness, it is also possible to see that there might be many other worlds. Little convincing proof can be offered for their existence, however, beyond the testimony of those who claim to have explored reality in its heights and depths. For those who cannot suspend disbelief, although they will not be able to appreciate the full extent of the Buddhist vision, there is a principle underlying this teaching that is equally relevant to our common human experience. Different people are in very different mental states and what they see is, to a large extent, a projection of their own minds and not something inherent in the objects of sense. It is in this more restricted sense that there can also be said to be different worlds corresponding to different psychological states. The six realms that we will now be examining can be understood either as objective dimensions of experience into which we may literally be reborn or as symbols for psychological states experienced by human beings.

If we look at the concept of projection in a little detail, this may help us to understand the six realms better. Projection is the psychological mechanism whereby we attribute to our surroundings and to other people feelings and thoughts that are, in fact, our own. We throw onto the world what is actually in us. In extreme cases of mental disturbance, for instance, the world is so overlaid with the projections of the person's mind that it becomes a completely different world from the one that others occupy. The most innocent scene can be filled with horrible demons and frightful dangers, and a friendly greeting may hold hidden menace. But projection is also a common fact of most people's lives. They see not only what their senses present to them but aspects of themselves. Nowhere is this more evident than in our dealings with other people. We attribute to them our own motives or see in them highly idealized qualities that they do not really possess. Since in our human world the objective element is relatively stable and enduring, it is easier to discern the discrepancy between projection and reality, although we by no means always do so. There are other worlds, according to Buddhist teaching, however, where objective content is more directly determined by subjective state. We are able, so to speak, to indulge in a hallucination in which we live and interact with other beings who have a corresponding hallucination.

Karmic conditionality itself is a process of projection, for we are constantly creating a world for ourselves that is the projection of our own volitions. At a more immediate – psychological – level, there are two main varieties of projection. Firstly, we project when we interpret the data of our sense impressions in terms of our own mental states – we fail properly to distinguish the subject from the object. People whose minds are dominated by fear see the innocent stranger as intent on attacking them. Cheats assume that everyone else is trying to cheat them. A variant of this type of projection is found in cases where people have strong feelings which, for one reason or another, they cannot admit, even to themselves. Since those feelings are energies that must find some expression, they are attributed to other people in whom they are often sternly disapproved of. Similarly, most people have a darker side to their personality, made up of those aspects they do not approve of or of which they are afraid. This 'shadow', as the psychologist C.G. Jung called it, is then projected onto others.

The second type of projection comes about not through the projection of our negative qualities, whether real or imagined, but through our own unrealized potential. When self-consciousness first differentiates itself from its surroundings it does so in a quite crude and rigid way. The resultant ego is narrow and lopsided since it contains only some aspects of individuality. What we conceive of as ourselves is but a small portion of the total possible energies of personality. Those aspects of a mature individuality that have not yet emerged into the full light of consciousness are projected onto others in idealized form. Thus, if we lack confidence and self-assurance we look to others as sources of reassurance and security. If we have developed the intellect at the expense of the emotions, we see in someone else the warmth and spontaneity that we do not have. This type of projection often occurs in sexual relationships when we 'fall in love'. It is also present in hero worship where the object of the projection – sporting champion, entertainment star, even political figure – is seen as possessing almost superhuman characteristics. These are really latent qualities which those who project could realize within themselves if they became fully self-aware. This type of projection is the result of alienation from the full energies of personality. The cultivation of a mature ego is the first task of the spiritual path, and so alienation must be overcome by what has been called *horizontal integration:* the drawing together in consciousness of all the energies of the mature personality. Only when we have withdrawn all these projections and integrated them into consciousness can we be said to be fully and truly human.

Projection of inner qualities goes beyond the horizontal plane, for rudimentary self-consciousness is not only alienated from the characteristics of full individuality but also from the whole range of consciousness, up to and including transcendental awareness. Self-consciousness contains the transcendental within it in the form of the evolutionary urge to attain higher levels. Latent spiritual and transcendental qualities also come out in projection, now of a vertical kind. The whole spiritual path leading to Buddhahood could be seen as a process of *vertical integration* of our projected higher potential.

Projection often has very unfortunate consequences, but it can also provide us with a means whereby we contact and integrate those unrealized qualities within us. While they are unconscious we have no knowledge of them at all. If we recognize our projections as projections, we have made them conscious although we are still separated from them. It is then possible gradually to withdraw the projection back into ourselves. Usually, of course, we fail to realize that we are projecting and we remain tangled up with the object. When that object is a person, we may well be in trouble for they will have designs and purposes of their own. We may, for instance, feel weak and impotent and will therefore project our own potential power on to some authority figure who may abuse the trust we place in him or her.

If we are going to take advantage of projection as a means of recapturing qualities from which we are cut off, we must be careful not to let our projection become caught up in real events. Otherwise, we may find that, even if we withdraw the projection, we are ensnared in its consequences whether we like it or not. Art has often provided the kind of neutral ground where the full passions may be expressed without the danger of entanglement. The artist uses the artistic medium to give full shape to the ideal qualities felt within. In the act of giving them expression, they become part of his own being. Buddhism provides a number of means for the vertical projection of the qualities within us, notably the worship of the Buddha image which is a representation of our own transcendental nature. If we are not engaging in this kind of process, there is nothing for the full force of our emotions to engage with and our development remains an abstract and bloodless ideal without any ardour to nourish it.

We will now examine, one by one, the six worlds and the beings who inhabit them. We will start, in this chapter, with the unhappy places of rebirth where suffering predominates. These are the projection of an immature consciousness that is dominated by greed, hatred, and delusion. They represent, in terms of an evolution of consciousness, blind alleys up which a distorted and unhealthy mind may go, producing for itself the concrete realization of its own nature.

The Realm of Hell

Pictures of hell in Buddhist tradition show strong similarities to the medieval Christian Inferno and the painful afterworlds of many other cultures. It is shown as a place of intense pain and torment where its victims are subjected to the most excruciating tortures, inflicted by the presiding demons. Flames engulf the whole realm, which is unbearably hot although, in the bottom reaches, there are regions of bitter cold which yield the worst sufferings of all. Hell consists of sub-planes, each of which specializes in a particular kind of pain appropriate to a certain kind of unskilful action. In popular Buddhism these are, all too often, described in considerable detail. There is, for instance, the hell of filth where the corruptors of the innocent wallow in slime while they are devoured by monstrous maggots. Murderers and torturers are spitted upon sharp spikes and their guts are pecked by birds with steel beaks. Perhaps we should beware of the literalism of such accounts, which sometimes amount to little more than crude superstition. Although Buddhism has never descended to hellfire preaching, the image of hell has sometimes been drawn in rather sharp detail. Such an emphasis may have a salutary effect, making some people consider the consequences of their actions more carefully, yet it may simply induce feelings of irrational fear and guilt. While for Buddhism the existence of hellish states is a plain fact that cannot be avoided, the image of hell should never be used to manipulate or to induce unwholesome mental states of gloom and despair such as may affect many people who have been brought up within churches where hell is emphasized, even to the very young, in all its ghastly detail. A genuine moral sense comes from self-confidence and maturity, not from terror.

Hell is probably not as orderly as it is often presented in Buddhist tradition, with a particular torment allotted to each unskilful deed. Perhaps we should not take the traditional depictions too literally. The basic features of hell are constant suffering and relentless pain inflicted by furious and vengeful beings. This kind of experience is, of course, to be met with even here on earth, but we must be careful not to assume that those who are the victims of intense suffering, whether through illness, injury, or oppression, are simply reaping the rewards of their past bad karma. That is an inhuman doctrine. Rather, the human realm itself has within it the possibility of great pain. Hell beings are to be found here on earth, however. They are those whose perspective is essentially paranoid. Everyone around them seems to be trying to do them down and they feel under constant threat. Their primary motivation is to eliminate or evade this menace and they are in a state of covert or open enmity with almost everyone they encounter. They suffer agonies of insecurity and feel the pain and humiliation of every imagined wrong or slight.

They see this torment as if it were inflicted upon them by their enemies who, they feel, are constantly trying to undermine them. In many cases, because of the way they behave towards others, they bring into being the enemies they at first only imagine.

We have already seen that hatred is the attempt to secure the ego-identity by excluding those objects that are considered to be threats. Human hatred is quite different from the aggression of an animal. When an animal inflicts harm it is an instinctive response, usually to preserve its immediate survival, and cannot be called hatred. Hatred is fed by the imagination and is the desire to cause another person pain and suffering, even to destroy them, because they pose a threat to us which is not merely physical but which strikes at the roots of our selfhood. Whether they have actually done something to us or we only imagine that they have, we feel weakened in our very being. The only way we can reassert our own identity is to retaliate. We may start off by reacting resentfully to someone over particular incidents but, sooner or later, a permanent attitude of hatred may develop. We no longer simply want to get our own back over those incidents – that is not enough any more. Regardless now of what the other person may do or say, we feel that we would like to see them suffer and we may be prepared to inflict pain on them ourselves.

In some cases, hatred hardens into a habitual mood as if the person carries within himself a permanent store of undischarged resentment, dammed up from the past. Not related to particular people or events, it has become an abiding attitude that is always looking for some outlet. Grumbling and complaining, backbiting and gossip are all ways in which such residual bad feeling is vented – and it can be much more vicious than that. This underlying negativity is so common that most human groups have an established enemy or 'out-group' against whom the hatred is expressed. Everyone in the group is united in their hatred of a particular person or class of persons. In families and other small groups one person may become the scapegoat and bear the burden of the residual hatred of the others. Similarly, many people find there is always one person who seems to undermine or annoy them. When the enemy of the moment is removed, however, a new one soon arises, as if they must always have someone to dislike, regardless of personal qualities.

The elimination of hatred from our minds is no easy task. By being mindful we can gradually restrict its expression and can check habitual negative states. By living happier, more fulfilled lives with friends with whom we share good feeling, we will feel confident and contented and therefore less prone to hatred. By actively practising the *metta bhavana*, we will gradually bring into being, more of the time, the love that drives out hatred. At the same time, we need to be careful that, in trying to get rid of hatred, we do not simply lose vitality. Because Buddhism is a non-violent teaching, it is sometimes thought that any vigorous words or deeds or any disagreements are incompatible with the Dharma. On the contrary, drive and energy, even perhaps a kind of anger, are essential to human growth. We need that sort of force to break through the many barriers, both internal and external, that we encounter in the course of our lives. This aggressive quality will never be directed to hurting others intentionally, however, but to breaking through to new levels of clarity and truth. For instance, in friendship we must be prepared to speak our minds frankly, even with a certain heat, if we feel our friend is wrong or that something stands between us and them. This 'positive anger', as it could be termed, arises from the frustration of healthy energies that then accumulate and burst forth, sometimes in a hot and emphatic way. With more skill and maturity, we will probably learn to express this positive drive in a less spectacular fashion. The point here is that the principle of non-hatred does not mean that we must always be meek and gentle in a rather bloodless way.

Spiritual life requires our full vigour and even a kind of destructiveness. We have to destroy everything within us that sweeps us back to lower forms of consciousness. The forces of greed, hatred, and delusion, the pull of the lower evolution, the inertia of ignorance: all these need to be resisted and overcome. Not only are these forces within us, they are also in the world around. Here, of course, we must be cautious, because it is in people that they are embodied. Our battle against the forces of ignorance must never be a battle against people, for that is completely contrary to the whole spirit of the Dharma. In the whole history of Buddhism, few, if any, wars have been fought in its name and persecution has been largely foreign to it. Buddhism teaches that evil must be combated by non-violent means. We should battle against everything that drags men down, using criticism, exhortation, influence, and whatever methods are ethically sound and cause no harm to others.

The need for a skilful cutting edge to our spiritual life gives us the opportunity to sublimate the hatred within us. We can put it to use. In the words of one Buddhist sage, Shantideva, we must use hatred to destroy hatred. We can be hot and sharp against what limits and binds beings, restricting them to lower states of mind. But although the truths we have to speak may be uncomfortable to some people, our aim should never be to hurt them, and we should avoid any action likely to cause violence to others, whether directly or indirectly. In this way, we can skilfully vent and tame the destructive force of our own latent hatred, while it still remains, at the same time as we actively work against the forces of darkness in the world.

If we do not learn to sublimate the hatred within us it will continue to exercise a controlling influence on our lives. If we allow it to dominate us it can make a hell for us, both here and now and in the states beyond death.

The fiery heat of the hells corresponds to the passionate intensity of hatred. The frozen hells are reserved for those in whom hatred has passed beyond the volcanic eruptions of ordinary passion and has become cold malice – the enjoyment in inflicting pain and suffering on others regardless of whether the victim has harmed us or not. This is probably the most unskilful state into which one can fall since it is one in which all feeling for others is completely deadened. The frozen hells are therefore at the very bottom of the whole system of worlds.

Although the traditional Buddhist depictions of hell bear a close resemblance to those of Christianity, the concept of hell differs from its Christian counterpart in two important respects: hell is not a punishment and it is not everlasting. Each of the worlds is the objectification of an individual's own mind in accordance with the natural workings of the principle of karma. No one judges, no one condemns. The figure of the Lord of Death in Buddhist mythology is the personification of death itself and the mirror that he holds up is our own conscience – our sensitivity to the feelings of others – which we often suppress but which stands revealed at death. (According to some traditions, the Lord of Death is Avalokiteshvara, the transcendental being who embodies the compassionate aspect of Buddhahood. This signifies the fact that even death, which most people see as the great catastrophe, when looked at in its true light, reveals the real nature of things. If only we would fully face up to death we would see not the glaring red eyes of a horrifying monster, but the compassionate smile of Avalokiteshvara.) Many people who have been close to death report having witnessed their lives passing before their eyes. In a similar way, at death one sees the deeds of one's past life reflected in the Lord of Death's mirror.

The momentum we set up determines the kind of world into which we will be reborn. Buddhism contains no conception of creator or divine judge – these figures are, it could be said, nothing more than the projections of our own hopes and fears, based upon our need for a reassuring father-figure who orders the cosmos. The universe is made up of processes that contain within themselves the laws governing their own functioning. The principle of karma is the law inherent in individualized consciousness and determines the effects that it will experience – resulting from its own volitions.

Every process is impermanent, and a particular state continues only as long as the conditions that have brought it into being are still present. Volitions based in hatred bring the experience of hell into being. When they are exhausted or counteracted by skilful volitions, one will disappear from hell and reappear in some other state that suits one's new karmic configuration. One will remain in the state of torment as long as there are undischarged karmic energies to keep one there. Tradition has it that a life in hell may extend over many aeons – perhaps this corresponds to the well-known experience of time dragging when we are suffering.

The Realm of the Hungry Ghosts

A desolate landscape stretches as far as the eye can see, a cold desert of rock and sand. A few leafless trees are the only protection against the biting wind, and a tiny, pale sun sheds a piteous warmth. A great river of brackish water flows slowly through the vast plain.

Groups of ungainly creatures huddle together for warmth beneath the skeletal trees. Their distended bodies are the colour of smoke and they appear insubstantial as if they were made of mist. Their arms and legs are spindly and frail and their heads are carried on long, thin necks, while their bellies are bloated, sagging masses that their legs can barely support. Tiny mouths, no thicker than a needle. are topped by round, staring eyes, filled with pain and longing.

An unquenchable thirst and perpetual hunger obsess these pathetic creatures. They stagger on their feeble limbs to the river's edge
but, as soon as their mouths approach the water, it recedes from
them. Even those who stand in the stream's midst cannot get a drop
into their mouths. The tortures of Tantalus are theirs. Those few who,
by chance, manage to swallow some meagre mouthfuls soon regret
it, for the water turns to liquid fire in their guts. One or two sparse
fruits grow on the trees but these, too, evade the reach of any
creature who, maddened with hunger, drags its enormous belly up
among the branches. Any that are eaten turn to swords and daggers,
piercing and slicing inside the stomach.

Driven by their overwhelming hunger and thirst, the hungry
ghosts live out their lives for no purpose other than food and drink.
Their weak limbs and pinhole mouths make it almost impossible for
them to gain any sustenance. And whatever they do manage to get
into their mouths causes them more pain than the torment of desire
that drove them to it. And so they live until the avarice and greed
that brought them to this world is spent.

The world of the hungry ghost is a kind of hell, constituted not so
much of physical torture – although there is some of that – as of the
pain of unsatisfied desire. Just as hell is the objectification of hatred,
so this realm is the reflection of a mind in which craving predominates. In our human world, there are people who are so possessed
by greed and longing that they live only to gather things to themselves. Even if they get what they want it gives them little pleasure.
No matter what they possess, they always feel that there is something missing. The realm of the hungry ghosts is built from this
attitude.

Craving is the longing to possess things in the belief that they will
make the ego more secure. Underlying it is a feeling of inner emptiness and insubstantiality. The immature ego is weak and incomplete
and does not have a very strong experience of itself, leaving an
uncomfortable feeling of vacancy and poverty. To feel real and substantial, the ego craves certain experiences, for experience absorbs
consciousness, giving an illusion of inner fullness and distracting
momentarily from the lack within.

The failure to fully experience oneself that underlies craving results from a kind of psychological warping at the time when an
individualized consciousness is emerging. In one way or another,

emotion comes to be minimized or excluded from self-awareness. Sometimes this is the consequence of repression, as when someone refuses to allow certain feelings into full consciousness because they have learned that they are 'wrong'. Certain sorts of Christian upbringing, for instance, can imbue a sense of guilt about the body and its sensations, particularly those of sex, and can lead to a refusal to acknowledge this kind of feeling. So when the emotion comes it is pushed out of awareness, leaving an inner blankness. Others, again, may have suffered so much unhappiness and pain, at some point in their lives, that they numb themselves to emotion. A development that is one-sidedly intellectual can have the same effect. In these ways, such people are left without much emotional life and left longing for some solid experience that will make them *feel*. The inner richness they lack is then projected on to the world outside. They imagine that, by possessing certain objects, by having certain experiences, or by being in certain kinds of relationships, they will gain the fulfilment they long for. They may feel pleasure at the point at which they get what they desire that may temporarily overlay the feeling of emptiness; but, sooner or later, it returns and a new cycle of craving begins.

The human hungry ghost is the miser who lives for money, the collector who is never content but must have more, or the addict. The drug addict is, perhaps, the archetype of the hungry ghost, barely alive to the world and concentrated solely upon the next dose – whose effects will soon fade away, leaving a longing for another. The hungry ghost is the addict, for addiction is a state of mind and one can be addicted to anything that is seen as a source of palliation for that restless inner longing. Whatever the object of addiction, it cannot give one satisfaction because what is longed for is an inner fullness, not the object itself. As soon as the brief respite the 'drug' brings begins to fade, one must have more.

Addiction can have many objects, but among the most frequent are other people. The addicted person is often neurotically dependent on others, seeking from them the emotional nourishment that should be found within. This extreme dependence is infantile and repetitive in character, for even if it is given, one soon wants more. Reassurance, approval, attention, security, all these may be sought in neurotic relationships. The unnatural attachment between parents and a grown-up child who is kept in a state of prolonged infancy is a not uncommon example of neurotic dependence. We also see it with especial frequency in sexual relationships. In this case the addicted partners are bound together, not by mutual respect and co-operation in raising a family, but by their neurotic needs; each seeks in the other the satisfaction of his or her own inner emptiness. When they cannot find what they seek, instead of learning their lesson they often blame each other for not giving it, adding resentment to craving. This form of addictive relationship is becoming more common, an aspect of the 'me generation', the children of the post-war period in whom affluence has encouraged appetite and whom rapid social change has made restless and insecure. Immature and self-centred, such people are really seeking to perpetuate with their sexual partner their infantile relationship with their mothers. It is a most unhappy and ugly phenomenon: two weak people, like shadows, trying to get something from each other that the other, too, lacks.

The circumstances of modern life, perhaps, encourage the attitude of neurotic craving because, in many ways, depth of feeling is undervalued. The ease and speed of communications have made people highly mobile, reducing stability and continuity. They do not have much opportunity to form deep connections with the people and places around them and therefore lack the satisfying depth of feeling that a more firmly rooted background can give. Again, modern life offers so many sensations and distractions that people are encouraged to fritter away their emotional resources. The result is a hollowness of feeling that breeds a neurotic quest for experience.

Neurotic desire has to be clearly distinguished from healthy need. The desires of the body are not, in themselves, cravings. Hunger and thirst are objective needs that arise from lack of nourishment and dehydration and, when we eat and drink, they are satiated. As anyone who has undergone a fast will know, one can remain perfectly happy even though deprived of food and feeling hungry. The case of sex is rather more complicated because a number of different elements are bound up in it. The immediate biological urge of sex, however, is not dissimilar to hunger and thirst, deriving from our physiological constitution. If we can satisfy these desires in a straightforward way that causes no harm to others, they are not neurotic. Unfortunately, food and sex are quite frequently distorted and abused and thus become the objects of neurotic craving. In such cases, there is a neurotic attempt to fill an inner lack by perverting desires that are not themselves unhealthy.

Healthy needs extend beyond the physiological plane. We have social needs that are not neurotic. We need, for instance, acknowledgement – to be seen and recognized by others. It is very hard to live in contact with other people if they never show any sign of having seen us as separate individuals. This need for acknowledgement of one's selfhood by others is quite different from the neurotic need for attention. The latter cannot be satisfied: the more attention one gives, the more will be devoured without any reduction in the craving. Like a vampire or leech, the neurotic sucks energy from those who allow him or her to fasten on to them. Someone who is given the human acknowledgement he or she needs very quickly becomes brighter and more cheerful.

Though the neurotic may indulge in sensual pleasures, he or she does not get much enjoyment from them. The emotional poverty of the neurotic prevents this, for the capacity to enjoy things comes from inner richness. Enjoyment is the contact between the object and one's own healthy emotions. When one is most contented one can enjoy the beauties of the senses. One is, then, satisfied with very simple pleasures and does not crave the sensory saturation that neurosis so often demands. Since spiritual growth is a growth of inner fullness, it is marked by an increasing capacity for enjoyment.

There is one final form of healthy desire in particular that needs to be clearly distinguished from the neurotic form: the attraction to spiritual ideals and to the people who embody them. That desire to evolve, to reach beyond our present level of consciousness, must be stimulated and intensified. Sometimes people do have a neurotic, appropriative attitude to what they consider to be the spiritual path. They see the spiritual life as a means of gaining power, or as an escape from themselves and their personal responsibilities. But the urge to develop is not narrow and personal, it is selfless and expansive. This desire is latent within everyone, covered over, more or less, by greed, hatred, and delusion. It is only by following it through that one will find the store of inner wealth that will finally dispel all craving.

The Realm of the Animals
In the realm of the animals, life is the life of the body. All endeavour is directed to the satisfaction of physical desires and the business of

self-preservation. This world is the objectification of the ignorant refusal to see beyond the needs of the body. The animals of the field and jungle are not ignorant in this sense since, being without self-consciousness, they are not responsible for the limitation of their understanding. Their ignorance is the ignorance of nature, not of individuals. The human animal, however, wilfully narrows his or her horizons and refuses to look at the meaning and purpose of life.

Animal-like humans are not neurotic like hungry ghosts, and no bottomless hunger drives them. Their bodily needs for nourishment, sleep, and sex are healthy and they get satisfaction and enjoyment from their fulfilment. But fulfilling those needs becomes their sole end. For them, human life has no other significance. However, although they are ignorant in that they fail to see any higher human destiny, they are not necessarily stupid in a practical sense. They may live very sophisticated lives, fulfilling complex jobs and surrounded by elaborate technology. They may have a very well-developed practical intelligence. But they have no ideals and for them there is nothing beyond themselves and the group for which they live.

Animals live without vision and without culture, in the sense of interests and pursuits through which they can cultivate their minds. Much of modern society is of this kind. Although there has never before been such a highly ordered civilization with such advanced technical capacities, remarkably few people, it seems, have any broad perspective on life and there is no widely-held common vision. In most other civilizations of the past, religion has been at the heart of all public acts and has provided the assumptions on which life was built. This is no longer the case in much of the world: Christianity in the West and other religious traditions elsewhere are decaying before the onslaught of consumerism – which might be called the 'philosophy' of the animal. In some way, this decay of old values is no bad thing, since much that was rotten or inappropriate is also cleared away. But, as a consequence, many people now live in a world of drastically restricted horizons and can only see the option of losing themselves in the animal-like pursuit of bodily gratification.

Whether human beings can literally be reborn as cats or horses, even as flies or fish, is a matter of dispute in Buddhist circles. The Buddha seems to have taught that they could (though in one scripture he speaks of rebirth as an animal as being the outcome of a systematic and sustained effort to act like an animal). On the face of it, it would seem unlikely that a human being could so utterly douse self-consciousness as to be reborn an animal. Perhaps, however, if one does persistently deny all creative tendencies within oneself and disregard the higher possibilities of human life, one's consciousness may gradually atrophy with neglect so that one is nothing but an animal. It is certainly possible to regress permanently from an adult to an infantile state, so it may well be possible to regress even more drastically to a preceding stage of evolution.

Whether or not humans can be reborn as animals, there are animal-like human beings. There are pockets of society where the level of culture is very low indeed and there is little understanding of man's potential. Neither the arts nor a higher philosophy lifts the gaze beyond the shallow concerns of everyday survival or the satisfaction of the needs of the body. Such pockets are not necessarily to be found among peoples living at the edges of the civilized world, they are to be found in the midst of many of our great cities. To be reborn into such societies is to be born an animal.

The Realm of the Titans

Knowing only war, the male titans live all their days in armour and rest with their weapons beside them, ready for battle. Each of these jealous gods cuts a ferocious figure, towering, thickset, and powerful, his skin a forbidding dark blue or green. His face is horribly ugly, knotted in a mask of fury, with bulging eyes and snarling lips. Again and again, in serried ranks, these giants rush upon the gods of the sensuous realm and try to grab from them their happiness and delight. They try to capture the heavenly tree that fulfils all wishes and, in their foolish envy, they begin to hack it down. But the gods rout them and they fall back in disarray. They immediately start to fight among themselves, each trying to gain for himself greater power in the ordered hierarchy of their armies.

The titanesses are one of the principal causes of dissension among the menfolk. They are no less jealous and acquisitive but they win their wars not by force of arms but by enchantment. For each titaness is as voluptuous and bewitching as any film starlet and knows how to captivate and charm her chosen victim. Like the sirens, the lamias, and Lorelei, she destroys those who fall into her power.

The inhabitants of this world seem to be descended, mythologically speaking, from one group of those gods who took part in the battle for heavenly supremacy recorded in the legends of Greece, Iran, and India. For this reason, I have called them by their Greek name although they should not be equated too closely with Atlas, Prometheus, Hyperion, etc. They are variously referred to as anti-gods, jealous gods, or angry gods, for they are godlike in their power and vigour although not at all in happiness and pleasure since they are driven by the misery of envy. Their longing to possess does not come from desire or greed, like the hungry ghosts. They want things because they begrudge others whatever possessions, achievements, or qualities they may have. The success of others makes them feel belittled, for their sense of self rests upon feeling themselves to be the centre of the universe, like a babe in arms. Whatever others gain, they cannot have, and this deprivation fills them with fury. The deep discontentment that others' good fortune breeds in them leads them to struggle vigorously, even violently, to grab it for themselves. In the myth they make war on the lower gods for possession of the wish-fulfilling tree that instantly grants all desires. The gods have gained this wondrous tree as a result of their good deeds done in the past. The jealous gods want to seize it without having laid the foundations for its enjoyment. Thus they try to cut it down and carry it off, severing the fruits of the tree from the roots that nourish them.

The male titan is highly competitive and tries to outdo others in every way so that he can maintain that sense of being the most important person in the world that is so essential to his identity. He always tries to be cleverer than others, or stronger, or richer, or more experienced, and so forth. Whatever they do, he must go one better. Such people are not uncommon in the worlds of politics or business – and in many other walks of life. Although they are always trying to prove their superiority, titans are very conscious of hierarchy and tend to form ordered power structures. They can relate to others only on the basis of dominance or submission, not as equals, and, where they can, they will dominate. Only where they feel that domination is not possible will they submit. The ranks into which they arrange themselves make for a very effective co-operation against a common competitor. But, as in any military dictatorship, each member is watching for others to weaken so that he can seize their power for himself. The hierarchy is not based on respect and honour but on fear and ambition. Backstabbing and conspiracy constantly undermine the stability of the social structure and new leaders are, all the time, pushing themselves forward.

The male titans compete through brute force or cunning. The females are equally competitive but they use their 'feminine wiles' to get their way. They manipulate their prey through their emotions and use sexual fascination to bait their traps. The titan seeks to reduce the world to his ordering and tries to turn it into a masculine hierarchy centring on himself, the Cosmic King. The titaness, in her attempts to be the most important person in the world, tries to influence others through her siren-like sexual charms or to form a vast family with herself as its Great Mother with everyone, male and female, brought back to a state of infantile dependence upon her.

These male and female titans represent the extremes of sexual polarization. Differentiation into sexes is a feature of all the worlds of the sensuous sphere, except some animals that are hermaphrodite or parthenogenetic. The higher gods are not divided into sexes but are androgynous. Dominating all the lower forms of self-consciousness, the split into male and female is an important factor in evolution which we need to understand if we are going to progress. Consciousness is closely bound up with the body and one of the these bodily determinants is sex. Although it is almost impossible to tell where biological conditioning ends and social conditioning begins, it cannot but be the case that our sex is a basic factor in forming our consciousness. We can explore this a little in the context of the titans as, amongst them, the polarity is highly exaggerated and clear – the consequence of a considerable distortion of self-consciousness. In the titans we can see that the masculine characteristics of initiative and drive have become brute force and desire for domination, while the healthy feminine characteristics of nurturance and care have been perverted into control and manipulation.

The titans and titanesses and their human counterparts are at the extremes of sexual polarity. Neither extreme is redeemed by any of the qualities of its opposite. Indeed, femininity in a man or masculinity in a woman would be considered shameful. Exaggeratedly one-sided and alienated from the complementary characteristics, the male titans are all brawn and aggression, establishing the dominance of their egos through their masculine drive and initiative. The females use their feminine emotionality and their sexual attraction to weave their own brand of control, a kind of perverted motherliness.

Identified almost entirely with their own sex and using its characteristics only to defend their distorted sense of self, the titans represent another of the evolutionary culs-de-sac into which consciousness can wander.

Because the male and female titans are so much identified with
their own biological sex, they have no experience of the psychological qualities associated with the opposite sex. Yet those qualities are
latent within them. The psychologically masculine have within
themselves the potential for femininity and, likewise, the feminine
conceal the masculine in themselves. If these qualities are not experienced consciously they are projected. This is also the main component in 'falling in love' in which the object of adoration is seen as the
embodiment of unrealized inner qualities. The more extreme the
polarization between those attributes that are expressed in consciousness and those that are not, the more intense the pangs of love
and the more complicated the relationship that ensues – for the
loved one is seldom the paragon that he or she first appears to be
and at the same time may have his or her own projections. Similarly,
the titans flounder helplessly in the toils of their own projected
expectations but continue to seek outside them the masculinity or
femininity which is, in reality, their own.

It is important to remember that human consciousness, although
initially conditioned by biological form, need not remain so. The
psychological characteristics that first emerge on the basis of bodily
gender can be rounded out by the process of horizontal integration
to include all aspects of a full individuality. The mature and healthy
ego unites qualities of both masculinity and femininity. The individual can take the lead, be resourceful and positively assertive, and
have drive and energy, and at the same time be sensitive to others,
careful of their needs, sympathetic to their sufferings, and receptive
to their words. Both the masculine and the feminine modes are
represented in his or her behaviour so that the individual seems to
be neither merely a man nor a woman but both and more. Male and
female biological character is transcended in the individual who
integrates both masculinity and femininity in one fully mature personality. Both men and women are capable of achieving the androgynous state and of passing far beyond it to Enlightenment itself.

The full integration of both psychosexual poles is no easy task,
reinforced as they are by the insistent demands of the body and by

the full pressure of social conditioning. To begin to work on our integration in this aspect we need to know where we are starting from. Human growth always begins with self-awareness and we must know our basic temperament and inclinations. In order to develop, we must take the raw material of our crude selfhood and gradually shape it into something finer and more complete. Thus we need to start with our biological qualities. In order to begin this task of horizontal integration we need a drive within us, a drive for *more*, that can be harnessed to our own development. The spiritual path is one that needs to be consciously undertaken; we need to want to undertake it, and to put considerable effort into it, if there is to be any movement towards a further, more integrated state. The quality of initiative or drive is therefore needed to start this process of integrating masculine with feminine.

To continue this process, these two poles will need to find expression in our lives. A creative outlet will encourage and express the masculine drives: work that challenges and calls up initiative and ingenuity, companions to encourage and stimulate, even a certain amount of healthy competitiveness – based on the desire to reach higher rather than merely to win. The feminine impulses also need to find healthy expression: to care for other beings in a metta-ful way, to respect those more developed, and to use any capacities in the service of genuine ideals. Neither function is at all dishonourable. The more masculine and the more feminine men or women should be encouraged to fulfil in a skilful way their basic psychological character. At the same time, unrealized qualities should be contacted and integrated into one harmonious whole.

Normal social conditions tend to reinforce sexual polarization rather than encourage an integration of the poles. In our own culture this is particularly evident in the glorification of romantic love, in which one's own unrealized qualities are projected on to another person. The increasing isolation of the family unit and the common belief that personal fulfilment is to be found in being part of a couple do not encourage the development of a balanced individuality. In the nuclear family, men and women are thrust into a mostly unrelieved proximity for which history has few precedents and which seems to breed psychological dependence and tends to reinforce existing psychosexual roles. For women and men to undertake that horizontal integration of masculine and feminine very different conditions are needed. Traditional Buddhist practice suggests that the spiritual interests of men and women are best served if they spend much of their time with their own sex. To begin with, without the powerful element of biological attraction, a principal distraction is removed. The subtle sexual by-play that is almost inevitable in a mixed atmosphere is often an annoying diversion when one is trying to concentrate on other things. But, more deeply, where those concerned have not reached the stage of integrated individuality, there is always a tendency to polarization and projection – and to falling in love. While this may initially be a harmless and enjoyable pastime, it hinders the process of integration.

We need to set up conditions in which the urge to serve and support is encouraged and directed to skilful ends, encompassing and going beyond the family, and where the energy of drive and initiative is used for the good of others. Both men and women need to be able to pass beyond their initial biological determination to an integrated individuality in which masculinity and femininity are merged. If this does not happen, biological maleness and femaleness may dominate consciousness and, if allowed to become accentuated and distorted, will result in rebirth among the titans.

8

Men and Gods

The Human World

The human realm is the world of everyday experience. It contains the whole animal side of human life: birth, mating, and death, the quest for food and shelter, and the struggle with the forces of nature. In it are all our technical productions: mighty cities, roads and communications systems, and complex agricultural and industrial developments. Included too are the social organizations mankind has evolved: tribes, city states, kingdoms, empires, and nations. It is the world of cultural achievements: languages, learning and scientific knowledge, arts and crafts. Finally, rooted in, but towering above, the human realm are the highest attainments of the human race: the great works of art and philosophy, the universal religions, and, above all, the true individuals who lead mankind beyond itself.

In the previous chapter, we examined the worlds of misery created by immature and distorted self-consciousness. In each, the burden of suffering is so great that there is not much energy available for developing higher modes of awareness. The agonized inhabitants of these realms are severely handicapped until they are no longer the victims of their past unskilfulness and until all their unwholesome volitions are exhausted. We will now concern ourselves with the two realms of happiness within the sensuous sphere. The inhabitants of these realms have healthily developed from embryonic individuality to maturity, where they stand on the threshold of new levels of spiritual awareness. These are the worlds of men and gods.

A human rebirth is considered the most favourable at the outset of one's spiritual life because it contains a balance of pleasure and pain. Constant pain, as experienced in the four lower realms, is demoralizing and numbs initiative. Persistent pleasure and success tends to breed complacency. Human life, containing both pleasure and pain, confronts us with the limitations of lower states of existence while allowing us the freedom actively to evolve our own consciousnesses. The human world is an axial point in the whole system of worlds: it is where the lower, biological evolution becomes the higher evolution of consciousness. Since human life gives us such rare opportunities for growth, Buddhism teaches that it is very precious indeed. We may not be born in such favourable circumstances again for many lifetimes, so we should take full advantage of them. We should not squander our life in careless living because we have failed to grasp its true significance.

Communication is the principal feature of the human realm. Communication, here, means more than mere flashing of signals and exchanging information. Many animals have ways of signalling to each other and, no doubt, the hell beings can howl their pain and fury to their fellow sufferers, the hungry ghosts can whimper their longings, and the titans can give commands and utter their battle-cry. But all these are solely concerned with themselves, having no feeling for, or real awareness of, those to whom they pass on their messages. Communication, in this special sense, involves a mutual recognition of individuality. Each party to the exchange can see the other, free from projections, as a separate person, and can enter sympathetically into the other's world. Each knows that the other is an experiencing subject and feels metta and appreciation of the other's special viewpoint. Where many animals look to others only as a source of herd-security, the hungry ghosts as objects of longing, the hell demons as threatening aggressors, and the titans as rivals, human beings can see others as individuals. Not only can they exchange with them facts about the world (although they have raised this capacity to a high level of exactitude and universality), but they can convey and recognize inner qualities such as love, courage, beauty, honesty, and understanding.

The human capacity for communication, in both its superficial and its deeper senses, makes possible the co-operation that brings about civilization and culture. This marks an enormous acceleration of the evolutionary process, for through culture is handed on to the future the stored experience of the past. The achievements, both technical and moral, of dead generations are retained in the various systems of transmission of a particular civilization. Epic poems, preserved in oral traditions, books, music, and works of art, all hand on to us what our ancestors learned. We need not recapitulate by trial and error the entire course of human civilization, but can learn from the past and launch ourselves from the highest achievements of our forebears. Of course, the collective memory embodied in these systems is selective and open to tampering, as recurrent book burnings demonstrate. None the less, in our own age as never before, a wealth of material is open to us. Data is stored in computer banks to which access can be gained from all over the world. The greatest of world literature has been translated into all the major world languages. Works of art can be seen in public galleries or enjoyed in inexpensive reproductions. The best of music is played by great performers in most major cities. With all this available to us in our human world, we may, if we choose to, deepen and extend our knowledge of physical nature and soar with the loftiest flights of the Imagination.

The human world comprises a number of different levels, corresponding to degrees of maturity both in the individual and in human culture. From the birth of a human being and the first emergence of true *homo sapiens*, through mature individuality, and on to the highest peaks of civilization – where man merges with the gods – is a long slow path. Several different stages could be distinguished through which healthy self-consciousness passes in its transition from the animals to the gods. For present purposes, we will divide that long passage into two and examine the developing individual and the positive group, on the one hand, and the committed individual and the spiritual community, on the other.

The dividing line between these two levels of humanity is the act of commitment to the spiritual life, in its broadest sense. We will be examining this crucial step in more detail in the next chapter but, for the present, in Buddhism, it is taken when an individual feels sufficiently drawn to the ideal of Enlightenment to place its pursuit at the centre of his or her life. One who has 'gone for Refuge to the Three Jewels of Buddha, Dharma, and Sangha', as this act of commitment is known in the traditional language, has started upon the Spiral Path. It is in the human realm that the Spiral really begins, so our examination of the second level of humanity belongs mainly to the next chapter. It could be said that the only true human being is the committed individual – the one who is inspired by the ideal of self-transcendence – for the development of mature individuality depends upon being able to look beyond one's own self-interest. There is a line of healthy development up to that point, however, that does not involve the distortions of immature self-consciousness that breed the hungry ghost, demon, titan, or animal. It is this process of development, the best of the human world, that I will describe below.

Before there is full individuality there is group membership; we are members of a group to the extent that we are not full individuals. If we have not fully differentiated our own thoughts and feelings from the views and attitudes of the society in which we live, if we have not become aware of the conditioning that has shaped our minds, and if we have not taken full responsibility for all our deeds, then we are still group members. To be a group member means to be shaped more by the pressures and views of those who surround us than by our own individual awareness. Just as a child is formed by parents, teachers, and other social influences and cannot really be said to have an independent point of view or be accounted morally responsible, so most humans cannot really be distinguished from the social group to which they belong. A child inevitably depends upon its parents for moral values and social education – this is, of course, normal and healthy. In the same way, many people need the support and security of the group and its norms until their own individuality has matured. The way in which the child matures depends, to a large extent, on the adults in his or her life; the way in which the individual matures depends on the group to which he or she belongs. We need, therefore, to distinguish between different types of group.

Groups may be analysed in terms of the six worlds. Whole societies, whole nations, may be broadly characterized as hungry-ghost-like, or titanic, or demonic, or bestial if, respectively, craving, envy, hatred, or ignorance are the predominant forces of the culture. The developing individual also lives in a group, but this time the group is of a positive kind. The main influences in that society tend towards the production of positive emotions and wholesome states of mind.

The positive group is what I shall call healthily pagan, pagan in the sense of unspoiled human nature or healthy, happy, human nature, such as we met in Chapter 4. Humanity is the axis of the Wheel and the Spiral; human beings possess a body that is the product of the long process of biological development and a self-consciousness that is capable of unfolding into Buddhahood. Neither aspect should be neglected. The pagan, in this sense, recognizes the natural forces both within and around himself or herself and allows them their appropriate expressions – but without them dominating or distorting the mind. There is none of the despising or hating the body that breeds repression and leads to the tortures of the hungry ghosts, who cannot admit to what they long for and can only crave some unsatisfying substitute. At the same time, instinctual demands do not entirely dominate self-consciousness, as they do with the animal who lives only to eat, sleep, and copulate.

Sex is the most commonly abused of the natural instincts because of its overriding power. Within the positive group, one finds sex is not regarded as 'dirty' or sinful. It is considered normal and healthy to have sexual feelings and the pleasures of sex are openly acknowledged, whilst not overestimated or raised to an all-consuming obsession. At the same time, its very strong and even disruptive force is recognized, for it can tear apart stable family life and undermine community harmony. A framework of custom and etiquette ensures that the sexual instinct has a healthy outlet, and that outside this it does not plague the mind or disrupt social relations.

The analogy to healthy pagans covers the positive group's wholesome attitude to the body in all respects. Pagans satisfy their bodily needs in a straightforward way and ensure that they are fit and physically healthy. They neither despise and torture their body nor indulge it. It is their vehicle for self-expression and the medium through which they act. In the human body we have the possibility of growth, so we need to guard and nourish the body with pride and care.

Soundness of mental attitude can likewise manifest itself in an elegant and pleasing way of dressing and adornment, avoiding the extremes of trying to attract attention by excessive display and of expressing self-hatred and neglect through untidy or unattractive clothing. In the same way, unspoiled human nature is in harmony with the natural world. It appreciates deeply the vitality in all things and responds to beauty and sublimity in the environment. With such an attitude one is careful not to waste or exploit the earth's natural resources.

The positive group should impart to its members a sense of self-confidence and assurance. Each can feel that he or she is valued and will have no sense of self-hatred or unworthiness. In this ideal group an atmosphere of trust in the culture and those that bring it to them can develop, with, therefore, much less of the suspiciousness and rebelliousness that many modern Westerners feel towards the civilization that has bred them. The positive traditions of the group will be valued and respected, and preserved with pride. The members will be able to believe in their culture and so to believe in themselves. They can, therefore, co-operate in a friendly spirit with other group members in communal economic, political, and social affairs. The collective energies of the group can be harnessed to positive ends: social enterprises that bring benefits to its members whether in material prosperity or in beauty and learning. A positive group has no need of a group enemy to channel surplus aggression, for all the community's vigour is used in a skilful way.

In the positive group the manners and customs that have evolved are there to guarantee harmonious and sensitive relationships between people. Social relations are, therefore, characterized by consideration and care, and each person knows what behaviour most fittingly expresses that friendly sensitivity in each situation. It also imparts a more basic code of ethics concerning abstention from murder, theft, sexual violence, etc. Since this model society is still a group whose members have not yet developed a natural ethical sense, that moral code needs to be sanctioned by a system of justice to punish and reward. Part of the responsibility of the members of the group is to know what their duty is as citizens. They will feel confidence that the laws of their group are just and will believe in the fittingness of the retribution that follows an offence.

All the influences of such a positive tradition as I have described are naturally upward. Cities would be built so that they were beautiful to look at and graceful to live in, learning and the arts would be encouraged, and pervading all the acts of public life would be a sense of idealism. In this arena, decisions would be taken not on the basis of sectional interests, each jockeying for position and power, but through a common regard for certain values, which transcend narrow personal wishes. The whole of society, if influenced in this way, would be raised up by a vision of a higher kind of life which all, at least to some extent, honoured and respected. Without that leaven of a higher set of values, the group can only fall back upon the interests of its members. Since these are bound to conflict sooner or later, strife will arise and the positive group will become a negative one: either demonic, titanic, bestial, or hungry-ghost-like. Without some generally accepted ideal, there can be no positive group.

An ideal cannot be manufactured – a vision cannot be artificially constructed – on abstract principles. A vision needs to be a living experience, vividly felt, washing aside all egoistic aspiration and dead values. A vision needs a visionary. There need to be people within the group, therefore, who have gone beyond the group; individuals who see the ideals clearly and who sufficiently embody them so that they may hand on the higher vision from which the culture of the positive group springs. The positive group needs leaders who are individuals with their own direct experience of truth, to gather itself around people who are individuals enough to have had their own experience of a higher level of consciousness. Only if the members of the group respect and are receptive to the wise in their midst will the sort of inspired culture outlined above come into being.

It is probably clear by now that Buddhism is not inherently democratic, much as many modern apologists would like it so. It is not, of course, aristocratic, in the usual sense of the term, nor totalitarian. It does not advocate the subordination of one part of the population to the egoistic wishes of another. Its 'political ideology' stems from its belief that human life has a purpose: to evolve as individuals to the goal of Buddhahood. It shows that different people are at different levels of development and, from common observation, only a few are highly developed in a spiritual sense. If decisions are based upon the opinions of the majority they run the danger of being founded on the lowest level of understanding. What most people want is likely to be what they consider to be in the interests of their own limited egos, not of some higher code of values. At the same time, Buddhism is not anti-democratic; it is certainly the case that the Western-style parliamentary democracies of the present day are the least offensive form of government to anyone who wishes to grow, since they impose little conformity of ideas. No particular form of government was, in fact, advocated by the Buddha. Whoever does exercise power, however they derive it, is simply urged to govern in accordance with moral principles and not with personal interest at heart. If those who govern have regard to the welfare of all the people, see that justice is impartially administered and ethically based, and encourage higher culture in general and the spiritual life in particular, honouring those who have given themselves to it fully, it is of secondary importance how their power is derived – so long as it comes without harm to others. Revolution, except in the most extreme cases, cannot usually be justified because of the disruption of the continuity of tradition and the violence it entails. It could be said that the principal issue of politics is not constitutional but moral and even spiritual. Without true moral and spiritual leadership, there can be no positive group.

The positive group is thus a network of people who have yet to achieve full ethical individuality and who have not committed themselves to the realization of the transcendental ideal. They rely on the moral sense or spiritual vision of committed individuals. Left to themselves, they are likely to fall back on their own limited self-interest, but they respond to the ethical guidance and reflected vision that is part of their cultural heritage. This allows them to act skilfully and encourages them to look beyond themselves. The worth of that tradition is guaranteed by the creative individuals who generated it in the past and their successors who now sustain it with their own renewed vision. The positive group in this way encourages a happy, vigorous, and friendly life devoted to ends greater than the individual. Above all, it urges and encourages all those who wish to go beyond the group to experience for themselves the transcendental reality that is the positive group's ultimate basis.

The spiritual community is, in principle, open to all those who have felt that impulsion to achieve a higher level of consciousness. Anyone can be accepted, regardless of their background or previous experience, as long as existing members of the spiritual community consider that their request is sincere and that they are able to carry out the commitment they wish to make. Although new members of the spiritual community may still have greed, hatred, and delusion swirling within them, they have decided that they want to function in a quite new way. They want to live ethically, not from fear of punishment or love of reward, but because they have some foreshadowing of the sensitivity and metta to all creatures that is the real basis of morality. They wish to develop higher states of consciousness and, in the end, transcendental insight. They also have some glimpse of the vision that inspires the spiritual community and they are prepared to open themselves fully to its influence. They want to develop friendships with others that are based, not on overlapping self-interest, but on mutual love and concern. They participate in the culture and tradition of the spiritual community that is at the basis of the culture and tradition of the positive group.

The spiritual community, or sangha in the context of this book, is the fulfilment of the human life and is its ultimate meaning. The positive group is kept in being by the sangha but it also provides a bridge over which those who wish may cross to the spiritual community itself. In a sense, it is only then that one is a full human being.

The Heavens of the Gods

Above the human world stretch plane upon plane of heavenly worlds, each one of greater subtlety and happiness than the one that lies beneath it. The lower of these god-worlds are still within the sphere of sensuous experience, but the higher are within the dimensions of archetypal form and of formless quality. Although the heavens collectively correspond to some degree to the ascending Spiral, we will be examining those of the sensuous sphere in this present chapter.

The Pali and Sanskrit words that are usually translated as 'god' come from a root meaning 'to shine'. The gods are the 'shining' or 'radiant' ones who live in unalloyed happiness and pleasure. It is traditionally recognized that such beings are heavenly and are also to be found on earth. There are heaven worlds into which one may be born as a god but it is also possible to live on this earth as if one were a god. Kings and princes seemed, in earlier times, to live a divine life, full of wealth and power, able to satisfy every desire. We have our own rich and powerful, today, who move in a sphere of opulence far removed from the ordinary man. (That many of them are notoriously unhappy is a sign, perhaps, that they are actually titans who have grabbed at riches and not gods who have attracted riches to them by their virtuous deeds!) Another sort of god on earth is the one who has spiritual attainment. The Stream Entrant and those beyond are resplendent with their transcendental knowledge and shine with the ideal qualities that they embody. They continuously experience the bliss of non-duality and they walk, like heroes, in full confidence and power. The world of the gods, properly speaking, however, is an objective dimension of existence into which any self-conscious entities may find themselves reborn.

God realms of the sensuous sphere, according to tradition, consist of six levels. The beings of the lowest are said to be able to interact with the human plane and are the benign spirits of folklore: fairies, dryads, naiads, and other nature spirits. Above these are beings of greater power and splendour who correspond, roughly, to the Greek Olympians – although they are of more blameless life. The highest planes are, respectively, occupied by the Contented Gods, the Gods who Delight in their own Creations, and the Gods who Delight in the Creations of Others. Each divine being has a physical body of a subtle substance that is not perceived by the ordinary human eye. They are very beautiful of form and noble of aspect. Everything they wish for immediately presents itself before them and they experience constant sensuous delight and satisfaction. The higher the realm, the more refined and satisfying are its pleasures. The gods of each world form a highly civilized society which is usually depicted as a royal court presided over by the king or chief god. They pass their time together in the enjoyment of beauty.

These gods of the sensuous realm are sexually differentiated, although at each level the difference becomes smaller. They do engage in sexual activity but, as the polarity between male and female relaxes, sex becomes more and more subtle. At the lowest levels, sexual gratification is by copulation, as among humans. Higher up, it is achieved by holding hands and then, progressively, by a smile, by prolonged gazing, and finally by a mere glance. At this highest level, masculinity and femininity are so closely united that if the eyes of a male meet even momentarily those of a female it relieves the tension that one-sidedness brings and gives all the pleasure of sexual release. Each rank of god is thus more highly integrated than the one below, and ascent through their levels marks the progressive overcoming of sexual polarization.

Since they share the same sphere of sensuous experience, albeit at the most rarefied levels, the gods are not so far removed from the human dimension that they are unable to interact with it. It is said that gods like to visit places of great natural beauty and are attracted to people who are happy and positive. They particularly like to be around those who are spiritually developed and are often said to shed a benevolent influence over them, like guardian angels. It is also claimed that humans can develop the faculty of seeing and communicating with these divine beings. Buddhism is not alone in this belief, for many other traditions tell of sages who can speak to the beings of higher dimensions. Since these gods are the embodiment of a higher level of consciousness, only those who have raised their own human minds to that same degree can contact them.

These gods, and those of the higher realms too, are all impermanent. Life for them is immeasurably long – the higher the realm, the longer the life – but they all must die when the pattern of volitions that made them gods has been exhausted. There are no immortal beings in Buddhist cosmology, extraordinarily long-lived as some gods are said to be. The gods are conditioned like any other inhabitant of the Wheel or Spiral. Not one of the gods is a creator, for the conditioned process has no beginning and was not created. Buddhism considers the idea of a single god who presides over the universe, whether the concept is presented in its crudest, anthropomorphic, form or in highly abstract philosophical theories, to be dangerous from an ethical and spiritual point of view. A god-centred universe is conceived of as containing an ultimate authority and thus may encourage moral irresponsibility since the god's commands are to be obeyed regardless of personal feeling. It also places a limit on human development since there is always an irreducible dichotomy between creature and god. For Buddhists, there is no limit to the evolution of consciousness and all dualities can be transcended. The gods, however refined their level, are always inferior to the Buddha since they still stand within the conditioned process and are caught in the framework of subject and object.

The god realms of the sensuous sphere are the objectification of an ethical consciousness. Those beings who usually function skilfully and who have achieved a natural moral sense act from increasingly wholesome volitions. In traditional terms, they 'make merit', that is, they build up a stock of positive volitional potential that will eventually bear fruit in pleasurable consequences. These they will experience in this life if they have not set up too much countervailing negative momentum in past lives, or in a future rebirth in a heaven world. If one can see that others have feelings like one's own and can feel sympathy for them, one will act ethically and will begin to accrue merit. This merit may be experienced quite quickly as life becomes more pleasant and smooth and opportunities seem to present themselves more and more readily. To an even greater extent, the consequences of merit will be found in the worlds of the gods, which are altogether more beautiful than Earth and lack most of its unpleasant features. The karmic results of skilful action are an increased feeling of well-being and ease and a more pleasurable sensuous experience.

That a more skilful way of life is likely to be accompanied by greater sensuous pleasure is a sign of the identity of ethical and aesthetic awareness, of 'goodness' and beauty. One whose mind is dominated by negative mental states will scarcely be able to appreciate the more refined delights of the senses. In this case pleasure is likely – for the most part – to be found in the release of pent-up tension, not in the enjoyment of proportion or harmony. The contemplation of sensuous beauty in its fullness is a pleasure for those with an easy conscience, for those whose wholesome mental states have some correspondence with the pleasing forms they perceive. The cultivation of the aesthetic sense needs to go hand in hand with the development of morality otherwise it will degenerate into mere connoisseurship – extensive technical knowledge without real appreciation – or into sensualism. The gods of the sensuous sphere are those who, by their goodness, are able to appreciate beauty.

The pleasures of the god realm hold out a danger. It is so enjoyable to live in the unalloyed delight of the senses that the gods and goddesses may lose awareness of who they are. It is as a result of mindfulness and skilful actions, moral efforts in the past, that they enjoy the bliss of the senses. But unless they continue to make an effort and maintain their self-awareness, gods and goddesses will gradually sink back to a lower stage of evolution or, at best, settle down where they are. For most of us this welcome danger lies in the future, but it holds a message for us, none the less. When we are happy and enjoying ourselves we tend to lose self-awareness and slip into unskilful behaviour. It is not that we should avoid happiness or that the gods should avoid the pleasures of their realm, but we need to maintain our consciousness of ourselves as developing individuals under the most pleasurable and the most painful experiences alike. It is all too easy for the god to slip into the forgetful rapture of the moment, giving no thought to climbing higher. It is easy, in the spiritual life, for complacency to set in.

9

The Mundane Path

The human world and the lower heavens correspond to the bottom steps of the Spiral Path, to which we will now turn. We will be examining each step of that Path by means of another chain of twelve links which is the Spiral counterpart of the cyclic chain at the rim of the Wheel. This time, the links do not form a circle but carry us upwards in a progressive order, leading away from the Wheel, and so breaking the endless circularity of its turnings. Each link in the Spiral provides the conditions for the arising of the succeeding link, which is at a higher level, surpassing it in happiness, clarity, and love. All these twelve links, from the lowest to the peak of Enlightenment itself, may be experienced in human life. The states of mind to which they correspond may also, at death, give rise to rebirth in worlds of ever greater beauty and purity. We will be exploring these steps on the spiritual path both in terms of subjective, inner experience and of the objective worlds that are their concrete expression.

The twelve links in the chain of progressive conditionality start with the experience of *imperfection* – a term usually translated as 'suffering', but really meaning much more than that, since it includes a deep existential experience of unsatisfactoriness. In dependence on imperfection, there arises *faith*, on faith, *delight*, on delight, *ecstasy*, and then, each unfolding out of the one before, *peace, bliss, absorption, knowledge and vision of things as they really are, disentanglement, dispassion, liberation*, and *recognition that the poisonous mental floods have been destroyed*. The first seven links, from imperfection to absorption, are the mundane path, since no Insight into reality has, as yet, arisen and whatever gains have been made can be lost. 'Knowledge and vision of things as they really are' is the point of Insight and, therefore, of Stream Entry. From here on, the links constitute the transcendental path. We will be following the mundane path in this chapter and the transcendental in the next.

The Spiral Path arises out of the Wheel for, endless as the cycle of links usually is, there is a point at which a gap opens up and we can escape. We have seen, in Chapter 6, that each link of the cyclic chain can be assigned to one of two phases. There is an active, *causal* phase that is established by our own volitions. The *resultant* phase follows inevitably from the momentum inherent in the causal phase. We have now a body, sense organs, and sense experience because of what we willed in the past; our present volitions are not responsible for our present experience but for our future experience. The whole cyclic chain consists of action and reaction between these two phases. In the twelve cyclic links, there are three points of transition between the two phases: where the causal phase in the past life gives way to the resultant phase in the present; where the resultant phase gives way to the causal, both in the present life; and where that causal phase gives way to the resultant phase in the life to come (see fig.4). The result inevitably follows from the cause; fuelled by the volitions, the Wheel must spin until its potential energy has been fully spent. Once the resultant process has unwound to its limit, however, further reaction is not inevitable. Only renewed unwholesome volition gives the Wheel another spin. The gap between resultant phase and causal phase, both in the present life, is the point on the Wheel where change is possible. That gap is between the link of feeling and the link of craving.

Pleasant and painful experiences come to us as the consequence of our psychophysical make-up. Usually, on the basis of those feelings, we crave what is pleasurable – or seems so – and try to cling to it, and we hate what seems painful and try to repel or destroy it. In this way, the causal phase is set up again. Feeling, then, is the last link in the resultant process, after which we begin a new round of volition that can either send us spinning upon the Wheel again or set our feet upon the Spiral.

There are different levels of feeling, and if we are not deeply aware of our feelings we will continue to react with unhealthy volitions. Our reactions are often based on relatively superficial likes and dislikes, even on immediate physical sensations of pleasure and pain. At a somewhat deeper level, our ability to imagine what is not immediately present to us gives rise to expectations and anticipations, hopes and fears. If we become dissatisfied at this level, it is because we want and expect more gratification from life and we are disappointed. We hope for better and we believe that we could be fully and perfectly satisfied if only we could achieve the right combination of circumstances. This attitude leads us to further craving and hatred as we throw all our energies into creating the ideal circumstances for our own limited individuality.

Imperfection

As we spin upon the Wheel, however, another kind of feeling may grow in us. Although we may be, in the more superficial sense, quite happy and may experience an abundance of pleasure of a sensuous or psychological kind, a deeper frustration begins to emerge. We begin to see that, in its very nature, worldly life is imperfect. It does, of course, offer very real pleasures, but they are always limited. Something always mars or spoils them, and they always come to an end. Whatever in the world we look to for any lasting security and happiness shows itself to be vulnerable. There is nothing we can fully rely upon: the happiest life contains some experience of pain and decay. We are never able to reach our fullest limit in enjoyment of any pleasure; something inside us remains unfulfilled, some constraint holds us back from complete happiness. Even, it is said, the most refined happiness of the highest god realm contains some faint trace of that constraint.

This growing sense of the imperfection of everything the world has to offer is not simply the disappointment that arises from frustrated ambition, nor is it the reaction of feeling cheated by life. If we feel this kind of frustration, we no longer expect to find perfection in worldly things. We have some faint intimation, some groping intuition, that real fulfilment is possible although we do not know where to find it. The things that we now do seem rather empty and meaningless, although we may have no problems in our relations with other people or in our work and we may be physically and psychologically perfectly healthy. We know that there is more to life than we now realize, and we are searching for its deeper meaning.

This feeling of imperfection is the natural expression of a consciousness that wishes to develop. Our self-awareness is the seed of transcendental consciousness and so cannot be long contained within the restricted circumference of the Wheel without our feeling cramped and confined. The nature of consciousness is to expand and, if that nature is not fulfilled, frustration and pain arise. The repression of this, the most fundamental of urges, has far more drastic consequences than the repression of the instincts, for it can leave us sour and embittered for a lifetime if we do not fulfil it. Many people feel this sense of imperfection or frustration: some simply lose it in the maelstrom of their own reactive impulses, others again are swept away by the pressures of the group in which they live that forces them to fulfil its conventional expectations; some begin their quest but are discouraged, sooner or later, by lack of any clear guidance or support and by the confusion of possibilities that confronts them. That call is not easily distinguished from all the other desires and longings that seethe within us, and it is harder still to find our way forward without any help or encouragement. It is not surprising that very many people who do experience at some time that sense of imperfection simply give up and carry on around the Wheel. Prevailing social attitudes and institutions scarcely encourage them to do otherwise. Yet that feeling of frustration with mundane life is not something to be drowned or cured. It should be honoured and cherished, for it is the entry to the path of the spiritual life.

Some who experience the imperfection of a limited life do go in quest of something more real. If they are fortunate, they encounter an embodiment of the ideal that gives them a glimpse, at last, of what they seek. It may be that a statue of the Buddha, if it is of high artistic merit, conveys to them the peace of the Enlightened state together with its deep understanding and strong sympathy for all living beings. Again, a book may succeed in communicating to them the truth for which they long. Or they may meet someone who impresses them with the human qualities that he or she has developed. In these and other ways, out of that noble sense of frustration, there emerges a new and real hope. In dependence on imperfection, arises faith.

Faith

In Buddhism, faith is a multi-faceted term of far broader significance than the English word conventionally conveys. It is not unreasoning belief but the wholehearted response of the total being to the Ideal. It is the surge of the Imagination beyond one's immediate experience to touch, and ultimately to grasp, the highest truth. Once faith has arisen, one knows what one must do. In the first place, faith is a direct, intuitive response. We respond to something that embodies the possibility of complete fulfilment and perfection. Whether it is a work of art, a person, or a book, the ideal it manifests corresponds to something in us. The transcendental consciousness latent within our own self-consciousness vibrates in sympathy with the transcendental reality mirrored in the object that fires our faith. Like is attracted to like and we are irresistibly drawn to what we feel reflects our own deepest nature. At first, faith may be rather vague and confused but it is none the less a very powerful emotion that lifts us up towards the Goal.

When it reaches its maturity, faith includes clarity of mind. The ideals in which one develops faith – in Buddhism these are the Buddha, Dharma, and Sangha – are understood rationally. An ability to accurately and intellectually understand the Dharma, and to investigate it with the intellect, is allied with an emotional response. No blind belief is required at all – indeed, an open-minded enquiry into the rational consistency of the Buddha's claim to Enlightenment may be necessary before faith can come to fruition. Faith must have sharpness and definition; we need a clear apprehension of the Ideal to which our intuition is responding. If there is not this more cognitive aspect to faith one can be very easily led astray. Faith may be confused with other, less healthy emotions so that, for instance, one's neurotic need for security may lead to placing inappropriate faith in gurus who like to have authority over others for their own neurotic reasons.

As faith is strengthened and sharpened by the emotions and the assessment of the intellect, it is further confirmed by experience. When faith is applied by following the Path, we will find that it is justified as we gain the benefits of the Dharma and see, by our own direct insight, some of its truths. Faith becomes yet more intense, being based now not only on emotional response and intellectual conviction but on the rock of confidence born of experience.

Faith is the first step on the spiritual path, the counterpart of craving which is the first step in a renewed round of the Wheel. That step away from the Wheel is not taken all at once. Every second of our lives, pleasant, painful, or neutral feelings present themselves to us and we have the choice of reacting with craving or responding with faith. If we crave, we deny our own higher destiny and identify ourselves completely with our present level of experience. Our longings for mundane pleasures run deep. If we feel faith, we see that pleasurable and painful sensations arise from conditions, and we start to fix our hearts on a happiness that is beyond conditions. We can thus respond to the feelings that arise during the course of our lives in a healthy way – enjoying the pleasurable, trying to remove the painful where possible, but less and less being intoxicated or overwhelmed by them because, for us, they do not contain the full meaning of life.

Gradually, we learn to recognize the conditioned nature of our feelings and to discriminate between our reactions of craving or hatred and our healthy responses of faith and metta. More and more of our energies are placed upon the Spiral until, with full Enlightenment, there is nothing of the Wheel in us at all. It is in the choice between craving and faith that the spiritual life consists. While we have yet to reach the point of Stream Entry, when the Spiral unfolds spontaneously, we need to direct all our efforts to discriminating the healthy from the unhealthy impulses within us. With unremitting mindfulness we can see clearly where our mind goes and so be able to act as skilfully as we can. Our initial efforts will probably only prevent us from committing the more obviously unskilful actions but, in time, our self-awareness will increase and we will be able to watch the ebb and flow of wholesome and unwholesome mental states within our minds before they ever reach the threshold of overt behaviour. In this way, the cyclic tendencies within us will gradually be starved and the Spiral will flourish.

This effort of mindfulness and mental discrimination is one of the active consequences of the arising of faith. Faith is not merely an appreciation of the Ideal but a desire to move towards it. Not only do we see the correspondence between Buddhahood and our own deepest nature but we want to make it a living reality – we want actively to develop our own consciousness. So we begin to practise by applying the teachings of Buddhism to our own lives, thus shifting ourselves from the Wheel to the Spiral. This requires us to consider the morality of our behaviour as we try to make our actions expressive of our new-found vision. We try to order our lives so that we are guided by the Ideals to which we have responded with faith. Faith, then, gives rise to ethics.

The active aspect of faith, the desire to realize the Ideals in one's own life, is called Going for Refuge to the Three Jewels: the act of commitment to the Buddha, Dharma, and Sangha. It is the expression of Going for Refuge and its acceptance by one's teacher and spiritual friends that formally constitutes one a member of the sangha – the spiritual community – understood in its broadest sense.

With faith, we take a leap beyond our old self and open up to a wider sphere of consciousness. When we acknowledge something beyond ourselves, we are no longer so tightly self-centred. We feel uplifted and inspired, and possessed by a new mood of generosity, because we are no longer so bound up with ourselves. Our feeling of inner wealth is such that it overflows to others, accompanied by a strong sense of gratitude to our teachers and spiritual friends. They have kept the Buddha's message alive and enabled us to find this Path that can fulfil all our aspirations and allay the emptiness and frustration of imperfection. The Ideals themselves, and those who embody them, therefore fill us with strong feelings of reverence and respect that we want to express in honour of their many wondrous qualities.

The cultivation and expression of these devotional feelings is of great importance. If they find no expression, like any impulse, they will wither and die. The more richly they are voiced, the more strongly they will rise, strengthening our faith. It is for this reason that, in virtually every Buddhist tradition, there are images of the Buddha before which people bow and make offerings or perform ceremonies with chanting and ritual. Often the shrines and the halls where they are situated, as well as the words and actions of the ceremonies, are very beautiful and deeply stirring, even if we do not know the precise significance of each sound and gesture. In this way, the emotions are drawn behind one's efforts to grow, providing the motive power that will move us forward. A theoretical grasp of the Dharma's formulations is not enough; we need to be emotionally involved. If we do not harness our emotions, they will simply fasten themselves to the objects of craving. Faith and devotion are the emotional aspects of the spiritual life and we need to take active steps to develop and extend them. Without devotional practices of some kind, it is likely that Buddhism will remain merely an intellectual pastime for us.

Faith, then, is the first step on the Path. It is the point where we contact the Ideal and commit ourselves to realizing it. We are carried beyond our own narrow self-interest and start to live more skilfully, to be more open-handed and to feel gratitude towards teachers and friends on the Path and devotion for the Three Jewels and their embodiments. This corresponds to the second level of the human world where the individual separates from the group and joins the spiritual community. The true human being is characterized by faith in transcendental ideals.

Although faith is the first step on the Path, it is not abandoned in the transition to the next. It develops and is strengthened more and more throughout the Spiral, underlying each succeeding link.

Faith followed through in active commitment begins to transform the individual. Our whole way of life is changed, our perspective on the world is different, our states of mind are on a new and higher plane, and we begin to experience a quite new sense of exultation and pleasure. In dependence on faith, arises delight.

Delight

When we live in a skilful way, in fulfilment of our faith, a sense of well-being and harmony arises – this is delight. Delight contains the inner satisfaction of knowing that there is nothing with which one need reproach oneself. When we have a clear conscience, we can feel fully at peace with ourselves. Because our aspiration is being put into practice, there is none of that sense of self-disgust and disappointment that comes from failing to live up to one's ideals.

Not only do we feel happy with ourselves, we are at ease with others – for there is also nothing for them to reproach us with. Our social difficulties often arise because of our defensiveness against the blame of others but, in the stage of delight, there is no corner of inconsistency that others can use to manipulate us. We feel psychologically secure and confident.

If we do not experience this sort of innocence, our minds tend to be clouded and distracted with guilt and self-reproach. We are then likely to be vulnerable to those who wish to exploit our weakness and we will feel uneasy when meeting people. Such guilt may be rational or irrational. Irrational guilt is the neurotic feeling that one has done something wrong – when actually one has only done something one feels guilty about although there is nothing truly immoral about it. As a result of their upbringing those who feel irrational guilt have learned to think of themselves as fundamentally sinful, so they have a permanent, underlying sense of guilt and fear of punishment. This, however, is a thoroughly unskilful state in itself and needs to be replaced by self-love and confidence as soon as possible. Rational guilt, on the other hand, is quite healthy and is our remorse at our genuinely unskilful behaviour. We have done wrong and we feel sorry for it. However, it is not skilful to remain too long in this state of remorse. We need, of course, to face up to our shortcomings and unskilfulness, but we should aim to resolve the feelings of guilt that arise as quickly as possible.

In Buddhism very great importance is attached to purging ourselves of guilt. First of all, it is important to acknowledge what we have done. This is best done by openly confessing it to teachers or spiritual friends who can appreciate that our action was really unskilful but who will remain positive in their basic attitude towards us. By making it open in this way, and by expressing our regret for what was done, we can feel our conscience to be clear once more. Sometimes, however, either because of the magnitude of the fault or because our conscience is very tender, confession may not cleanse our hearts and we may still feel guilty. Then devotional practices of various kinds are recommended that stimulate feelings of faith and will eventually induce a more positive state of mind. Of course, a crucial part of confession and of the devotional ceremony is a firm commitment to avoid such behaviour in future.

Delight is the perfect absence of any moral conflict or guilt. Not only is there a subjective feeling of happiness and ease but objectively one experiences the karmic fruits of skilful actions. Merits will bring their benefits. On death, one in whom this stage predominates will be reborn in the heaven worlds of the sensuous sphere and will enjoy the subtle sensuous delights they afford.

The pursuit of the Spiral Path brings joys from the start, but they swell ever greater the higher one climbs. An integrated ethical life forms the basis for a deeper psychical integration in which all the conflicting energies are harmonized and unified in an experience of overwhelming happiness and pleasure. In dependence on delight, arises ecstasy.

Ecstasy

With this link we step, for the first time, beyond the sphere of sensuous desire into the realm of archetypal form. The succeeding three links take us through all the archetypal levels together with those of the formless realm. Both of these are the spheres of meditation; the states of mind that constitute them are quite different from those of ordinary consciousness. Language is strained to its limits in trying to convey something of these sublime heights. None the less, these states are quite within the reach of any practitioners who apply themselves systematically to the practice of meditation.

Meditation has two primary, related effects when one first engages upon it: it integrates all the energies of the psyche and it leads to more and more positive emotion. The stage of ecstasy comes about as all psychological conflict and tension is resolved and the subconscious impulses are released and absorbed into full consciousness. This gives rise to intensely pleasurable physical sensations and an even more light and zestful joy than was known in the stage of delight. Much of the time we are mentally divided and our energies are scattered over a number of different interests and preoccupations which are not formed into one harmonious pattern. To further complicate the matter, we are often not fully aware of, or are confused about, our own motivations. It is as if we are not one single person but an assembly of different personalities – some of which may be in direct conflict with one another. We can seldom call upon our full emotional and mental resources for any task. For most, if not all, of the time we operate with a fraction of our total potential and we do not experience the richness of a life lived wholeheartedly. It is a striking fact that many of the great artists and inspired figures of the past seem to have enjoyed superabundant energy and to have been capable of an eagerness and enthusiasm that most of us lost in childhood.

In order to bring about the horizontal integration of all these sub-personalities within us, we must apply mindfulness and self-reflection, getting to know ourselves more deeply and fully. Meditation, positive work that is 'Right Livelihood', spiritual friendship, all help in this key task of drawing together the fragments of the personality into one balanced individuality. But, above all, it is having a vision and being devoted to its realization that pulls our energies together. Just as all the struggling factions in a nation are united by the common desire to prevail against an aggressor, so we need something beyond our own selves to which we can dedicate ourselves. To bring every aspect of being into harmony, such a goal cannot afford to be one-sided or contain any trace of unwholesomeness. That Ideal is Enlightenment. At the stage of ecstasy, our faith in the Three Jewels and our active pursuit of a skilful way of life bear fruit in the resolution of all conflicts and tensions and the release of subconscious energies into the strengthening current of faith. It is only a high purpose that can mobilize the full force of the human heart.

Conflicts and tensions are not merely mental events, they find expression in the very posture of our bodies. The anxious woman hunches her shoulders against the blows of fate, the angry man clenches his teeth and holds himself ready for attack. Our predominant emotions permanently shape our muscles into what the psychologist Wilhelm Reich called 'character armour'. As psychological tension is resolved in the integrated state, this rigidity begins to break down and nervous energy locked in the musculature can flow more freely. The melting of these blockages and the resulting release of physical vitality is experienced in sensations of actual bodily pleasure. The extent to which the rapture is felt depends upon the amount of previous inhibition and tension – it may be very strong indeed. Buddhist psychological analysis enumerates five levels of ecstasy. First, there is the 'lesser thrill' which is strong enough only to raise the hairs of the body. Then comes the 'momentary rapture' which shoots intense but brief currents through the frame, like flashes of lightning. The 'flooding rapture' washes through the body, ebbing and flowing like the waves of the sea beating upon the shore. 'Transporting rapture' is said to be so powerful that the body may actually levitate! The 'all-pervading rapture' brings the process to its culmination and is likened to a ball full of air, for the sensations of ecstasy have become so pervasive and enduring that they fill the entire system.

These progressive levels of ecstasy are but more intense forms of the kinds of physical manifestations that powerful emotion often excites. When we are very deeply stirred by something – art or nature, acts of heroism, or our communication with another person – tears may start in our eyes or we may find ourselves shaking uncontrollably. These are not signs of weakness or lack of self-control, but evidence that something has moved us so profoundly that the emotions cannot be contained within the boundaries of normal expression and seek some more immediate discharge. Such rushes of emotion are not uncommon in meditation and people may find themselves weeping, shaking, or laughing quite involuntarily. These may all be manifestations of ecstasy and they are characterized not only by sensations of physical release and pleasure but by very strong feelings of happiness. All one's psychological energies flow more and more powerfully behind one's faith and one feels complete and whole, deeply satisfied to be engaged in the best and noblest task that a human being can undertake.

The deeper the ecstasy becomes, the more the purely mental experience predominates and so, in dependence upon ecstasy, there arises peace.

Peace

Sooner or later the process of horizontal integration is completed and all the energy locked in tension and subconscious conflict is released. The experience of physical ecstasy therefore subsides and the exhilarating joy becomes steadier. The fact that there is no longer the thrilling pleasure of rapture does not mean that the ensuing state is less happy, rather is it even more so, but the happiness is of a more refined nature, passing beyond the body, which can no longer contain it. At this stage, awareness of the body recedes altogether and the world of sensuous experience is left entirely behind. One dwells in a state of complete ease and tranquillity. The mind is light and clear, very receptive and pliant without rigidity or prejudice. No tremor of negative emotion disturbs the profound and invigorating calm in which one is immersed.

In this state of deep peace, the emotions flow more and more powerfully in one swelling flood yet, at the same time, they grow ever more subtle and delicate. So, in dependence on peace, arises bliss.

Bliss

Having used up all the available superlatives for happiness and positivity, it is hard to describe a state that is happier and more positive still – and we are only halfway up the Spiral chain. But this is what bliss is: the happiness of peace raised to a yet higher degree. The process of vertical integration is now drawing up energies from a far deeper level, energies of inspiration and creativity that enhance the powerful current of emotion which, since it first bubbled up from the spring of faith, has gathered into a force that sweeps all before it in one gigantic tide of happiness. All the other positive emotions are present too: an all-embracing metta, radiating to all creatures; a sympathetic compassion for all who suffer; a rejoicing in the happiness and virtue of others; gratitude and devotion to those more developed. No element of personal prejudice or predilection mars the perfect equanimity of this love.

Vertical integration continues until all the forces of mundane consciousness are flowing together so that, in dependence on bliss, arises absorption.

Absorption

Nothing is excluded from consciousness. The total energies of the whole being are united in full awareness and brought to bear upon a single point. Everything is focused, in perfect equipoise, at the highest level of refinement. The mind is exalted and enjoys sublime happiness. It is fresh and zestful, sharp and clear, concentrated in pure awareness. Subject and object are now so fine and vibrate so closely together that it is hard to distinguish one from the other. The mind has been brought to its very peak of mundane excellence. It is from this point that the great leap takes place into the transcendental for, in dependence on absorption, there arises knowledge and vision of things as they really are.

The link of absorption represents the culmination of that stage of the Path that is primarily concerned with meditation. As we noted in Chapter 2, the Path has three principal phases: morality, meditation, and wisdom. Faith and delight are connected primarily with the stage of morality; ecstasy, peace, bliss, and absorption with meditation; and the remainder of the chain with the cultivation of transcendental wisdom. Since the practice of meditation is one of the central methods of the spiritual path, we will now examine it in a little more detail.

The purpose of meditation is to help us develop systematically the higher states of consciousness. Their aim is to bring about that highest link of the mundane path: absorption. There are other meditation techniques that are directed to the cultivation of Insight, but we will not be concerned with these since they imply that absorption has already been achieved. The logic of our chain of spiral evolution seems to tell us that we should only start practising meditation when we have perfected the phase of morality comprising the first three links of imperfection, faith, and delight.

In fact, human development is never so neat and orderly as such a formula suggests. We are not so much at one particular stage on the Path as spread out over a whole area of it. Our predominant experience, for instance, may be one of imperfection but we have periods of faith, even of delight, and there may be brief moments when we feel the first thrillings of ecstasy. We cannot really go very much further than the link that is, as it were, our base and we must beware of trying to run before we can walk, but the attempt to bring into being a stage a little higher than the one we are now on will help us to consolidate the lower levels. We must, however, put our main efforts into perfecting the lower levels, otherwise our practice of the higher ones will be useless. So even though some practice of meditation may be beneficial before morality has been made firm, unless we try to make our lives more ethically sound, meditation will not get us very far. Many people who are at the stage of 'looking for something' may try meditation. It will certainly help many in their quest although, sooner or later, they must develop faith and commit themselves otherwise they will find they can go no further.

The two basic techniques of meditation common to many schools of Buddhism are concerned with the cultivation of positive emotion on the one hand and concentration on the other. Positive emotion will, of course, be reached through concentration, and concentration through positive emotion – we have seen that the higher mental states are characterized both by happiness and integration. There is some danger, however, that we will develop in a one-sided way unless we attend to both: concentration may become rather dry and even alienated from feeling, and feeling may be too vague and imprecise with a tendency to distraction. Although each implies a slightly different line of development, the general principles for both techniques are the same.

When one first sits down to meditate, although all the external conditions may be ideal it soon becomes apparent that there are inner forces that are going to make it very difficult to carry out the simple process of counting the breath. These mental tendencies are known as 'hindrances' because they prevent one from becoming concentrated on the object of meditation. The hindrances are five in number and the first is *sensuous desire*. Much of one's mental activity is devoted to fantasy about various things. When one first tries to meditate, it can be quite a shock to become aware of the persistent tendency of one's mind to dwell on certain longings and preoccupations. These fantasies may be quite pleasant but they stop one from letting go of sensuous experience altogether and entering the higher dimension of archetypal form. *Hatred*, the second hindrance, similarly absorbs one in thinking of the evils of one's supposed enemies and in dwelling upon the revenge one is going to mete out to them. *Sloth and torpor* are the states of dullness and lethargy that afflict many when they try to meditate. They fall into a drowsy reverie and may even go to sleep. This state is usually induced by mental conflict going on beneath the surface of consciousness, starving the mind of energy. *Restlessness and anxiety* cause our minds to flit from topic to topic so that we never settle down to meditate at all. The last hindrance, *doubt*, is the chronic inability to commit ourselves to anything – even to the meditation for the one session. We are unwilling to push everything aside and put ourselves wholeheartedly into following the technique.

These five – craving, hatred, sloth and torpor, restlessness and anxiety, and doubt – must all be temporarily laid aside so that we can concentrate on the breath. While we are meditating, we keep on returning to the breath no matter what happens. As soon as we notice that we have wandered under the influence of one or another of the hindrances, we bring ourselves back to watching the breath. The more skilful our lives are and the happier we are, the easier it will be for us to rid ourselves of the hindrances.

If we can avoid too much distraction by the hindrances, we will be able to carry out the meditation practice. If we are doing the 'Mindfulness of Breathing' exercise mentioned in Chapter 2, we first focus upon the breath very much as we would upon any object, watching it and trying to feel it as fully as we can. After a while, the whole experience becomes more subtle. The breath is no longer a gross physical sensation to us; it seems very light and delicate, even and steady. It becomes fascinating and pleasurable to sense the flow of air into and out of the body and to feel the mind becoming still and calm. At this point we pass from *trying* to meditate to meditation itself. We move from the sensuous sphere to the sphere of archetypal form. We become completely engrossed in the breath and pass through a sequence of four stages of absorption that take us to the pinnacle of the mundane chain of conditionality.

Stages of Absorption

The first absorption is the stage of *horizontal integration* when all the energies of the conscious and subconscious are unified. There is, here, some subtle discursive mental activity, usually connected with the object of concentration, but it is relatively peripheral to the mind and attention is almost wholly on the breath. Feelings of ecstasy, as described in the section on ecstasy (p.166), course through the body and strong feelings of joy and bliss possess one. In the next absorption, the *stage of inspiration*, the process of vertical integration begins and one feels as if one were being nourished with creative energy from some higher source. Ecstasy and bliss are stronger still, and the one-pointedness of mind has become so fine that all discursive thinking has ceased. The mind is luminously clear but no thoughts disturb its tranquillity. The third absorption is the *stage of permeation*, in which the mind is completely immersed in that higher dimension of awareness which, in the previous stage, appeared only as an outside source of inspiration. All trace of the sensuous world has receded from consciousness and one moves in the sphere of pure form. Ecstasy has ceased because the reservoir of unresolved energies has been exhausted, but the bliss and happiness are greater still and the mind is more sharply focused than ever. The breath has now faded from attention – not because the mind has wandered but because it has, as it were, 'passed beyond' the breath. The fourth absorption is the *stage of radiation*. One experiences a state of equipoise and balance that is also dynamic. The powerful positivity of one's mind, passing beyond the bliss of the previous stages, now seems to radiate in great waves of love and well-wishing, a kind of aura of beneficial influence. Although there are other, higher states of absorption that belong to the sphere of formlessness, they are but further refinements of this fully concentrated stage of radiation, for there are no more energies to unify – integration is complete. The experience of these absorptions is a vitally important one, since it is only an integrated and refined mind that is capable of seeing reality. If we do not have this basis, whatever insight we may gain will only pertain to the intellectual aspects of our personality. For an insight to transform us, it must be backed by the full weight of our purified and unified mind in which reason and emotion are drawn together and resolved in the faculty of Imagination.

The worlds that correspond to these sublime states of consciousness are themselves sublime. They all belong to those spheres of archetypal form and formlessness that lie beyond the sensuous sphere. Each of the worlds of archetypal form, surpassing the one below it in beauty and delight, does have form but it is of a subtle kind, communicating itself not by means of sense organs but directly to the mind. Here we may contemplate beauty not clothed in any earthly clay, but in its pure, ideal form. Not that such forms are abstract, but they pass beyond sensuous definition. Perhaps the nearest we can get to imagining such an experience is to conceive of a world constructed of beams of light, rainbows, subtle perfumes, and chords of music. The formless sphere is even more subtle, for not even the pure form of the archetypal world can be perceived. Here we are in contact with the most refined essences of experience: infinite space, infinite consciousness, 'no-thing-ness' – in which we go beyond the differentiation of experience into particular objects – and 'neither perception nor non-perception', in which subject and object are so closely merged that we cannot find words to describe the experience. It is to these spheres that we gain access through meditation once we have passed through the less subtle visionary experiences corresponding to those of the gods of the sensuous sphere. The gods on these higher planes are born here as a result of their development of meditative states in previous lives. They are as beautiful and pure as the worlds they inhabit. They are androgynous, perfectly integrating masculine and feminine qualities. No sexual activity is found here because the gods have transcended sexual polarity and joyfully experience within themselves the play of opposites that humans seek in sex.

Immeasurably exalted though the highest stage of absorption – and the beings who inhabit it, human or divine – may be, it is still mundane. It is still possible for evolution to be reversed if the conditions that have brought it about are exhausted and no new merit is accrued. The mundane part of the Spiral is maintained only by constant effort and mindfulness, for the Wheel is still more powerful within one than the Spiral unless it is supported by conscious striving. So strong are the powers of ignorance within us that most people would be incapable of making headway against them on their own. They need the full co-operation and encouragement of the environment and people who surround them. Ugliness, brutality, and confusion make it hard to develop positive emotions. Hatred and enmity, or indifference and scorn, from the people we live and work with soon wear down all but the strongest. We need a world that is beautiful and peaceful and companions who share our faith and who have more experience on the Path than we have. Without these, we are liable to fall back again and again. No one should underestimate the effort required for the spiritual life – although neither should one underestimate its rewards. If we truly wish to ascend the Spiral, we need spiritual friendship. Without it, even those gods of the highest world of formlessness may slip back into lower states of being. Only with the transcendental can one no longer fall back and progress be assured.

10

The Transcendental Path

After John Milton's death, an acquaintance reported that he had met nobody who could, with any certainty, ascribe motives to Milton's actions. We judge others by what we know and particularly by what moves us. We cannot, therefore, easily assess those greater than us because their psychology is differently based and does not fit into any mechanical pattern. Their deeds spring from deeper sources, fed by the Muses and the forces of creative imagination. Their personality does not have that rigid structure that makes its motions predictable or easy to analyse. Those who have transcendental attainment are even harder to fathom. They are said to resemble three beings – a ghost, a madman, and a child: a ghost, because they appear out of nowhere so that one cannot tell by what agency they arrived; a madman, because their actions will not conform to the logic of convention and seem to make no sense; and a child, because they have all the wholeheartedness, energy, and spontaneity of youth. The Buddha himself compared those great beings who have passed the point of no return to strange monsters swimming in the ocean's deep. They live in a quite different medium from us, the medium of Truth, and we cannot properly discern them. All we see is a dark fin breaking the waves, from time to time, or a silver flash beneath the swell. These few glimpses and the wonderful stories that voyagers tell are all we have to picture them by. It is of these great beings, moving in the waters of the Dharma, that we must now attempt to form some impression.

Up to this point, the stages of the Spiral Path we have considered have consisted in the progressive refinement of the distinction between subject and object. Experience is still divided into self and world, but the self is now very light and open and the world is very subtle and beautiful. Self and world, though distinct, are in harmony and vibrate closely together. Morality has removed the grosser negative emotions, and meditation has unified consciousness, purified it of the remaining taints, and given it strength and sharpness. The mind can now see the real nature of things and so, in dependence on absorption, there arises 'knowledge and vision of things as they really are'.

Knowledge and Vision of Things as They Really Are

For the first time, the veil of delusion is lifted and reality is faced directly. This is not merely intellectual understanding but *vision*, backed by the full force of the intensified emotions and one-pointed mind. Until this link, we have not seen things as they are at all but distorted and perverted by the greed, hatred, and delusion within us. This leads us, as we have seen, to see the world as made up of stable entities, forming desirable objects that we think can give us some deep and lasting satisfaction. Moreover, we think of ourselves as isolated units, egos that are fixed and unchanging. Having made the great evolutionary advance of dividing self from other, we attach ultimate significance to the division we have made. Even at the state of absorption, this is our basic attitude, albeit highly sublimated. But now things are seen as they really are: impermanent, insubstantial, imperfect, and ugly.

I hope I have already sufficiently stressed that everything conditioned is part of a process whose essential nature is change. Nothing, however vast and long-lasting, is exempt from this universal law. Probably no one would deny its truth, at least as regards the things of this human world, although most of us act as if it were not so. We behave as if we ourselves were going to live for ever and we expend much time and energy in the service of things that are even more perishable. Some people maintain that there are higher beings and states that are eternal. This Buddhism denies, asserting that, throughout all the levels of existence, even among the highest gods, nothing is permanent and there is no supreme being who stands exempt from the law of change.

Going one step further, one who gains this level of Insight into things as they really are sees that what we usually perceive as things or people are, in reality, compounds – innumerable particles bound together in complex patterns. We label these formations as objects or people for the sake of practical convenience, but then we go on to attach an absolute metaphysical reality to our own labels. A tree has no reality apart from the sum of the attributes that present themselves to our senses. It is like a pointillist painting, a cloud of dancing atoms, molecules, and perhaps more subtle forces in constant motion. Even these particles are, of course, not realities but are themselves compounded of smaller units that can be subdivided further. When we analyse any object, we can never come to a substance beyond which our analysis cannot penetrate. We can never find anything conditioned that has an underlying substantial reality. We are, ourselves, constituted of parts, as we have seen in examining the five heaps that make up the psychophysical organism. All things, whether subject or object, are processes linked together in an intricate network of mutual conditions.

That all conditioned things are imperfect follows from the preceding considerations. Conditioned things are fleeting and insubstantial and cannot be sources of ultimate satisfaction or reliance. There is, of course, pleasure to be gained and happiness to be enjoyed but, within the sensuous world, that pleasure is inevitably mixed with pain and suffering. Even in the higher worlds, there is a subtle pain or frustration since consciousness is limited and confined by the constrictions of that conditioned world. Only to be beyond all worlds whatsoever gives lasting satisfaction in the experience of true perfection. One who has Insight has no illusions that conditioned experience can provide that perfection.

Finally, conditioned existence is seen as ugly. There is nothing within it that is worthy of our full approbation. Such experiences of beauty as we do have are more or less pale reflections of an ideal beauty that cannot be found within the mundane. The pursuit and appreciation of beautiful things is, in fact, a search for a beauty that lies beyond the objects – in the transcendental itself.

With knowledge and vision of things as they really are, one sees that conditioned things are quite different from what one normally conceives them to be. The ordinary man is distracted by the bright surface of the world and mistakes this for reality. Of course, the objects and people of this world are real in the sense that we can perceive and interact with them, but we do not see them as they really are. Insight now reveals our previous error. But it also reveals that, as it were behind the conditioned or within its depths, there lies unconditioned reality. That reality is the ultimate nature of both the world and the self. The unconditioned is glimpsed as being permanent for, since it is empty of conditions, it is beyond change. It is seen as ultimately real although it has no fixed characteristics by which it can be defined – even the categories of existence and non-existence cannot apply to it. It is perfect and complete and is the source of the only abiding happiness and fulfilment there can be. And it is Beauty itself, the satisfaction of all desires and the fount of all pleasure. Since it is transcendental, it cannot be caught by words that inevitably limit it in defining it. It can only be perceived by the direct penetrative Insight that this stage represents.

The mundane path finds its consummation here. The stirrings of intuition that were faith have been confirmed by direct vision. At this point, one no longer moves forward with great personal effort based on strong intuition and backed up by reason, but knows for oneself the real nature of things. Although the person who has reached this point may still function, and function very effectively, within the world, he or she is not entirely of it any more. This person is now a transcendental being, not a worldly one. This is the point of no return at which one enters the stream that flows on to full Enlightenment and cannot be turned back.

Though this radical change in the orientation of one's being has taken place, there still remain within the forces of greed, hatred, and delusion. Although the Wheel has been overcome, it has not been extirpated and it still exercises a strong, though never decisive, influence. The remainder of the transcendental path consists in the gradual eradication of its every trace. The vision has been glimpsed but now the whole being must be transformed so that it becomes its perfect expression. The Stream Entrant begins to move away from the worldly within him or her, and so, in dependence on knowledge and vision of things as they really are, there arises disentanglement.

Disentanglement

Conditioned things having been seen for what they are, there are no longer any illusions about them. Quite naturally, old attachments based upon those false conceptions just fall away. No real effort is required to do this; they simply do not hold the same interest as they used to. Just as a child leaves behind, without really noticing that they have gone, the toys that he or she once cried and fought for, so at this stage one withdraws from the worldly things that previously engaged all one's energies. This is not a mood of grim and moralistic asceticism but a natural movement that arises out of the experience of the supreme happiness and beauty of the transcendental. It is a joyous and serene detachment, not a sense of being aloof and isolated from others. No longer clinging to people out of craving, one is all the more capable of feeling love and compassion for them. As the Path progresses, metta and compassion become the dominant emotions that underlie one's actions. One becomes, more and more, quite simply a manifestation of compassion.

Disentanglement marks the changing basis of one's involvement with conditioned things. It gives way to an even deeper and steadier detachment as, in dependence on disentanglement, arises dispassion.

Dispassion

So powerful, now, is the effect of Insight that one is not stirred by worldly things at all. One feels, not indifference, but an equal love for all things. Based in the transcendental, nothing can disturb the perfect calm and firm tranquillity of one's being.

This great stream, flooding towards Enlightenment, continues at more and more subtle levels and so, in dependence on dispassion, there arises liberation.

Liberation

So far, the force of Insight has reached the limits of the conditioned. Beings at this stage have been liberated from the psychological forces that bind and constrict the mind and give rise to craving and hatred. But now the most subtle of barriers is attacked, that is the bonds of the most finely-woven wrong views. Liberation here is liberation from the dualism of conditioned and Unconditioned. From our worldly point of view, there is, most certainly, a conditioned and an Unconditioned. When we come to experience the true nature of each, however, we find that that distinction was made merely from our own point of view, although very much to our spiritual advantage. When we see the conditioned in its depths, we realize that it has no fixed or definable nature. It is as if one is gazing at smoke billowing from a chimney: one can never capture its essential shape because it does not have one. It is nothing but a constant flow of ever-changing forms. Our mind can never grasp or fix it and must simply stand back and enjoy the rich variety of its configurations. The smoke is empty of all definable characteristics. In reality, all conditioned things are like this. We may arbitrarily define them as trees, or neighbours, or whatever, but their real and essential nature we cannot grasp. They are empty of such characteristics and it is that Emptiness that is their inmost nature.

Emptiness, in this most profound sense, is not a black hole of nothingness, but the ultimate unboundedness of things, the fact that nothing can ever finally be tied down. Emptiness is, therefore, infinite potentiality, limitless creativity. If we look deeply into the heart of any object or, more especially, any person, we will see this Emptiness that is absolute creativity. Everything, seen as it really is, is the perfect expression of transcendent potentiality. This is the true nature of the conditioned. The Unconditioned, too, is devoid of characteristics, indefinable, and cannot be grasped by the mind. It too is characterized only by Emptiness. The conditioned and the Unconditioned are both empty. If one looks at the conditioned one sees, in its heart, the Unconditioned, and if one looks into the Unconditioned there is the conditioned. With liberation, one is freed from that subtle delusion that leads us to separate the one from the other although, it must once more be stressed, it is a delusion from that exalted perspective alone – not from ours, for we have far grosser delusions to deal with first. One is liberated then from both the conditioned and the Unconditioned. One's mind is almost identical with the potent Emptiness – that Full Emptiness as it has been called – and there is but a hair's breadth that separates one from it.

The final barrier that then stands before complete liberation is the very concept of freedom itself, even of Emptiness. One must be freed of freedom, see that Emptiness is empty. All thoughts and views, even the categories of Buddhism itself that have carried one to this point, must be abandoned in the full and direct experience of reality, unmediated by any concept or image. The last trace of any distinction between self and world must be relinquished. In this way, in dependence on liberation, there arises recognition that the poisonous mental floods have been destroyed.

Recognition that the Poisonous Mental Floods have been Destroyed

This last link in the evolutionary chain is the point of Enlightenment. Buddhahood is devoid of all negative tendencies whatsoever; the poisonous mental floods that spring from the defence of our ego and intoxicate us, filling our lives with their noxious vapours, are completely dried up.

There are three of these mental floods, the first of which is the poison of *craving for sense experience*. This is that familiar longing to fix and confirm the ego by sensuous pleasures, as without their tangible experience we feel weak and insubstantial. The Enlightened person dwells in the utter security of the transcendental and has, therefore, no need of such hollow sanctuary as the senses afford. He or she is able to use the senses, even to enjoy them, but has no neurotic need for their pleasures. Then there is the poison of *craving for existence* on any plane, in any world. The ego craves some definite state, some world in which it can define itself against everything else. Beyond self and other, Enlightened beings have no need of such embodiment, although they choose to function through a body and in a world in order to help others to gain freedom. They have also extinguished the most basic poison of all, that of *ignorance*, the refusal to see things clearly out of fear that our ego will be overwhelmed. With a mind absorbed in Truth and a heart in bliss, the Buddha has nothing to fear from non-dual awareness. Not the faintest trace of any tendency towards the Wheel is left in such a one, even in its most rarefied form.

This stage is not only one of destruction of all negative tendencies; it is one of recognition that that is what has happened. The Enlightened individual knows that the poisonous mental floods are dried up, quite clearly, without any self-aggrandizement or inflation – knows that he or she is Enlightened. But we have passed beyond the power of language to describe this experience.

The whole of the transcendental path, indeed the complete evolutionary spiral, can be traversed in a single human lifetime. Those beings who die at any of the stages on the Path short of full Enlightenment, however, will be reborn according to their level of consciousness and to the extent of the influence that the Wheel still has on them. We will now examine the four kinds of transcendental being and the rebirths that await them.

Transcendental Beings

Stream Entrants are those in whom vision has first dawned. They have, of course, already traversed the mundane path and so combine the qualities of steadfast morality and firm faith in the Three Jewels with that burning vigour, delicacy of feeling, and sharpness of mind that the absorptions perfect. They are full of love and good will and have unfailing positivity. The Stream Entrant is said to have broken the first three of ten fetters that tie us to the conditioned: the fetters of personality-view, doubt, and attachment to external observances and ethical rules as ends in themselves. These are the grosser veils of ignorance that blind us to the full radiance of reality. *Personality-view* is the opinion that either there is an unchanging soul or spirit that survives death, or the personality is identical with the body and, therefore, ceases at death. These two, eternalism and nihilism, make it impossible to see the real nature of things as an ever-changing process. This can be called the fetter of habit, for it is the tendency to see things in a fixed, habitual way without recognizing that every-thing is constantly coming into being and passing away. We even see ourselves like this, as if we always are and always will be the same.

Doubt as a fetter does not mean the careful refusal to accept something until sound evidence has been presented, but a chronic unwillingness to make up one's mind about things. One prefers to remain in perplexity and continues to throw up objections long after conviction would have been reasonable. Such doubt is emotional in basis. It is our reluctance to clarify our mind on any issue because we will then have to act upon whatever conclusion we have reached. So we waver and dither and never really move. This has been termed the fetter of vagueness, for the doubter refuses to clarify his or her mind and likes to keep things woolly and undefined. The Stream Entrant, by contrast, is able to be wholeheartedly behind his or her Insight.

Attachment to external observances and ethical rules as ends in themselves is that tendency to superficial practice that constantly threatens those who follow the Path. Instead of observing the precepts in order to develop the underlying ethical sensitivity that they express, we keep them as if they were a list of rules. Instead of meditating in order to develop higher states of consciousness, we merely sit for a few minutes out of habit or to keep up appearances. What start out as important and useful practices and guidelines become quite external activities whose true meaning is lost. This is the fetter of superficiality: we just go through the outer motions without looking for the inner meaning. Precepts, spiritual exercises, ritual, and ceremony *all* have an important place in Buddhism and are very effective means of spiritual development but, unless they are performed with an awareness of what is being done and why, they may actively hinder us. Stream Entrants have broken through these fetters and, it is said, will gain Enlightenment within seven human rebirths. They may also be reborn into higher realms, from time to time, but they can never again be born in any of the four worlds of suffering.

The *Once-returner* is the next of the transcendental beings. Such a one has, and surpasses, all the qualities of the Stream Entrant and, in addition, has weakened the next two fetters: *sensuous craving* and *aversion*. Even at this exalted level these basic negative emotions are still present and, though their power is considerably weakened, they still exert their baneful influence. The Stream Entrant has broken the fetters of confused understanding but the emotions are far harder to transform. The Once-returner has sufficient of the cock, the snake, and the pig within to bring him or her back to the human world one more time, from which full Enlightenment will be gained.

The *Non-returner* finally breaks the fetters of sensuous craving and aversion that the Once-returner merely weakened. With all the bonds that bind to the sphere of sensuous experience broken, there is no longer rebirth in any of its worlds. There are, however, still subtle illusions and tenuous cravings that bind the Non-returner to the worlds of archetypal form and formlessness. Within these higher heavens, he or she will traverse the remaining steps of the Path and reach Enlightenment.

The *Enlightened* are the last in this series of four transcendental beings. They have broken the remaining five fetters that tie one to the conditioned, even at its most rarefied. Those who have reached this stage have destroyed the two fetters of *craving for experience in the worlds of archetypal form* and *of formlessness*. The desire to achieve and settle down in one of these states is said to correspond to the longing of the theist to dwell in heaven with God. But the Enlightened break through even this most attenuated manifestation of duality. They break also the fetter of *conceit* which, in this context, is the last trace of attachment to ego-identity, which the Non-returner still has. The fetter of *restlessness* is the almost imperceptible disturbance produced by a last, faint dividing line between subject and object. This, too, is finally dissolved in the all-pervading bliss of transcendental non-duality. The last fetter is the chain of *ignorance*. In the mind of the Non-returner there is still a very thin veil covering the full radiance of reality, the most refined delusion of subject and object. This, too, is torn aside and the Truth shines forth, absolutely clear and unobstructed.

One who has attained this state is no longer reborn, but this does not mean that they do not exist. It is said that when an Enlightened person dies, they neither exist nor do they not exist – nor both, nor neither! They pass beyond our comprehension. There is nothing within our experience by which we can grasp the nature of their being. Our language is built out of our common experience in the sensuous world. It can never adequately describe the Enlightened ones, for whatever we say about them, if taken literally, can be misunderstood since Enlightenment utterly transcends the mundane whose language we must use. We can, for instance, describe the state negatively as an absence of all unwholesome emotions, the destruction of those poisonous mental floods and of the Wheel with all its forces. Sometimes, Buddhism resorts to a steady denial of all the categories of thought, saying that Enlightenment is not this, not that, so that we are forced to stop trying to understand with our intellect alone and use some deeper, more intuitive faculty. But this does not tell us what the state actually is and may lead us to suppose that it is simply a complete vacuum. We can try using superlatives, describing it as the state wherein all the most positive qualities that we revere are raised to their highest degree. This has the virtue of giving us the image of Buddhahood as something eminently desirable but introduces the danger that we may think of it as being merely the best of the mundane rather than being on another level altogether. Sometimes paradox is used, forcing us to join two contradictory ideas together so that we must intuit something that transcends them both. Perhaps the most effective means of conveying some flavour of the Enlightened state is by appeal to the Imagination through the use of symbols and poetic images. It is this kind of communication of the ultimate goal of human existence that we will be encountering in the next chapter.

11

The Mandala of the Five Buddhas

The potential for Enlightenment lies deep within us. It exists not as a mere abstract possibility, but as an experience within us, an experience of an upward momentum or pressure. It could even be said that, from an absolute point of view, we are transcendental beings who do not recognize our own true nature. Our ultimate essence is constantly trying to manifest through us, pushing aside the egoistic personality that fights desperately for its own narrow survival. This is, fundamentally, what it is to be human – to have within the twin currents of the Wheel and the Spiral; to be cut off, not only from elements of our psychological make-up but also from our deeper spiritual and transcendental nature. We need, in other words, both horizontal and vertical integration. Whatever we lack in our inner experience, we project onto our environment and its inhabitants. And so we invest sense objects and other people with the qualities of the transcendental – with permanence, substantiality, perfection, and beauty, qualities that they, being conditioned, cannot possess.

Projection, we have found, can lead to terrible confusion and pain, for the object of our projection is not seen as it is and our lives are built upon illusion. But projection also brings us into contact with the qualities that we have projected and so gives us the opportunity to draw them into our consciousness. Let us take the example of someone who has developed a rather one-sided masculinity, projecting femininity on to some other person, and perhaps using the act of falling in love with that person to make up for a lack of inner femininity. The danger is then one of becoming tangled with that other person to their mutual disadvantage. But if he (or she) can catch his projection in the mirror, say, of poetry, and prevent it from attaching itself to its original object, he may make it fully conscious, first of all, as something outside himself and then, within. Similarly, if we can head off our projection of those qualities that are really transcendental from the world around us we can begin to incorporate them into consciousness or, rather, see that they are ultimately the basic nature of our own minds and of the entire universe.

In vertical projection, we select either people, physical objects, or visionary symbols as the screens upon which to throw our images. When we project onto people, the danger arises that they may take advantage of our projection. Thus, if we fall in love, the object of our affections may exploit or manipulate our infatuation – or may fall in love, too. Rather than recapturing our latent qualities, we may end in a confused emotional tangle or trapped in conventional domesticity. Similarly, if we project idealized spiritual qualities onto people who do not in fact possess them, they may use our devotion for their own private purposes as many modern gurus so clearly do. If, on the other hand, the objects of our projection are worthy of the confidence we place in them – that is, if our projection corresponds to their actual qualities – then they will help us, in our communication with them, to draw out the same latent virtues in ourselves. This aspect of projection is part of the very important principle of spiritual friendship that is one of the keys to human growth.

Physical objects may be the vehicle for our projected potential. A lump of clay or wood fashioned into the likeness of a seated man – a statue of the Buddha – may be a focus for very genuine feelings of devotion. As far as the devotee is concerned, the figure is the Buddha – although, at the same time, he or she knows that it is but a statue. The more devotion we can experience and the more readily we can feel that, when we bow to the statue, we are bowing to the Buddha himself, the more deeply we will contact our own inner potential for Buddhahood. Some schools of Buddhism have taken advantage of this faculty of vertical projection onto physical objects by developing a very beautiful and effective system of rituals using a rich variety of symbolic implements and forms.

Visionary experiences, in which we see archetypal figures enacting myths which have deep spiritual significance, are also projections of the vertical kind, this time using the inner eye of imagination. Some forms of Buddhism have raised this aspect of spiritual practice to a very high level indeed. A system of figures of Buddhas and other beings has evolved which represents, in symbolic form, the transcendental in its myriad qualities. The contemplation, in imagination, of these figures allows us to project more and more of our own inner nature. They are very beautiful, made of bright and clear colours, richly dressed, and adorned with jewels, glowing with brilliant light and so, as we see them more and more vividly, our own sense of beauty is stirred and we are lifted up the mundane links of the Spiral. But the figures are also significant, they carry implements and make gestures that have a transcendental meaning so that the more cognitive aspect of imagination is also aroused. The figures embody both Beauty and Truth, and we are led on by our fascination for them until we project not only the spiritual within us but the transcendental also. At this highest point, the figures are not just beautiful and rich in meaning but they express reality itself. We have seen, as it were, through the form and colour to the Emptiness beyond which is our own true nature.

Of the Buddhist schools that utilize these symbolic forms, each has its own system which varies in detail from the others, although the basic principles are the same for all. There are many hundreds of these figures, each representing transcendental reality from a somewhat different point of view. Thus the figures each embody a quality such as wisdom, compassion, energy, and so forth, all aspects of the Enlightened mind. In a sense, the entire assembly of forms is one figure, viewed from different perspectives in the same way that the many facets of a cut jewel refract the fire at the centre in its own surface. Every figure contains all the others and, in its turn, is contained by them.

The Mandala

All the Buddhas and other transcendental beings arrange themselves in a kind of sacred circle, called a mandala in Sanskrit. A mandala is a harmonious and symmetrical network of archetypal forms placed in a circle about one central figure; it represents the dynamic totality of the Enlightened mind in all its various dimensions.

We are here concerned with the Mandala of the Five Buddhas, which consists of one Buddha seated at the centre of the circle with four others at the cardinal points. In a sense, each of the four outer figures is but an aspect of the central one, drawing out his many endowments. At the same time, each of the five encompasses all the others and each becomes himself the centre of a sub-mandala with his own surrounding figures, elaborating yet further his own particular qualities. In principle, this process of unfoldment could go on indefinitely, each figure emanating more figures which are, at the same time, aspects of the one central figure and themselves the totality of the Enlightened mind. The beings in the Mandala are engaged in a kind of exuberant dance that suggests the infinite creativity of Enlightenment and its perfect completeness and harmony.

The Mandala is set in the midst of space, which is perceived as a clear blue sky stretching to a luminous infinity in every direction. It is surrounded by a threefold wall through which we must pass if we are to glimpse the Buddhas themselves. The innermost wall is a wall of lotus flowers. Lotuses are a very common symbol in Buddhist iconography, not only because they are magnificent when in full bloom. Though their roots are nourished by the mud at the depths of a lake yet they stand clear of the water, pure and undefiled by the dirt from which they have grown. They suggest, therefore, growth from a grosser to a finer level, and thus purification. In other contexts, as when they form the thrones for the Buddhas in the Mandala, they indicate transcendence, for the lotus stands clear of the earth and water that nourished it and blossoms in the clear radiance of the sun. So, to pass through the wall of lotuses, one must be pure. One must have practised morality and one must be purged of all unskilfulness. A wall of thunderbolts meets us next. The thunderbolt is a very rich symbol indeed, often used as the active counterpart of the more soft, receptive qualities that the lotus flower suggests. A thunderbolt is irresistibly powerful and is said to be itself indestructible; yet it can destroy everything in its path as it flashes from the sky. It comes, therefore, to represent, among other things, unshakeable determination, the kind of commitment to realizing the Ideal that allows nothing to stand in its way. One must have this kind of dedication to enter the Mandala. Finally, there is a wall of flames, for flames transmute: they consume gross material substances and change them into the heat and smoke that billow upwards from a fire. Thus flames represent the transformation of every particle of our being. We must die to our old selves, be swallowed up in the fire of spiritual practice, so that we can be reborn within the Mandala.

Akshobhya

We enter the Mandala from the east, the direction of the rising sun. Before us is Akshobhya, the Imperturbable, the blue Buddha in his realm of Complete Joy. His skin is the dark blue of the tropic sky at midnight, deep and mysterious, dark yet luminous. He sits, as do all the Buddhas, in lotus posture, his legs crossed, and he is adorned with silk robes of the same dark blue as his body, covered in golden embroidery. On his head is a golden crown with five crests, delicately worked and covered in jewels. He wears a necklace of gold, and other ornaments on his arms and feet, and his whole body glows with brilliant light so that he is surrounded by a shining aura. His left hand rests in his lap while his right touches the earth before him. This gesture recalls the legendary incident before the historical Buddha's Enlightenment when he was challenged by the personified forces of evil to state his right to be seated on that spot where all the Buddhas of the past had sat. The Buddha touched the ground before him in this way, calling the Earth Goddess to witness that he had been making his spiritual effort for innumerable lifetimes so that he had a firm basis of ethical and meditative experience. The gesture suggests confidence, deep-rootedness, and the same kind of determination that the Buddha manifested at the moment before his attainment of Enlightenment. In the palm of his left hand Akshobhya holds a thunderbolt, symbol of irresistible conviction and commitment and of a power that penetrates to the very heart of things. He is seated on a great blue lotus that is supported by two blue elephants that stand with massive strength.

Each Buddha is the head of a 'family' of transcendental beings which are further refractions of the aspect of Enlightenment that he embodies and which arrange themselves around him to form a new mandala within the greater one. Akshobhya is head of the Thunderbolt family whose qualities are penetrative wisdom and the destruction of all barriers and obstacles. Many members of the family are shown in 'wrathful' form – powerfully built, surrounded by flames, and with faces glaring with anger – which draws out the associations of strength and positive destructiveness of this clan. All these subsidiary figures are Bodhisattvas (a term we will explore in detail in the next chapter) or Buddhas. Briefly, a Bodhisattva is a being who has dedicated himself or herself to the attainment of Enlightenment for the sake of all beings, out of deep compassion for the suffering by which he or she is surrounded. The Bodhisattvas of the Mandala are of such lofty attainment that they come to represent Buddhahood manifesting itself as an active force in all the worlds of the conditioned. The chief Bodhisattvas connected with Akshobhya are Vajrapani and Kshitigarbha. Vajrapani, the Thunderbolt-bearer, represents the unconditioned dynamism of Buddhahood. Kshitigarbha is the Bodhisattva who enters the realms of hell in order to help its denizens gain liberation – representing the extent to which active compassion is prepared to go in order to help beings.

Each Buddha is the embodiment of a wisdom, the five together constituting the full depth and range of Enlightened awareness. The Mirror-like Wisdom shines from the heart of Akshobhya as a pure, dazzling white light. Just as a mirror reflects an absolutely faithful image of the object before it, so Akshobhya's wisdom sees things exactly as they are without distortion or interpretation, perfectly objectively.

If we take any feature of conditioned experience and contemplate it deeply enough we will find that it opens out into the transcendental. Similarly, the figures in the Mandala not only express all transcendental qualities but also correspond to every aspect of the mundane. Each of the five Buddhas therefore represents one of the five heaps into which human experience may be divided (form, feeling, recognition, motivation, and consciousness) in purified form. Some Buddhist schools have worked out an elaborate network of these alignments that reveal to us the ultimate identity of the mundane and the transcendental. Akshobhya's quality of firmness, solidity, and objective awareness corresponds to the more stable and objective elements in our experience – to the heap of form. The passion of hatred, with its destructiveness, corresponds in purified form to the thunderbolt aspect of this blue Buddha – his quality of bursting through all barriers and obstacles to the heart of Truth. He is also therefore associated with the realm of hell that is the manifestation of hatred.

Ratnasambhava

Following the track of the sun, we come next to the southern quarter of the Mandala in which we see the Buddha Ratnasambhava, the Jewel-Born, in his realm, the Glorious. He is golden yellow, like a field of ripe corn in bright sunlight, and he, too, is richly dressed in royal robes and jewellery and is crowned with a five-pointed crown. His left hand rests in his lap and he reaches forward with his right hand in the gesture of giving. His open palm contains a jewel – the wish-fulfilling gem that instantly grants all desires. This is the 'triple gem' of Buddha, Dharma, and Sangha, the threefold Ideal that alone can ultimately satisfy us. He sits on a golden lotus throne which is supported by two powerful yellow horses. The horse, to a nomadic people, means wealth, and in many cultures it has been a sign of aristocracy. It also suggests a journey – a spiritual voyage such as that on which the Buddha-to-be set forth when he left his life at home, riding on his faithful charger. It often, too, signifies a messenger bringing news from distant places – just as the Tibetan Buddhist 'windhorse' carries the message of the Three Jewels on its back, to all beings.

In the Jewel family, of which Ratnasambhava is the head, is Ratnapani, He Who Holds the Jewel in his Hand, and Jambhala, a strange figure who squeezes a mongoose with his left hand so that it vomits forth jewels – a kind of Indian cornucopia.

A yellow light shining from Ratnasambhava's heart is the light of the Wisdom of Equality. Everything is perceived as having the same fundamental nature – which is Emptiness. Beneath the external differences of things is one underlying reality – not a substantial entity but a principle of absolute creativity that underlies all things. It is this basic nature that Ratnasambhava sees. He sees the creative wealth inherent in all things and the transcendental beauty that pervades the entire universe – he could even be called the Buddha of Beauty just as Akshobhya could be called the Buddha of Wisdom. Ratnasambhava's wisdom corresponds to the heap of feeling, since the Ideal Beauty that he embodies is the transcendental counterpart of pleasure. Because he sees all things as having one underlying nature he does not compare himself with others – he therefore transcends the passion of pride. Pride is the failing of the human realm, for self-consciousness can, all too easily, degenerate into self-conceit. Ratnasambhava's realm is therefore aligned with the human world.

Amitabha

In the western quarter, the Buddha Amitabha, Infinite Light, presides over the realm Sukhavati, the Abode of Bliss. He is deep red, the colour of the setting sun, and richly adorned. His hands are folded in his lap in the gesture of meditation and in them is cupped a red lotus blossom. He sits on a red lotus throne which is upheld by two peacocks, their shimmering fans uplifted. The peacock was thought to derive the brilliant hues of its plumage from the poison of the snakes on which it was said to feed – a symbol, therefore, of purification and transformation.

Amitabha's family is the Lotus family, which contains many deeply revered Bodhisattvas and Buddhas, the most well-known of whom is Avalokiteshvara, the Lord Who Looks Down, the quintessential embodiment of compassion. The family also contains two historical figures: Gautama Shakyamuni, the founder of the Buddhist tradition, and Padmasambhava, the great teacher who established the Dharma among the Tibetans, by whom he is known as the 'Second Buddha'. Amitabha has a kind of special jurisdiction over our own era and, since he is the Buddha of the west, perhaps over the Western world as well.

Amitabha represents, above all, love – the active compassion that shines in the glowing red of his body. A ray of red light, the Discriminating Wisdom, beams from his heart. The Mirror-like Wisdom sees everything as it is and the Wisdom of Equality sees everything as having the same Emptiness as its fundamental nature; the Discriminating Wisdom sees each and everything as unique with its own minute particularities. Amitabha's love is not mere generalized goodwill; it is a burning compassion, sensitive to the individual needs of every creature. This wisdom corresponds to the heap of recognition that is the faculty whereby we recognize things and set them off from their surroundings. The intense emotion of compassion is the transcendental counterpart of craving, which is a strong attachment to particular things. Craving is the poison that drives the hungry ghosts and so their world is aligned with Amitabha's realm, Sukhavati.

Amoghasiddhi

The Buddha of the northern quarter is Amoghasiddhi, Unobstructed Success, who dwells in the Realm of Accumulated Actions. He is green in colour and raises his right hand in the gesture of fearlessness, conveying confidence and serenity. In his left hand, resting in his lap, he holds two thunderbolts crossed – a symbol of immense power in which two forces are united, each of which is irresistible, indicating a transcendence that harmonizes all fundamental polarities, such as that of subject and object. His throne is supported by two strange creatures called shang-shangs. These are composite animals, a bird up to the neck, from which sprouts the upper body of a man who clashes two cymbals as he flies.

Amoghasiddhi's family is the Action family, which has among its members the Bodhisattva Vishvapani, He Who Holds the Universe. Also in this clan is Sarvanivaranavishkambhin, He Who Destroys the Hindrances.

The green radiance from Amoghasiddhi's heart is the All-performing Wisdom. Wisdom is no passive quality, it is not merely the ability to see things clearly. It is also the knowledge of what needs to be done, what actions will bring about the fulfilment of all beings. It is a very mysterious power, able to see connections and interrelations invisible to ordinary cunning, so much in tune with the fundamental rhythm of the universe that it can act with complete confidence of success. This wisdom is very subtle and Amoghasiddhi's movements are barely perceptible as he fulfils his aims. The end to which his efforts are always directed is the highest happiness of all creatures. Amoghasiddhi, since he is the Buddha of Action, corresponds to the heap of motivation, for his compassionate activity is the transcendental counterpart of volition. The poison of envy leads to very aggressive and competitive behaviour, all undertaken to surpass or confound rivals. Amoghasiddhi's activity is even more vigorous but it is directed to the welfare of others. The world of the titans, who are motivated by envy, aligns with his realm.

Vairochana

In the centre of the Mandala is Vairochana, the Illuminator, and his realm is the All-Pervading Circle. He is, in a sense, the sum of all the Buddhas and combines all their qualities. He is therefore pure white, since white light is a blend of all colours. Each of the Buddhas is the idealization of an aspect of Enlightenment, particularly as exemplified in the career of the historical Buddha. Thus Akshobhya sums up that determination and steadiness that Gautama displayed when he touched the earth to call the Earth Goddess to witness. So Vairochana is the idealization of what might be termed the central function of a Buddha, the teaching of the way to the transcendental. The occasion that has come most closely to represent this in Gautama Buddha's life is the teaching of his five former ascetic disciples immediately after his Enlightenment. This is known as the First Turning of the Wheel of the Dharma. Probably this eight-spoked golden wheel which has come to symbolize the Dharma was originally a solar disc in Indian tradition, and it later came to be considered an attribute of kingship. The king was the one who occupied the position of the sun in society and so he held the sun-wheel as a symbol of his authority. The Buddha occupies that same position in the universe from a spiritual point of view. He is the source of the nourishing light of Truth and, when he turns the Wheel of the Dharma, it sends forth golden beams which illumine the hearts of men, darkened by ignorance. So Vairochana, the Illuminator, is the ideal form of this teaching function of the Buddha and, like a great sun disc, he holds the Wheel of the Dharma to his heart and turns it so that it burns ever more brightly. Vairochana is a kind of transcendental Sun King, blazing at the centre of the Mandala. His white lotus throne is supported by two great lions, for the lion is the king of beasts and, it is said, when he roars all other beasts fall silent. The Buddha's teaching is a lion's roar because all lesser teachings are silenced by its depth and grandeur. The family of Vairochana is the Buddha family and its principal member is Manjushri, the Bodhisattva of Wisdom.

The blue light that shines from Vairochana's heart is the Wisdom of the Sphere of the Dharma. The whole of existence, from the lowest hell realm to the most refined heaven, is seen as Truth. Wherever one looks, whatever one contemplates, one is faced by the Dharma. The transcendental is perceived as non-different from the mundane, the mundane as non-different from the transcendental. At one and the same time, with the Wisdom of the Sphere of the Dharma, conditioned things are seen as objects and people – but also as Empty, as manifestations of Absolute Reality.

The heap of consciousness that illumines the objects of perception is the mundane equivalent of the transcendental wisdom of Vairochana, the Sun of Truth. The absolute brilliance of his awareness corresponds to the darkness of ignorance. The gods, who are at the summit of mundane existence as Vairochana is of all reality, are separated from the transcendental only by their ignorance of the real nature of things, and so their world aligns with Vairochana's realm.

That realm is the All-Pervading Circle, a kind of circle without centre or circumference, for though Vairochana represents centrality and kingship, it is of a transcendental kind. The centre is everywhere, at every point in the universe, for transcendental awareness is not identified with any particular place in space or time. Though he is at the heart of the Mandala, he is also at every other point within it – and outside it.

The Five Buddhas in their Mandala with their attendant Bodhisattvas present in symbolic form all the qualities of Enlightenment. The contemplation of their shapes and colours, their various emblems and figures, will help us to project more and more of the transcendental qualities within us. The more vividly the Mandala is seen and the more beautiful and brilliant the whole vision appears, the nearer to reality will we approach. In the end, the Five Buddhas are not really to be found in their symbolic forms. By going beyond their shapes and colours we can arrive at their very essence. To see the Five Buddhas in their true form, one must see the transcendental face to face – one must gain Enlightenment.

12

The Bodhisattva and the World

In the infinite blue sky of absolute space, the Buddha Amitabha sits, poised in the perfect peace of transcendental meditation. His body glows the fiery red of the setting sun, an aura of universal love that penetrates the entire universe. On his calm features is the faint smile of ineffable bliss, mingled with highest wisdom and compassion. From his heart, a ray of ruby light shines forth, out into the furthest reaches of the cosmos. At the end of this piercing beam, the glorious figure of a young prince manifests itself. His skin is pure white, the colour of virgin snow when the sun first gleams on its surface. He is dressed in richly coloured silken robes, embroidered with golden flowers. On his head he wears a crown with its five wisdom crests, and the jewels of the six perfections adorn his body. His finely proportioned figure is strong but lithe and graceful. His features have all the fineness of wisdom and the fullness of compassion. His eyes are clear and penetrating and filled with tears. He is Avalokiteshvara, the Lord Who Looks Down in Compassion, the Bodhisattva of Compassion, and he weeps as he beholds the manifold sufferings of all the beings in the six realms and three spheres of existence.

As he gazes down at the universe, he feels utterly helpless. Transcendental being though he is, he cannot help everyone. So intensely does he enter into the individual agony of every creature that his body cannot absorb or express the power of his emotion, and it bursts into fragments. His head splits into eleven pieces, each of which forms another head, searching yet more intently for beings in need:

one faces in the direction of each of the four cardinal and four intermediate points, one to the zenith, one to the nadir and one in the centre. No being, however minute, goes unnoticed. His shattered body sprouts a thousand arms that fan out in a great circle around him. In the palm of each hand is an eye, the eye of transcendental awareness that sees each creature with complete clarity. In each of the hands is an implement: a weapon, book, jewel, food, fire, whatever is needed to help any being to grow beyond suffering. The hands reach out to every corner of every world, however remote, bringing the aid appropriate to each individual. Tirelessly, joyfully, Avalokiteshvara works, his eleven heads seeking out suffering and his thousand arms bringing relief. Although he feels the pains of every other being as if they were his own, yet is he inseparably immersed in the supreme bliss of transcendental realization and, though he works without ceasing, inspired by his bottomless compassion, he feels his work to be a joyous play. He vows that he will not cease that playful activity until the last being has been helped to pass beyond suffering.

Avalokiteshvara in the Six Realms

Even now, Avalokiteshvara considers that more must be done, and from his heart he radiates six beams of light: white, green, red, dark blue, light blue, and yellow. Each of the rays enters one of the six realms of existence and there manifests a Buddha who comes in a guise appropriate to the beings to whom he appears. In the realm of hell, a dark blue Buddha brings ambrosial ointment which he pours on the hell beings, soothing their sufferings. In the world of the hungry ghosts, a red Buddha bears food and drink that will at last give them true nourishment. Among the animals, a light blue Buddha appears carrying a book that gives them the culture and vision to lift them beyond their instincts. In the world of the titans, a green Buddha wields a flaming sword. It is the sword of wisdom and he shows them how to fight ignorance and darkness. Into the human world comes a yellow Buddha wearing the orange robe of a monk and holding a begging-bowl and staff, teaching them how to lead the spiritual life. Finally, a white Buddha plays a lute to the gods. His tune is the melody of impermanence which wakes the gods to the transience of their pleasures.

Avalokiteshvara manifests himself at every level of existence and brings to every single living being the means for liberation – if we will only take it. His compassion is at once completely universal and impartial and, at the same time, responsive to the particular needs of every single individual. His field of activity is infinite space and his era is eternity. He never ceases to help all living beings to gain Enlightenment. He is the true Bodhisattva.

The image of the six manifestations of the Bodhisattva Avalokiteshvara, the Buddhas who appear in the six realms of the Wheel of Life, is of very profound significance and provides us with a suitable symbol around which to synthesize all we have discussed so far and bring it to its culmination. The image tells us something about the spiritual needs of beings in the various worlds. In each, the needs are different and the Bodhisattva responds in an appropriate form. Even within our human world, people are of varying temperaments and types and so have different spiritual requirements. There is, in principle, but one Path, for the same Ideals, the same ethical values, the same truths hold good for everyone. But the outward form which that one principial Path will take will vary from one individual to the next. Buddhism has always applied this truth and developed new ways of expressing the one eternal Dharma in each new culture and age. Moreover, Buddhism presents, even within one school, fashioned for a particular time and place, many different approaches so that each person moves forward from his or her particular point of contact with the Dharma. Some people respond more to meditation, others to study, and for others it is work for the Dharma that draws them. While all aspects of spiritual life must eventually be brought into harmony, initially it is likely to be one or another that attracts. The Dharma, though universal in its appeal, is individual in its application. It is not an abstract set of quasi-mathematical theorems but a living communication between the Enlightened mind and the individual unenlightened being. Avalokiteshvara does not impose his preconceived notions of growth upon the beings he encounters or try to fit them to the procrustean bed of his dogmas. He sees beings as they are and he gives them what they need in order to unfold for themselves their own inner potential.

To the hell beings he brings soothing balm for their sufferings. Someone in that state of extreme hate needs very careful handling. One must guard against their tendency to see a threat where none is intended and, if possible, some objectivity must be introduced into their experience. In this way, they will be able to recognize their own hatred as the source of their pain and frustration. But, first of all, the Bodhisattva relieves their agony. Wherever there is suffering, whatever its source, he tries to remove it because excess of pain so dominates the mind and numbs awareness that it is almost impossible to rise to any higher level. Only when the agony has abated will it be possible to absorb the Dharma. So the Bodhisattva soothes the fury of the demon, removes the torments that torture him, and then teaches him the Dharma.

The hungry ghost is filled with neurotic longings, but the objects craved cannot nourish; indeed, they only increase the pain. Suffering from a sense of inner emptiness, the hungry ghosts try to fill this hole with external gratifications. The Bodhisattva brings substantial food that brings nourishment. He then helps them face up to their own emptiness and recognize what they really want. If the desires are simply repressed instinctual needs, they need to learn to satisfy them in a healthy way; if of a deeper nature, they can find fulfilment for them in the Dharma.

The animal is totally immersed in the body and has no wider perspective on life than food, sex, and sleep. Avalokiteshvara's emanation brings it a book, representing culture. He awakens beings in this realm to the life of the mind and heart, to beauty and the Imagination. For the first time, they raise their heads from the grass on which they are grazing to see the limitless expanse of the sky. From this new perspective they begin to see that life has some meaning and that they have a destiny.

The titans, in their intense envy, battle and intrigue to dominate and to possess the wish-fulfilling tree. They must be met with a power they will respect, so the Bodhisattva appears as a warrior brandishing a sword. Yet he does not harm anyone with his weapons. He teaches the titans to channel their inordinate energies into the battle for spiritual development and to use their might not to destroy but to cut through confusion and ignorance and to reveal the Truth.

In the human world, there is communication and co-operation so that culture can come about. But that culture can easily be perverted so that the human world degenerates into one of the worlds of suffering. There must be a higher aspiration if the human state is to endure. Human beings must commit themselves to following the spiritual path, so the Bodhisattva appears in the guise of a full-time follower of the Dharma and encourages others to go for Refuge to the Three Jewels and to lead a life based upon them.

The Bodhisattva approaches the gods on their own terms. Lapped already in pleasure, they respond to the beauty of the melody he plays upon his lute. It has, perhaps, a haunting quality. It is lovely, but it can never be caught and savoured to eternity: the music flows on, but eventually it comes to an end. Just by listening to it the gods are reminded of mortality, for in their extreme happiness and delight they hardly notice the passing of time. They are shaken from their complacency and spurred to reach yet higher on the spiral of evolution and to change the brittle pleasures of heaven for the permanent bliss of the transcendental.

The Bodhisattvas in each realm represent the transcendental within the mundane. Whatever our state of mind, whatever the world we occupy, Enlightenment is still there. If we only could see clearly enough or enter the full depth of things we would see them as they really are. And if we see the conditioned as it is, we also see the Unconditioned. Each world, looked at with the eye of Truth, is fundamentally Empty, the field of limitless potentiality. Within each and every world, there is the Bodhisattva.

Not only do the Bodhisattvas signify this Unconditioned principle immanent within the conditioned world, they represent the evolutionary force inherent within all consciousness. As we have seen, it is part of the basic nature of consciousness that it seeks to expand to higher levels. Because we fear for the loss of our present level of self-consciousness, we fight against that tendency to grow with all the vigour of greed, hatred, and delusion. Our efforts are directed to preventing our own growth, it seems! Among all the forces, however, that have shaped the world in which we find ourselves, forces generated by our own past volitions, there is, at least, some trace of the urge to transcend. This is the force that drives consciousness at every level to go beyond itself. Self-consciousness is driven to go beyond the boundaries of subject and object at its lowest levels, and then to move beyond each new, more refined duality. The spiritual path essentially consists in this process of self-transcendence at higher and higher levels until self is finally fully transcended in Enlightenment. This force is the Bodhisattva within each being.

The Bodhisattva is the link between the mundane and the transcendental; the drive within the mundane to fulfil itself in the transcendental. But also, as the emanation of Amitabha, one of the Ideal Buddhas of the Mandala we met in the last chapter, the Bodhisattva is the movement of the transcendental towards the mundane. The Bodhisattva within us is aided in the upward struggle by the Bodhisattva from without who, as it were, descends to pull us up by an outstretched hand. In this sense, the Bodhisattva is a being who, motivated by compassion, strives to lead others on to the Path.

Bodhisattva is a Sanskrit word that means 'Being of Awakening'. This is variously interpreted as the being who is set upon gaining Enlightenment or the being whose basis is Enlightenment. The Bodhisattva, properly speaking, is one who has vowed to gain Enlightenment for the sake of all beings. He or she does not see Enlightenment as a personal goal at all, but as a basis from which to help others. The Bodhisattva is motivated not only by experience of the imperfections of the world and by faith in the Three Jewels, but by feelings of sympathy and compassion for others. This is no mere mundane altruism. It is not just an ability to empathize with others based upon healthy self-love. Admirable as that certainly is, this compassion goes far beyond it. The true Bodhisattva no longer makes any distinction between self and others. At this level one has seen through the dichotomy of subject and object to the extent that one feels the sufferings of others as keenly as one's own. The concern at this level is only with the removal of suffering – without troubling to distinguish whose suffering it is. Here the qualities of wisdom and compassion are united. Wisdom breaks the barriers of subject and object and compassion acts for the welfare of all.

Friendship

We have, so far, viewed the spiritual path mainly in terms of psychological states and of worlds. It could also be looked at from other points of view – for instance, in a sociological perspective or as a system of practices and exercises. Using the figure of the Bodhisattva we have another, very important, way of seeing the whole Path, this time in terms of our relations with other people, for as well as the archetypal forms of Bodhisattvas we have already met, we can also see the Bodhisattva Path as one that we can tread. Although traditionally the Bodhisattvas and the Stream Entrants are seen to be pursuing different spiritual ideals, close examination suggests that the Path of the Bodhisattva is the same spiritual path that the Stream Entrants tread, but what the Bodhisattva teaches us is that our spiritual development must take other people into account. In the first place, our lives are so bound up with other people that we can scarcely develop unless we consider and work upon our relations with them. Ultimately, one cannot be fully at peace while others suffer. No man, truly, is an island and spiritual development consists in realizing our interconnectedness with others on ever deeper levels until we are identified not with the ego at all but with the whole field of consciousness.

We have seen that the evolution of our relations with others begins in the group, the human equivalent of the animal herd. The group provides its members with the important benefits of security and support, but it demands conformity with its conventions. Such a group may be positive or negative. In the former case, it encourages healthiness and happiness in its members and is upheld by a higher vision. The negative group holds together only out of the overlapping self-interest of its members, and unwholesome mental states predominate within it. Within either kind of group, relationships are based upon need. The group member belongs more to the group than to himself or herself. The group member's consciousness, by and large, is an expression of the group's consciousness. From immersion in the network of needs that is the group, mature individuality slowly emerges.

The individual has identified himself or herself as a separate awareness from others. He or she is, therefore, for the first time, able to feel a genuine disinterested friendliness, rising above immediate self-interest and appreciating the separate being of others. More especially, since there is awareness of self not only in the present but in the past and the future as well, he or she is aware of having a continuity of identity and therefore can enter into enduring relationships with others based upon mutual good will. Friendliness becomes friendship.

True friendship is based upon self-awareness, and full self-awareness contains an awareness of the urge to go beyond that is in all consciousness. Real friends are, therefore, aware of themselves and each other as developing individuals whose lives are based upon an ideal. Without that vertical dimension the friendship will usually be based upon mutual self-interest and soon falls to the level of the group. Friendship, in its full sense, is therefore spiritual friendship, based upon common commitment to growth and development. The cultivation of such friendships is one of the principal aspects of the Path and one of its principal delights. The Buddha is reported as saying, on one occasion, that spiritual friendship is the whole of the spiritual life.

The first aspect of spiritual friendship is metta. Usually we pick friends because of shared interests or some sort of temperamental affinity between them and us. Metta teaches us to go beyond that and to see other people apart from our conditioned predispositions. With metta we can feel good will for any conscious entity and so are capable of friendship with anyone who is sufficiently an individual to form friendships. Spiritual friendship responds to the spiritual potential in the other person, is attracted by his or her positive qualities. Friendship, it has been said, is the mutual recognition of the virtuous and cannot be known by the vicious.

Friendship does not blossom overnight, for it takes some time for two people to get to know each other. It is by communication that friends are made – communication in the sense of that mutual awareness and openness that we have already noted. As friendship develops, the parties to it can reveal more and more of themselves to each other and be themselves more fully. Since true friendship is based upon ideals, it will be possible to relate freely to one's friends at one's best and highest while ordinary acquaintances might have no appreciation of those ideals and might even ridicule them. Our spiritual friends will place these ideals at the heart of their lives and spiritual commitment will underlie all our communication with them. In this way, vision is intensified and reinforced. Where one person is less developed than the other, that person is raised up by contact with the spiritual friend. His or her own latent qualities are activated by experiencing the exemplification of those virtues by the friend. In this vertical sense, spiritual friendship forms a chain running from the highest to the lowest levels of the spiritual path. The more developed give their friendship to the less developed, drawing out their spiritual potential, and the less developed respect them and value the friendship they receive. From the Buddhas and Bodhisattvas down to those who feel the first stirrings of a desire to develop, the whole Path is linked by friendship.

This great network of friends, stretching from one end of the Path to the other, is the sangha, the spiritual community, in its widest sense. All those who share a spiritual vision share, in a sense, the same world and they have more in common with their fellows on the Path than with those who inhabit the same physical world as they do. They are all trying to go beyond themselves, to give up their limited ego-sense – not by regressing into the unconscious harmony of the group but by joining together in a fellowship which is on a level where self and other merge.

It is often made into a concrete reality for practitioners by means of the formation of a particular order or community as a living embodiment of the ideal of sangha. Those who have joined such a community try, in their relations with one another, to transcend themselves and to experience a level of consciousness in which their egoistic interests are merged in mutual love and respect. It could even be said that they aspire to a kind of 'collective consciousness'. I do not mean here the submersion of individuality in an undifferentiated sea of unconscious group identification; rather that the members of the sangha try to share individually in a common state of consciousness that transcends the individual. By their care and concern for one another, by their communication, by their work and practice together, they each try to go beyond themselves to realize a true spiritual community. For sangha, in its highest sense, is the fellowship of those who have transcended the distinction between subject and object. It is the community of the Stream Entrants, the Once-returners, the Non-returners, the Liberated Ones, the Bodhisattvas, and the Buddhas. They dwell in a state of consciousness in which self and other are merged in a non-dual awareness to which our normal categories of understanding do not apply. They are, each of them, completely unique individuals but they are also all manifestations of one unconditioned reality. It is this transcendental community that the members of the sangha seek to bring about on earth by their love and co-operation with each other.

Other people are our principal pathway to self-transcendence. They are part of the objective aspect of our experience, yet they are themselves subjects who will not easily bend to the dictates of our egos. If we enter into friendship with them and join with them in a spiritual community, we must consider their needs and desires as much as our own. This means we must go a little beyond ourselves.

The more intensely we can harmonize with them, the more we will transcend ourselves until eventually we will go beyond subject and object altogether. This is the Bodhisattva Path.

The Novice Bodhisattva

The Path of the Bodhisattva is divided into two major phases: the stage of the novice Bodhisattva and that of the Bodhisattva of the Path. The novice feels the urge to self-transcendence and has faith in the Three Jewels and in the Bodhisattva Ideal itself. Novices want to go beyond themselves so that they can, like Avalokiteshvara, become the manifestation of compassion let loose in the world. As yet, however, these are aspirations, though noble, and not realities. They must work hard upon themselves in order to bring them about. They strive to cultivate six virtues that are, in the true Bodhisattva, natural qualities, spontaneously expressed.

There is, first of all, the virtue of *generosity*. They strive to overcome their tendency to meanness and egoistical self-seeking by giving in many different ways. They give material things to those who need them, and their assistance in time and energy; and, wherever they can, they give the Dharma or, at least, help to provide the conditions under which others may find the Dharma. Whatever the situation they find themselves in, they try to act creatively, giving freely of themselves. In this way, they begin to go beyond themselves.

The next virtue they try to cultivate is *morality*. They cultivate that sensitivity to others which is completely natural to the full Bodhisattva, by applying the ethical precepts to their lives as closely as they can. Their behaviour is not only moral in the broadest sense but it is civilized. Their interaction with others is decorous and considered, and they are polite and dignified in their actions.

Novice Bodhisattvas try to practise *patience* as the next virtue and attempt to overcome their reactive hatreds and cravings. They will thus not blame others for their own misfortunes and strive to feel no enmity for those who cause them harm. They forbear to seek vengeance and do not try to assert their own ego against that of others. Patience in this sense also has the aspect of receptivity to other people, being able to listen to them and, if possible, learn from them. Similarly, the novice Bodhisattvas are always ready to absorb spiritual truth, however much it may undermine their own present understanding. They are co-operative and amenable, able to work with others and to drop contention on trifling matters. They have what have been called the feminine virtues – an ability to respond with warmth and to care for and help others.

Energy is the virtue that, as it were, balances patience. It has been called the masculine quality of initiative and vigour, that in the novice Bodhisattvas actively seeks the good. Since the spiritual life can only occur on the basis of effort, energy is indispensable to growth. It is the drive to self-transcendence, the positive urge that takes us beyond ourselves. It also expresses itself in work, particularly for the sake of the Dharma.

The novice Bodhisattva cultivates *meditation* as a virtue, systematically training the mind to experience more and more positive states, trying to raise consciousness so that he or she dwells for some time each day in the state of absorption.

Becoming a Bodhisattva of the Path

Wisdom is the last and most crucial virtue that the novice tries to develop aided by all the other virtues. It is specifically courted by the study of the doctrinal formulations of the Dharma and by meditations that are directed to Insight. It is the dawning of Wisdom that turns novice Bodhisattvas into Bodhisattvas of the Path. With the eye of Wisdom they see that all things are ultimately indefinable, unconditioned, and Empty. They themselves are Empty, all other beings are Empty. They see that the basic nature of all reality is that ungraspable openness that is called Emptiness. Once more, it is not a blank nothingness but such a plenitude that all our ordinary categories of thought diminish and belittle it. Based in Wisdom, they now strive to convert all the virtues into transcendental perfections, the spontaneous expressions of their Insight into non-duality. They give perfectly out of their immediate and heartfelt response to need, without any preconceived idea of themselves as a donor or of the recipients as beings to whom they are giving – they do not even have an idea of an act of giving. They are equally the giver, the receiver, and the gift. They have the perfection of morality because they act spontaneously out of Wisdom without any idea of trying to cultivate precepts or etiquette. Their behaviour is naturally moral. They are perfect in patience. They feel no anger towards those who harm them because they are as much concerned for the wrongdoer as for themselves. They have to make no effort to curb or control reactions

– they simply have none. They have the perfection of energy because, by now, evolution works through them, they have to make no effort in order for it to manifest. Their energy arises freely and without limit to help living beings. Perfect meditation is theirs because their mind is always calm and balanced, always one-pointed and refined. They no longer struggle to become absorbed – absorption is their natural medium. And they have Perfect Wisdom, the realization that all things are empty, which raises virtues to perfections.

The historical Buddha, Gautama Shakyamuni, is said to have pursued this Path of the Bodhisattva over innumerable lifetimes during which he cultivated and perfected each of the virtues. Countless aeons before the life in which he gained Enlightenment, the story goes, he made his great vow before the Buddha of that era. This vow arises in all Bodhisattvas when they become Bodhisattvas of the Path and it represents their spontaneous response to the sufferings of all beings. They feel, very deeply, their interconnectedness with all life and they vow that they will gain full Enlightenment for the sake of all. They see that spiritual life is not a matter of personal development alone but of bringing the entire universe to perfection. Their perspective is the infinitude of space and the endless sequence of time and it involves all living creatures. The story of the Bodhisattva career of the historical Buddha is told in a series of tales. Some of them are, quite clearly, folk stories, like Aesop's fables, but the general emphasis of all the stories, whether they are taken as literal records of the Buddha's previous lives or not, is clear. In each incident the Bodhisattva goes beyond himself, and in going beyond himself he leads other beings with him.

Buddhist history is filled with great teachers and sages who showed those same Bodhisattva qualities in full measure – people who, sometimes under very difficult circumstances, led their fellows on the Path to Enlightenment. Indeed, it is that Bodhisattva spirit that has kept Buddhism alive to this day, not as a set of scholarly philosophies or exotic customs, but as a living network of spiritual friendships in which individuals are developing. The ideal of the Bodhisattva has inspired and still inspires countless men and women to see their own development and the welfare of others as two aspects of one Path. While they work vigorously to raise their own consciousness, they also devote themselves to helping others. The Bodhisattva Ideal has thus found expression in the lives of many human beings. Many have, as novice Bodhisattvas, tried to bring about those six virtues in their own conduct. They have assiduously cultivated feelings of metta and deepened their spiritual friendships, participating in that sangha-consciousness that transcends but does not negate the individual. They have also worked directly for the welfare of others. Some have, in this way, broken through to a new level of wisdom, the level of the Bodhisattva of the Path. Their virtues have become perfections and their active compassion has sprung from their transcendental insight.

Archetypal Bodhisattvas
The Bodhisattva principle, as we have seen, also finds expression in archetypal form. By that process of vertical projection, figures have been envisaged which are the personification of the essential qualities of the Bodhisattva. Existing on the loftiest plane of Enlightenment, they embody the active nature of Enlightenment as the force of good in the world. There are four principal Ideal Bodhisattvas who are revered in some Buddhist schools as the archetypes of the Bodhisattva's virtues.

Avalokiteshvara, the Bodhisattva of Compassion, with his eleven heads and thousand arms, we have already encountered at the beginning of this chapter. Like all Bodhisattvas, he is represented not only in visual form but also as a mantra. A mantra is a sound-symbol that carries the qualities of Enlightenment just as does the shape, colour, and gesture of the visual image. The mantra *is* the Bodhisattva in terms of sound. It does not really mean anything, or rather what literal meaning it has is scarcely relevant. It has its effect by virtue of the associations it has gathered to itself in the course of centuries. (The mantra of Avalokiteshvara is the famous *om mani padme hum* which is sometimes translated as 'om, jewel-lotus, hum', *om* referring to absolute reality, the jewel being the jewel of Enlightenment and the lotus the mind, and *hum* being absolute reality as manifested in the conditioned world.)

Manjushri, the Gently Auspicious One, is the Bodhisattva of Wisdom. He, too, is a young prince of great beauty, decked in silks. On his head is the crown of the Five Wisdoms and on his body are the jewelled ornaments of the six perfections. His body is a fiery orange colour, 'like a lion's eye', and from him there glows a resplendent blue aura. He is seated in the cross-legged posture and his right hand is raised aloft, wielding the flaming sword of wisdom whose razor-sharpness cuts effortlessly through all confusion and ignorance. It is the sword of non-duality that slices away suffering and imperfection. With his left hand, he presses a book to his heart, the book of Perfect Wisdom, the highest knowledge that there is. Manjushri is a kind of Buddhist Apollo, although on a far loftier, transcendental plane, for he is the patron of all arts and sciences, the bringer of culture and learning. His mantra is *om a ra pa cha na dhih.*

The Bodhisattva of energy is Vajrapani, the Bearer of the Thunderbolt. He is often depicted in wrathful form to emphasize the force and positive destructiveness of the transcendental, bursting through all barriers, annihilating ignorance and burning up all limitations. He is an enormous, dark blue figure with a barrel chest and massive arms and legs, rippling with heavy muscles. He stands stamping his right foot upon a prostrate corpse and raising in his right hand a golden thunderbolt as if to hurl it. His left hand is held to his heart in a gesture of teaching. His face is scowling and his three bloodshot eyes glare in rage. His teeth are pointed and drip blood. Around his body is an aureole of flames. Although the transcendental being has nothing but love for every member of the universe, to those who are completely identified with their own ignorance and who do not wish to grow his uncompromising honesty and unfailing energy appear terrifying and threatening. Even this horrific figure of Vajrapani is, in reality, the calm and serene Buddha, sitting in perfect peace. His mantra is *om vajrapani hum.*

Tara, the Saviouress, is the female Bodhisattva of Compassion. She is said to have been born out of a lake formed by the tears of Avalokiteshvara as he wept for the sufferings of the world. She is a beautiful young princess, a delicate jade-green in colour. She sits with her left leg drawn up in meditation and her right leg stepping down into the world to save living beings. Her left hand holds to her heart the stalks of three lotuses whose pale blue flowers are at her left shoulder; one in bud, one half open, and one in full bloom, symbolizing the different stages of maturation of beings. Her right hand is extended before her right knee in the gesture of generosity. She symbolizes the very quintessence of that sympathy for all creatures that is the Bodhisattva's nature. Her mantra is *om tare tuttare ture svaha.*

The career of the Bodhisattvas, in their path from the earliest efforts of the novice to the complete Enlightenment of a Buddha, may take many, many lifetimes. During their careers, Bodhisattvas will try to help as many other beings as they can. The more advanced they are, the more beneficial and widespread their aid will be. They will each gradually form around them a field of influence that will raise up all those who are open to it. In the final stages of their careers, each Bodhisattva creates a kind of ideal world by the power of his or her own compassionate volitions. Everyone who makes spiritual contact with the Bodhisattva and who is receptive to him or her will be reborn in that world called a Pure Land. In it everything is favourable to development and nothing hinders or obstructs. It is the perfect environment for the leading of the spiritual life for one is always in the presence of the Bodhisattva whose pure land it is and who now becomes a Buddha. Everywhere in the Pure Land one hears the Dharma, and the only beings there are members of the sangha. All bodily and psychological wants are immediately satisfied merely by wishing for them and the whole world is of exceptional beauty and purity. It is like the highest of the heaven worlds suffused with the influence of the transcendental.

The Bodhisattva on the threshold of Buddhahood creates a Pure Land at a very high level of refinement. The human Bodhisattva, whether novice or of the Path, tries to create a Pure Land on Earth. More especially, he or she works with others, with the sangha, to create the best possible conditions for growth here and now by trying to bring into being a movement of people who are inspired by the vision of the Three Jewels. He or she tries to establish the institutions in which people can live and work together on the basis of those ideals and tries to bring about a culture that carries the perspective of the spiritual path to as many people as possible. All his or her efforts are directed to forming a new society that has spiritual evolution as its central value.

The Bodhisattva does not work alone but seeks out and co-operates with others who share this vision. Some may see it more brightly and clearly and willingly follow the Bodhisattva's guidance. Others who are less spiritually mature, the Bodhisattva leads and encourages as best he or she can. With all, with this total sangha, the Bodhisattva is united in bonds of friendship and mutual self-transcendence.

This is the Buddhist life. It is an unending yet joyous struggle to unfold the best and noblest qualities from within oneself. It is an ever-deepening harmony with one's spiritual friends and fellows in the sangha so that one moves with them as if all were different manifestations of a single higher consciousness. And it is the heroic effort to draw as many people as possible onto the Path so that they may fulfil their own innermost nature. The Buddhist life, in the end, is the truly human life, a life dedicated to the transformation of self and world.

Further Reading

Edwin Arnold, *The Light of Asia*, Windhorse, Birmingham 1999

S.T. Coleridge, *Biographia Literaria*, Everyman, 1997

Edward Conze, *Buddhism: Its Essence and Development*, Windhorse (forthcoming)

Edward Conze et al., *Buddhist Texts Through the Ages*, Oneworld, Oxford 1995

Francesca Fremantle and Chögyam Trungpa (trans.), *The Tibetan Book of the Dead*, Shambhala, Boston and London 2000

Herbert V. Guenther, *Philosophy and Psychology in the Abhidhamma*, Shambhala, 1976

Joseph Head and S.L. Cranston, *Reincarnation: The Phoenix Fire Mystery*, Theosophical University Press, 1994

Kamalashila, *Meditation: The Buddhist Way of Tranquillity and Insight*, Windhorse, Birmingham 1999

Bhikkhu Nanamoli, *The Life of the Buddha*, Buddhist Publication Society, Kandy 1992

Stanton Peele and Archie Brodsky, *Love and Addiction*, Sphere, 1977

Sangharakshita, *The Bodhisattva Ideal*, Windhorse, Birmingham, 1999

Sangharakshita, *Going for Refuge*, Windhorse, Birmingham 1997

Sangharakshita, *Human Enlightenment*, Windhorse, Glasgow 1993

Sangharakshita, *Mind Creative and Reactive*, Windhorse, Birmingham 1995

Sangharakshita, *The Priceless Jewel*, Windhorse, Glasgow 1993

Sangharakshita, *A Survey of Buddhism*, Windhorse, Birmingham 2001

Sangharakshita, *The Three Jewels*, Windhorse, Birmingham 1998

Francis Story, *Rebirth as Doctrine and Experience*, Buddhist
    Publication Society, Kandy 1998
Subhuti, *Sangharakshita: A New Voice in the Buddhist Tradition*,
    Windhorse, Birmingham 1994
Subhuti, *Bringing Buddhism to the West*, Windhorse, Birmingham
    1995
Vessantara, *Meeting the Buddhas*, Windhorse, Birmingham 1998
Vessantara, *The Mandala of the Five Buddhas*, Windhorse,
    Birmingham 1999
F.L. Woodward (trans.), *Some Sayings of the Buddha*, Buddhist
    Society, London 1974

INDEX

The Windhorse symbolizes the energy of the enlightened mind carrying the Three Jewels – the Buddha, the Dharma, and the Sangha – to all sentient beings.

Buddhism is one of the fastest-growing spiritual traditions in the Western world. Throughout its 2,500-year history, it has always succeeded in adapting its mode of expression to suit whatever culture it has encountered.

Windhorse Publications aims to continue this tradition as Buddhism comes to the West. Today's Westerners are heirs to the entire Buddhist tradition, free to draw instruction and inspiration from all the many schools and branches. Windhorse publishes works by authors who not only understand the Buddhist tradition but are also familiar with Western culture and the Western mind. Manuscripts welcome.

For orders and catalogues contact

WINDHORSE PUBLICATIONS	WINDHORSE BOOKS	WEATHERHILL INC
11 PARK ROAD	P O BOX 574	41 MONROE TURNPIKE
BIRMINGHAM	NEWTOWN	TRUMBULL
B13 8AB	NSW 2042	CT 06611
UK	AUSTRALIA	USA

Windhorse Publications is an arm of the Friends of the Western Buddhist Order, which has more than sixty centres on five continents. Through these centres, members of the Western Buddhist Order offer regular programmes of events for the general public and for more experienced students. These include meditation classes, public talks, study on Buddhist themes and texts, and 'bodywork' classes such as t'ai chi, yoga, and massage. The FWBO also runs several retreat centres and the Karuna Trust, a fund-raising charity that supports social welfare projects in the slums and villages of India.

Many FWBO centres have residential spiritual communities and ethical businesses associated with them. Arts activities are encouraged too, as is the development of strong bonds of friendship between people who share the same ideals. In this way the FWBO is developing a unique approach to Buddhism, not simply as a set of techniques, less still as an exotic cultural interest, but as a creatively directed way of life for people living in the modern world.

If you would like more information about the FWBO please visit www.fwbo.org or write to

LONDON BUDDHIST CENTRE	ARYALOKA
51 ROMAN ROAD	HEARTWOOD CIRCLE
LONDON	NEWMARKET
E2 0HU	NH 03857
UK	USA

ALSO FROM WINDHORSE

KULANANDA

THE WHEEL OF LIFE

The Wheel of Life is an ancient symbol of tremendous spiritual significance. It is a graphic representation of the Buddhist understanding of life, a mirror held up to the human heart. Within its depths we see the forces that limit and bind us. We see the happiness and the suffering we create for ourselves. We see the chain of ingrained habits that makes us who we are. But, looking deeper still, we begin to see the way to freedom.

84 pages, with illustrations
ISBN 1 899579 30 3
£5.99/$11.95

VESSANTARA

MEETING THE BUDDHAS:

A GUIDE TO BUDDHAS, BODHISATTVAS, AND TANTRIC DEITIES

Sitting poised and serene upon fragrant lotus blooms, they offer smiles of infinite tenderness, immeasurable wisdom. Bellowing formidable roars of angry triumph from the heart of blazing infernos, they dance on the naked corpses of their enemies.

Who are these beings – the Buddhas, Bodhisattvas, and Protectors, the 'angry demons' and 'benign deities' – of the Buddhist Tantric tradition? Are they products of an alien, even disturbed, imagination? Or are they, perhaps, real? What have they got to do with Buddhism? And what have they got to do with us?

In this vivid informed account, an experienced Western Buddhist guides us into the heart of this magical realm and introduces us to the miraculous beings who dwell there.

368 pages, with text illustrations and colour plates
ISBN 0 904766 53 5
£14.99/$29.95

JINANANDA

MEDITATING

This is a guide to Buddhist meditation that is in sympathy with modern lifestyle. Accessible and thought-provoking, this books tells you what you need to know to get started with meditation, and keep going through the ups and downs of everyday life. Realistic, witty, and very inspiring.

128 pages
ISBN 1 899579 07 9
£4.99/$9.95

SANGHARAKSHITA

TIBETAN BUDDHISM: AN INTRODUCTION

A glorious past, a traumatic present, an uncertain future. What are we to make of Tibetan Buddhism?

Sangharakshita has spent many years in contact with Tibetan lamas of all schools, within the context of a wide experience of the Buddhist tradition as a whole. He is admirably qualified as a guide through the labyrinth that is Tibetan Buddhism. In this book he gives a down-to-earth account of the origin and history of Buddhism in Tibet, and explains the essentials of this practical tradition which has much to teach us.

As the essence of Tibetan Buddhism is revealed, it is shown to be a beautiful and noble tradition which – and this is the important thing – can help us contact a sense of beauty and nobility in our lives.

144 pages, illustrated
ISBN 0 904766 86 1
£8.50/$16.95

TEJANANDA

THE BUDDHIST PATH TO AWAKENING

The word Buddha means 'one who is awake'. In this accessible introduction, Tejananda alerts us to the Buddha's wake-up call, illustrating how the Buddhist path can help us develop a clearer mind and a more compassionate heart.

Drawing on over twenty years of Buddhist meditation and study, Tejananda gives us a straightforward and encouraging description of the path of the Buddha and his followers – the path that leads ultimately to our own 'awakening'.

224 pages, with diagrams
ISBN 1 899579 02 8
£8.99/$17.95

VESSANTARA

THE MANDALA OF THE FIVE BUDDHAS

The mandala of the Five Buddhas is an important Buddhist symbol – a multi-faceted jewel communicating the different aspects of Enlightenment. Meeting each Buddha in turn, we start to awaken to the qualities they embody – energy, beauty, love, confidence, and freedom.

By contemplating the mandala as a whole we can transform ourselves through the power of the imagination, and experience the majesty of the mind set free.

96 pages, with colour plates
ISBN 1 899579 16 8
£5.99/$11.95